P9-CEZ-252

UNCOVERING
FASHION

fb

UNCOVERING FASHION

*Fashion Communications
Across the Media*

MARIAN FRANCES WOLBERS
Albright College

FAIRCHILD BOOKS
New York

Executive Editor: Olga T. Kontzias

Editorial Development Director: Jennifer Crane

Development Editor: Rob Phelps

Associate Art Director: Erin Fitzsimmons

Production Director: Ginger Hillman

Senior Production Editor: Elizabeth Marotta

Copyeditor: Tracy Grenier

Cover Design: Erin Fitzsimmons

Cover Art: © Art + Commerce

Text Design: Nicola Ferguson

Page Composition: Tom Helleberg

Copyright © 2009 Fairchild Books, A Division of Condé Nast Publications.

All rights reserved. No part of this book covered by the copyright hereon may be reproduced or used in any form or by any means—graphic, electronic, or mechanical, including photocopying, recording, taping, or information storage and retrieval systems—without written permission of the publisher.

Library of Congress Catalog Card Number: 2008926797

ISBN: 978-1-56367-615-4

GST R 133004424

Printed in the United States of America

TP18

To Hella Rose,

and

in memory of Marian Hodkin Marr

Contents

Extended Table of Contents   *ix*

Foreword   *xvii*

Preface   *xix*

Introduction   *xxiii*

Acknowledgments   *xxv*

PART I: FASHION COMMUNICATIONS— *A Layered Look*

CHAPTER 1: Fashion Information from the Inside Out   *3*

CHAPTER 2: Understanding Raw Materials   *25*

CHAPTER 3: Laboring for Fashion: Influences from the Industry   *43*

PART II: FASHION COMMUNICATIONS—
The Business End

CHAPTER 4: Details, Details   *71*

CHAPTER 5: Becoming Fashion   *103*

CHAPTER 6: Out There for All to See   *121*

PART III: FASHION COMMUNICATIONS—
Representation in the Media

CHAPTER 7: The Big C: Creativity   *151*

CHAPTER 8: Evolution of the Fashion Magazine   *171*

CHAPTER 9: Dynamic Wording—The Art of Describing Fashion   *189*

CHAPTER 10: Visuals That Speak   *215*

CHAPTER 11: "With This Page (Ad, Script, or Whatever!), I Thee Wed"   *239*

Afterword   *263*

Resources and Recommended Readings   *267*

References   *273*

Credits   *281*

Index   *283*

Extended Table of Contents

Foreword   *xvii*

Preface   *xix*

Introduction   *xxiii*

Acknowledgments   *xxv*

PART I: FASHION COMMUNICATIONS—
A Layered Look

CHAPTER 1: Fashion Information from the Inside Out   *3*

Chapter Objectives   *3*

Accessing Core Information   *5*

How to Become a Style Dissector   *7*

Practice: Adopting a Research Mind-set   *11*

Create a Garment Profile   *11*

Locate Your Wardrobe's Origins   *20*

Start a Fabric and Embellishments Bank   *20*

"What's It Made Of?" Challenge   *21*

Dissect Style   *22*

Key Terms   *24*

CHAPTER 2: Understanding Raw Materials   *25*

Chapter Objectives   *25*

Entertainment as the Brother of Invention   *27*

Blending Function with Form   *28*

The Four-Theories Ad Challenge   *30*

New Twists on Old Materials   *32*

Practice: Digging Up the Facts of Fashion   *33*

Master Raw Materials and Inventions   *34*

Challenge the Experts   *37*

Deconstruct an Outfit   *40*

Create a Compare and Contrast Presentation   *40*

Write a Short Definition-Style Essay (150–400 words)   *40*

Key Terms   *41*

CHAPTER 3: Laboring for Fashion: Influences from the Industry   *43*

Chapter Objectives   *43*

The Triangle Waist Company Fire   *44*

Lessons from the Triangle Disaster   *45*

Evolution of the U.S. Fashion Industry   *46*

Big Business   *49*

Communicating within the Industry   *50*

Wordsmithing in the Fashion Trade Publications   *53*

Creative Copy Definitely Counts   *60*

Practice: Scanning the Range of Resources   *62*

Subscribe to Trade Publications   *64*

Visit Unfamiliar Web Sites   *64*

Do Some Fieldwork   *65*

Look into Labor   *65*

Key Terms   *67*

PART II: FASHION COMMUNICATIONS—
The Business End

CHAPTER 4: Details, Details   *71*

Chapter Objectives   *71*

Fashion Communications on the Job   *81*

    The Outreacher   *83*

    Road Warrior   *86*

    "Follow That Script!"   *91*

    ThePlanner   *93*

    From Actor to Super   *96*

Practice: Communicating the Details   *97*

    Create a Detail Quiz (Group Task)   *97*

    Examine a Press Kit / Create a Press Kit   *99*

    Conduct an Interview (Individual Assignment)   *100*

Key Terms   *101*

CHAPTER 5: Becoming Fashion   *103*

Chapter Objectives   *103*

Follow the Leader   *104*

    Trendsetting in the Information Age   *105*

    Trendspotting   *106*

The Magazine Makes Fashion   *114*

Practice: Fashioning Fashion   *117*

    Uncover the Influence of Historical People   *117*

    Discover the Influence of Materials (Objects and Fabrics)   *117*

    Find Out Underlying Motivations for Fashion Adoption   *118*

    Examine Fashion in Print over the Decades   *118*

    Conduct a Comparative Analysis of a Fashion Item with
        a Focus on Fashion Communication   *119*

Key Terms   *120*

CHAPTER 6: Out There for All to See *121*

    Chapter Objectives *121*

    The Many Fields of Fashion *123*

        Marketing *123*

        Sales *123*

        Advertising *126*

        Public Relations *127*

        Promotions *133*

        Branding *134*

    Old Codes and New Codes *135*

        Presence *143*

        Relativity *143*

        Currency *143*

        Communication = Democratization *143*

    Practice: Exploring the Do's and Don'ts of Getting Out There *144*

        Explore the "Oops" Effect *144*

        Keep a Group's Activities Secret *144*

        Surf for Resources *145*

        Brand It *146*

    Key Terms *147*

PART III: FASHION COMMUNICATIONS— *Representation in the Media*

CHAPTER 7: The Big C: Creativity *151*

    Chapter Objectives *151*

    Fundamentals for Fashion *152*

        Creativity and Originality *154*

    What Are the Elements of Creativity? *155*

        Inner Vision *158*

        Curiosity *160*

        Inspiration *161*

`   Ability   *162*

    Environment   *164*

  Communicating Fashion in Fresh Ways   *166*

    Brainstorming   *166*

  Practice: Creating Original Fashion and Communicating Original Ideas   *168*

  Brainstorm and Present Ideas   *168*

  Key Terms   *170*

CHAPTER 8: Evolution of the Fashion Magazine   *171*

  Chapter Objectives   *171*

  Agents of Change   *173*

    Examples from June 2007 *GQ*   *174*

    Examples from Fall 2007 *Elle Accessories,*
      Your Fall/Winter Shopping Guide   *176*

    Examples from December 2007 *Glamour*   *176*

    Examples from December 2005 *Vogue*   *176*

  Choices, Choices, Choices   *177*

    Giving People What They Need   *178*

  Practice: Understanding Magazines as an Intersection of Art and Commerce   *185*

    Pursuing the Philosophy of Fashion Magazines   *185*

    Getting Real with a Magazine Content Count   *186*

    Debate It!   *187*

  Key Terms   *187*

CHAPTER 9: Dynamic Wording—The Art of Describing Fashion   *189*

  Chapter Objectives   *189*

  Where Fashion Is the Focus   *191*

  Shifting into Excellent Gear   *202*

    What Good Writers Do   *202*

  Spoken Fashion   *203*

    Speaking Adjectives   *204*

    Tailor Your Writing to the Task   *206*

  Practice: Do Close Readings for Place and Purpose   *207*

Writing Sample 1   *208*

Writing Sample 2   *209*

Writing Sample 3   *210*

Writing Sample 4   *211*

Writing Sample 5   *212*

Writing Sample 6   *213*

Writing Sample 7   *214*

Key Terms   *214*

CHAPTER 10: Visuals That Speak   *215*

Chapter Objectives   *215*

Enduring Design Principles   *218*

Visual Decisions   *231*

Finding Images   *234*

Sticking with What Works   *234*

Practice: Sharpening Visual Skills and Understanding   *237*

Tracing the River   *237*

Digital Pix—Blindfolded   *237*

Create a Hangtag and Bag   *237*

Make a Cover!   *238*

Design a Magazine or Catalog Page Spread   *238*

Key Terms   *238*

CHAPTER 11: "With This Page (Ad, Script, or Whatever!), I Thee Wed"   *239*

Chapter Objectives   *239*

Word and Image Vows   *240*

Trends in Verbal-Visual Interplay   *242*

A Crash Course in Web Site Excellence   *243*

Web Site Pre-Construction Checklist   *243*

Examining Successful Sites   *243*

The Four C's   *254*

Careers in Fashion Communications   *254*

Practice: Becoming an Expert Matchmaker   *255*

    Taking Aim at Consistency   *255*

    Four C's Web Site Analysis   *260*

    Make a Crazy Collage   *261*

    Do a Fashion Review   *262*

    Compare and Contrast Web Sites   *262*

Key Terms   *262*

Afterword   *263*

Resources and Recommended Readings   *267*

References   *273*

Credits   *281*

Index   *283*

Foreword

Fashion is very important. It is life enhancing and,
like everything that gives pleasure, it is worth doing well.
VIVIENNE WESTWOOD

Words are Marian Wolbers's tools of the trade. My tools are the elements of design, which, like words, can speak. The methods of communication differ but the desired outcome is the same: to bring forth that spark of creativity found in everyone and invite it to enlighten the individual and the global community of this new century of technology.

Uncovering Fashion brings together the broad spectrum of fashion, from the raw materials to the finished silhouettes on the runway and in the retail store. The courses I have taught over the years include: Fundamentals of Textiles, History of Costume, Draping, Flat Pattern, Fashion Retail, Visual Merchandising, Basic Construction, Boutique Management, and Art Wearables. I have taken my students to international fashion competitions in South Africa and Belgium, and I represented the United States when Italy sponsored the first international symposium on window dressing (visual merchandising) targeted toward the training and employment of students. My daily contact with students for more than 25 years has led me to believe that a practical textbook focused specifically on fashion communications has long been a missing element in the educational field.

Uncovering Fashion guides the reader to develop a sixth sense of idea sharing that embodies the various components of fashion—art, design, architecture, legalities, and more—across the wide range of communications media. Marian Wolbers is able to weave all these components from cross-pollinated thoughts and ideas and has pulled them into an articulated whole. The author fuses thoughts and ideas, fragmented or whole as they may be, and transforms them into a journey of creative thought that must be experienced rather than imagined.

Wolbers illustrates the "how to" of fashion communications with clear, concise instructions and examples so students can gain full comprehension of the communication skills required in the fashion industry. Included in this book are historical examples that illuminate the present and concrete verbal-visual directives that are easily put into practice. *Uncovering Fashion* is the first text that includes the legal aspects related to plagiarism, intellectual property, and copyright issues. The inclusion of this information preserves the integrity of not only the author of any work but of the students as well, and it provides a safeguard for all concerned. Issues of intellectual property have become an issue that must be addressed, especially with the emergence of advanced technology and collaborative efforts.

Real-life situations are presented in profiles throughout the book. These profiles give students the true picture of various aspects of communications in the fashion world. There are interviews with individual designers, writers, museum curators, small business owners, retailers, photographers, and bloggers. The reader can gain practical and usable insight from these vignettes. Their inclusion provides information that would pique anybody's interest no matter what their profession.

Marian Wolbers has authored a book that is truly necessary for fashion programs anywhere or for anyone who seeks to develop communication skills. I feel privileged to have written the foreword for this groundbreaking text.

Connie Heller-Horacek
Professor, Albright College
Reading, Pennsylvania

Preface

As I gathered my thoughts for this text, my mind traveled back over the strangely meandering path that informed my own awareness of fashion, a sensibility that dates back to early childhood.

At age five, I sat at my grandmother Marian Marr's knee in a child's chair at her New Hampshire farmstead, learning my stitches. Grammy had been a seamstress all her life, traveling from house to house in a horse-drawn carriage, hand sewing entire wardrobes for families or elaborately crafted wedding gowns embellished with hundreds of pearls. Like the Tirocchi sisters described in Chapter 3, my grandmother kept up with fashion trends by making numerous trips to Boston and bringing the latest styles and fabrics back to her fashion-hungry clientele. She was a wonderfully skilled dressmaker; her services were booked for two years in advance by the time she was 18. She designed and made every single costume my mother wore as a young dancer and her very tailored (1940s) college wardrobe. My mother was also a talented seamstress, but her passion lived in dance performance and dance education. This may explain why my grandmother devoted her attention toward me and became determined to make me into a dressmaker like herself.

Alas, I was prone to heaving huge sighs of relief (privately, of course) after all the threading, darning, and delicate stitching sessions. By the time I was six years old, I would finish my sewing lessons and head straight to the front parlor to sit under the baby grand piano. There I read books, wrote in my diary, and penned letters to my friends back home in New York. The seamstress aspect did not stick with me, but I have vivid memories of nearly every one of my grandmother's gowns, dresses, and suits. They hung in an enormous walk-in closet that completely defied the outward appearance of my grandparents' farmhouse in Temple, with its Jersey cows, woodstove, homegrown squash, and hand-cooked cherry jam. I can still see the glittering jewelry with which Grammy accessorized her outfits, along with her stylish shoes, hats in hatboxes stacked five-high, lamb's wool and beaver fur coats, and colorful jackets made of serge, tweed, and about 14 other fabrics.

It would take too long to tell the whole story, but here are some of the formative experiences and hands-on training that led to this book: Around age 16, I attended Barbizon School of Modeling in Philadelphia. In my 20s, I worked as a photographic and cosmetics model in New York City, at Saks Fifth Avenue and Bloomingdale's, and in Japan, primarily Tokyo, but also in Hiroshima, Osaka, and Kobe. I wrote professionally for Time, Inc., Rodale, and other publishers. For these publishers, I wrote mostly for books and magazines, but I also wrote for newsletters and corporate publications. I did public relations for a major maternity wear retailer in North Carolina, creating *Maternity World News,* which covered maternity fashions and health. I formed a funky art wearables T-shirt/sweatshirt company called What Is Art? I wrote numerous fashion articles and blocks of clothing catalog copy and a fun magazine column called "Cheap Chic," and I served as the CEO of One Love for the Tennisseur, an exclusive line of fashionable tennis wear. This tennis wear line was the brainchild of my brother, George, a tennis pro and a man of remarkably astute design, communications, and marketing talents.

There is so much more, including a long immersion in photography. There's all the magazine and book and Web site editorial experience that exposed me to working with dozens of amazing individuals, including art directors, production editors, artists, photographers, photo editors, writers, fact-checkers, graphic designers, publicists, advertising teams, and copywriters.

As a college instructor, I am still working with dynamic people. Now it is my colleagues and students who are constantly teaching me what fashion communications is all about.

It is my fondest hope that instructors will find this book useful as a springboard for their own approaches to the topics covered within these chapters. The Practice sections can be done either in class or outside of class, in a computer lab, library, or dorm room. The tasks engage students both as individuals and as members of groups, giving them practical experience in teamwork, a skill required in fashion communications environments. I hope students find this textbook helps them hone their critical thinking skills, boost their creativity, and explore all the media forms that serve the strange and magical deity called fashion.

Marian Frances Wolbers
January 2009

INTRODUCTION

What Is Fashion Communications?

The dynamics of fashion depend on visuals: When we see something we like, we respond to its color, line, form, and eye appeal. In that sense, fashion communicates by itself—without words or added graphics. However, the world of fashion demands much more than the mere presence of garments, accessories, and footwear. Fashion involves a wide range of communications, including words—printed, spoken, and electronically transmitted. Those words may serve alone or with images and designs that enhance and illustrate their meaning. Of course, images and designs that explain, explore, enhance, or sell fashion may depend on words to make a point or answer a question.

The term "fashion communications" refers not only to monthly fashion magazines like *Vogue* and *Harper's Bazaar* but also to every facet of information relating to fashion. Fashion communications can be found on multiple levels, from the names of the colors at the dye factory to the latest runway reviews posted on fashion Web sites.

The full range of fashion communications and the wide variety of venues for fashion expression will unfold in the chapters that follow and will focus on three key arenas: business and trade, promotions and publicity, and representation in mainstream media. Included in each chapter are profiles and interviews of individuals and companies, as well as suggested assignments and exercises. The Practice sections are located at the end of each chapter and are designed to help students develop the critical thinking and creative skills necessary for mastering the unique language of fashion.

Acknowledgments

I extend deep gratitude to the visionary Olga Kontzias of Fairchild Books, Fairchild Books' Development Editor Rob Phelps, my "editorial right hand" Kerry Boderman, writers Hella Rose Bloom and Claudia Strauss, fact-checker Bernadette Sukley, and teaching mentor Connie Heller Horacek. I would also like to thank Fairchild's Editorial Development Director Jennifer Crane, Senior Production Editor Elizabeth Marotta, Associate Art Director Erin Fitzsimmons, and reviewers Don Brewer of Sierra College, Pandora Neiland of IADT Seattle, and Barbara Dyer, of Florida State University.

A very special thanks goes to all the companies, institutions, and individuals who graciously gave interviews, artwork, permissions to reprint, expertise, commentary, and editorial and moral support to make this project a reality. These parties include: Albright College fashion students, Allen Abbott, Jacquie Atkins, Mary Baskett, Jon Bekken, Carmen Jewel Bloom, Kenneth Bloom, Rosemary Brutico, Alberto Cacicedo, and Ed Christian. I would also like to thank the Cincinnati Art Museum, James Cucinotta, John Dever, Susan Faeder, Kim Gilde, Robin Givhan, Annie Leibovitz, Chris Lindland, Zomi Bloom Nigh, Michele Obi, Madelyn Shaw, Jill Smith, and Bill Thomas.

part i

FASHION COMMUNICATIONS— A LAYERED LOOK

UNDERSTANDING THE NUTS AND BOLTS—THE PRACTICAL ELEMENTS—OF fashion is crucial to effective communication.

Chapter 1, Fashion Information from the Inside Out, explores the basic need for clarity in information, starting from the ground floor of the companies involved in fashion, with references to historical precedents. Thinking more deeply about the origins of attire in the most practical sense helps fashion communicators grow accustomed to recognizing the many layers involved in assembling fashion information.

Chapter 2, Understanding Raw Materials, also takes a historical focus. The chapter also examines technology and its repercussions, the realities of construction elements underlying fashion essentials, and the impact of science and invention. Understanding the materials used in creating garments and accessories leads to fashion communications that are richer in verbal description and illustrative power.

Chapter 3, Laboring for Fashion: Influences from the Industry, discusses fashion from a perspective that includes the wide range of people who comprise the fashion workforce, including workers, industry journalists, and others of varying levels of influence, who typically receive little attention and yet are vital to the smooth functioning of the system. Consideration of the methods that persons in the industry have historically used and currently use to communicate with each other gives fashion communicators important insights regarding avenues of information.

CHAPTER ONE

Fashion Information from the Inside Out

"The insides are as magnificent as the outside."

GEORGE SIMONTON

fashion designer, describing haute couture

CHAPTER OBJECTIVES

The information presented in this chapter is designed to help you understand:

- The multiple levels encompassed by fashion communications, starting from the ground floor of the manufacturer's facility on up.
- The importance of observing historical precedents in fashion.
- The basic, clear need for accurate information in the fashion industry.

Ideally, after reading this chapter, you will:

- Think more deeply about the origins of attire.
- Recognize that many layers are involved in putting together fashion information.

Where does fashion come from? Does it come from the Paris runway, or from young people on the hippest streets of Tokyo?

How do people get their information about fashion? Do they get it from photos in a magazine? Designer Web sites? A store rack?

How is fashion communicated in society? The red carpet at the Oscars? A cell phone photo?

In the twenty-first century, becoming informed about fashion is infinitely more complex than such simple answers as "the runway" or "magazines." The **information revolution** has brought access to fashion words and images to the masses. People in Western countries simply assume the existence of information about fashion. They rarely think deeply about how that body of knowledge reaches the public.

One hundred years ago, information connections were more evident, more tangible, and more traceable. This was because fashionable dress was dictated by certain powerful, well-established forces of wealth and artisanship. At this point in history, there were millions of Americans working in cotton fields, textile mills, dye houses, fiber mills, tanneries, and apparel factories (Figure 1.1). They raised sheep for wool, made thread, and embroidered labels. Some people were dressmakers who worked at home, in a shop, or traveled from town to town, creating wardrobes on commission. Some people were tailors. The dressmakers and tailors usually strove to keep up with fashion trends, and they often carried fashionable fabrics and designs from the cities out into the countryside.

With the advent of **prêt-a-porter**, or market-ready, factory-finished clothing, thousands of garment workers swung into action, creating standard-size pieces of clothing that were deemed modern, acceptable, and desirable by the populace. Many people in cities were directly acquainted with at least one assembly-line worker who was connected to the garment trade. It was not unusual to hear "My mother works in a silk mill" or "My uncle fixes knitting machinery."

Today, fewer and fewer Americans know what a sewing machine looks like; in fact, many Americans have never held a needle and thread in their hands. It is not surprising that the average person cannot find the vocabulary with which to describe the garment he or she just bought. Today's consumer might not know what country a garment came from, or who designed it. For these consumers, the hangtag and label (sewn in or stamped on) solve that problem and give the consumers the information they need. The information on a hangtag includes: size, fiber(s) or other materials used in construction, the company name / designer name, the country where the garment was manufactured or assembled, and the price. A separate label carries laundering details. Sometimes, safety information is also included as required by law (e.g., whether or not a material is fire-retardant, or whether a long tie string should be kept away from babies).

Interestingly enough, the classified ads you find in a newspaper and the listings on career Web sites like *www.monster.com* do not usually list job openings for "Fashion Communicators," the people who make sure that fashion-related information gets to the public. Occupations in fashion communications are difficult to describe because fashion communication occurs on many levels, from the idea in a designer's mind to the factory floor, to the many media used to bring fashion information to the public. Fashion communications is not an easy career to define.

The term **fashion communicator** is a general, two-word phrase that encompasses the entire range of persons whose lives and/or livelihoods have an effect on how fashion gets presented and represented, promoted and demoted. *Fashion* is itself a broad and deep field, one involving style and apparel but not restricted to it; *communications* is a field that basically covers everything from whispering to speechwriting.

Figure 1.1   Checking threads, Catoir Silk Mill, Catasauqua, PA.

Fashion communications at its very best requires full comprehension of individual styles, looks, and apparel, from the bottom up and from the inside out. Each style, each look, each piece of apparel that adorns the human body invites the fashion communicator to trace an item back to its origin. Being able to account for the goods that comprise the physical manifestations of fashion constitutes an integral part of discovering how fashion can best be communicated to society at large.

ACCESSING CORE INFORMATION

Information is the bedrock of all communications. When it comes to the field of fashion, a common misconception exists that the type of information involved is 99 percent visual. At every level, fashion communicators concern themselves with a fashion language that is characterized by descriptive information derived from the source of the garments or accessories themselves.

When it comes to the pinnacle of design, **haute couture**, a term that literally means "high sewing" or "high fashion," the average person benefits from definitions and details that explain why haute couture is as compelling, and as expensive, as it is.

Journalist Lauren Sherman discussed this subject in an article she wrote for *Forbes* on June 28, 2006. *Forbes* is a publication whose readers are potential investors in haute couture creations:

> *Haute couture.* The French phrase, which literally means "high sewing," is tossed around casually these days, into fashion magazine headlines and onto the labels of irreverent knitwear brands. But in fashion parlance, haute couture is something very specific: a garment that is completely custom-made, from impeccable lining to hand-stitched hem. Not only is the dress **bespoke** [custom-made], the fabrics and embellishments are of the highest quality, and the tailors, seamstresses, embroiderers, lace makers, and other craftspeople who spend hundreds of hours assembling these pieces are the most skilled in the world.

With this introduction, Sherman establishes that the particulars of each designer creation are critically important. She points out that a Versace dress, for example, may take four months to complete, and then she describes the exact materials and other original features that serve to make a dress distinctive:

> Take one in particular, a 1920s-inspired gown made of dove grey chiffon. Decorated with delicate metal decals and a beaded fringe, it carries more than 50,000 Swarovski crystal beads, and took more than 150 man-hours to assemble. It's priced accordingly at around $90,000. (Sherman 2006)

Thanks to this **verbal description**, a fashion enthusiast is given the sort of core information he or she needs to make a judgment about an haute couture garment. Of course, since haute couture garments come directly from design houses, the designer and his or her staff are primarily responsible for providing the information needed for accurate fashion communications.

For **ready-to-wear** markets, information is available from a much broader range of sources. Manufacturers themselves are one obvious source. On the industry level, at least in the United States, one baseline source for general apparel manufacturing information is the federal government. The U.S. Census Bureau reports regularly on the numbers of people who are fashion designers, garment factory owners, apparel workers, and more (Figure 1.2). Table 1.1 presents **U.S. Department of Labor** statistics from the *Occupational Outlook Handbook, 2008–09 Edition*. You can also use the Internet to search under keywords like "apparel manufacturers" or "accessory manufacturers." Internet researchers will see that the Web sites these searches generate are the tip of a very large iceberg. It takes some degree of experience and expertise to discover the Web sites that contain the most valuable information.

The best fashion communicators go to great lengths to learn as much as they can about the garments, designers, and trends they are publicizing. The more knowledge they have, the more effective their efforts are at presenting that information to the public.

How to Become a Style Dissector

How can fashion communicators get to the source of style? How can fashion communicators access core information for a better understanding of fashion's underpinnings? Often, the process of discovery requires fashion communicators to assume a child's curiosity.

Think about the following scenario, a scenario unrelated to fashion: Somewhere in America, a third-grade teacher is asking her class, "Where do you think peas come from?" Some of the students will immediately answer, "The grocery store." Those are the kids who accompanied Mom or Dad to the frozen foods section, where peas and carrots are neatly packaged in plastic bags, staying hard and cold from store to home freezer, until heated up for the dinner plate. A few of the students know better. They will answer, "Peas come from a farm." "They come from a plant." Now the discussion is rolling. More questions emerge. "What kind of plant? A tree, or a bush, or a vine? Do peas grow on the ground or in the ground?" Finally, the discussion can evolve into the science lesson that the teacher had planned all along: about plants, soil, leaves, nutrients, water, sun, chlorophyll, photosynthesis, insects, and more. The complexity and wonders of the world become an open road for discovery.

A century ago, a question about where peas come from would not have been so hard for students to answer. The sons and daughters of farmers and backyard vegetable growers would already have known well what a pea pod looked like and felt like.

So what do peas and photosynthesis have to do with fashion?

Because modern society has become so detached from the sources of the goods they buy, and because people have come to assume that clothing magically makes its way into stores and eventually onto their bodies, fashion communicators must go the extra mile

TABLE 1.1   TEXTILE AND APPAREL WORKERS IN THE UNITED STATES

The information below comes from a government report in the U.S. Department of Labor's *Occupational Outlook Handbook, 2008–09 Edition*. Textile, apparel, and furnishings workers held 873,000 jobs in 2006. Employment in the detailed occupations that make up this group was distributed as follows:

OCCUPATION	NUMBER OF WORKERS
Laundry and dry-cleaning workers	239,000
Sewing machine operators	233,000
Pressers, textile, garment, and related materials	77,000
Upholsterers	55,000
Tailors, dressmakers, and custom sewers	54,000
Textile winding, twisting, and drawing out machine setters, operators, and tenders	43,000
Textile knitting and weaving machine setters, operators, and tenders	40,000
Sewers, hand	23,000
Textile bleaching and dyeing machine operators and tenders	19,000
Textile cutting machine setters, operators, and tenders	19,000
Extruding and forming machine setters, operators, and tenders, synthetic and glass fibers	18,000
Shoe and leather workers and repairers	16,000
Fabric and apparel pattern makers	9,200
Shoe machine operators and tenders	4,100
All other textile, apparel, and furnishings workers	24,000

Manufacturing jobs are concentrated in California, North Carolina, Georgia, New York, Texas, and South Carolina. Jobs in reupholstery, shoe repair and custom leatherwork, and laundry and dry-cleaning establishments are found in cities and towns throughout the [United States]. Overall, about 12 percent of all workers in textile, apparel, and furnishings occupations were self-employed; however, about half of all tailors, dressmakers, and sewers and about a quarter of all upholsterers were self-employed. *(Bureau of Labor Statistics, 2008)*

to know the specifics of dress. They must always strive to educate themselves about the particulars of textiles, man-made and natural materials, and embellishments in order to create a personal database of information from which to communicate well.

The main method for deepening comprehension is dissection, a strategy for examining something in detail. In a science class, you might dis-sect an object by looking at its

Figure 1.2   Many garments are constructed overseas.

smaller parts. The strategy is similar in fashion. You might dissect a garment by examining the materials that comprise it. Thus, **style dissection** is the process by which people examine fashion in great detail. Style dissection starts with dissecting language as well as images. Images are a critical part of fashion information. However, all images eventually need words to describe them.

To be most efficient in mastering the language of fashion, it helps to remember that:

1. Clues lie in language construction. Taking everyday words apart—everyday words like *fashion* and *communication*—is an exercise that lends itself to thinking more deeply and strengthening some of the key skills required for effective fashion communications. These skills include accuracy in description, appropriate power (in word and image), and dynamic reflection of the core concept intended (Box 1.1).

2. Asking the question "Where does _____ come from?" is a critical first question for style dissection.

3. History invariably plays a part. Understanding the origins of attire in the most practical sense, from the field to the factory and beyond, familiarizes fashion com-municators with the many layers involved in putting together information. That history may involve an artistic movement, a religious dictate, the cinema, ecology, scientific advances, or many other fields of study.

4. Case in point: A close look at a **fashion classic**, the khaki, reveals a rich history that begins with the word "khaki" itself. A classic is an enduring style or fashion item, in this case "characterized by simple tailored lines" (*Merriam-Webster's 10th Edition 1993*). Khaki pants or slacks have become a mainstay of summer wardrobes for many Americans, both male and female (Figure 1.3). Extending beyond summer and warm weather wear, khakis have also made their way into school wardrobes in many public and private schools from north to south, east to west. So, the appropriate question to ask is: "Where do khakis come from?"

BOX 1.1

EXAMINING WORD ORIGINS

Nothing beats a good dictionary for a good definition—but not just any dictionary will do. Buying a hardcover dictionary that includes word origins is crucial to boosting your knowledge of words, and it is a valuable tool for all online research. For example:

"Where does the word *fashion* come from?"

Fashion is both a noun (a thing) and a verb (an action word). The word can be traced back to the Latin word for "to make" or "to do," which is *facere*. This word evolved into Middle English forms, including *facioun*, or *fasoun*, meaning "shape" or "manner." More definitions entered the dictionary over time. One *Webster's* version (10th edition) gives this verb form: "to make or construct usually with the use of imagination or ingenuity." As a noun, *Webster's* defines fashion as "prevailing style (as in dress) during a particular time" and/or "a garment in such a style."

"Where does the word *communication* come from?"

Like many other English words, *communication* can be followed back to Roman times when the verb *communicare* meant "to impart" or "participate." *Communicare* can be traced to the word *communis*, or "common." Thus, communications refers to sharing or presenting information in order to get a message across, with mutual understanding as the underlying goal.

5. In Profile 1.1, the owner of Bills Khakis describes how good communications practices drive sales of that company's classic trousers. A sense of history is important to this company, so its Web site carries a special page devoted to that topic.

6. Fashion involves almost every aspect of culture, including agriculture, science and technology, mathematics, foreign languages, and art. The discovery process leads to subjects like horticulture and biology, sheepherding and animal husbandry, industrial

Figure 1.3 Public schools have increasingly adopted khakis as part of their school uniform.

advances and laboratory research, gemology, linguistics and psychology, sociology and anthropology, history, business, and philosophy. The list of disciplines of scholarship and inquiry that are connected to fashion is endless.

Fashion communications as a topic contains a natural richness. Its effectiveness depends on a well-developed bank of knowledge.

PRACTICE: ADOPTING A RESEARCH MIND-SET

These research-focused activities call for analytical approaches to thinking about fashion more deeply, from the inside out.

Create a Garment Profile

Follow a garment from start to finish. The garment may be a swimsuit, belt, sweater, or any other specific fashion item, past or present.

(*continued on page 19*)

THE KHAKI MAN: AN INTERVIEW WITH BILL THOMAS OF BILLS KHAKIS

Bill Thomas's office is in a rehabilitated brick building with gorgeous hardwood floors and lots of natural light. On the day of this interview, the L-shaped desk area with computer was cleared of paper, but along one side of the floor, a most interesting array of catalogs, books, fabrics, and more were arranged in neat piles. Sporty, but luxurious, men's jackets were hanging against a window, waiting their turn for attention from the busy owner and creative director of Bills Khakis (*www.billskhakis.com*).

The "History" page on Bills Khakis Web site uses storytelling to deepen customer appreciation and build loyalty.

What a beautiful office! I like the evidence of creativity, too. If your office were spotlessly clean, I would be wondering . . .

Well, I'm not proud of this "creative mess." [Laughs] In fact, I need to clean it up. It's not good. Organization in a business is critical. And I'm not by nature a well-organized person, not to the level I need to be. That's a fault. It doesn't come naturally to me.

But you need things, items, around as part of the creative process. You need to sort through things, right?

When you're in a creative frame of mind, your mind doesn't want to take the time to be organized because it can't go there. But I suppose that it's not unusual for someone who's in more of a creative role to be not as organized as someone who's in a managerial role.

Is that why a creative guy like you hires other people?

[Laughing again] Well, more and more people join your effort because they realize how desperately you need them.

Khaki pants *do* undergo changes from year to year, don't they?

Well, that's what actually is unique about ours. Our tagline, our trademarked tagline, is "We made Bills better by not changing a thing." So it's what doesn't change about Bills Khakis that is the core and crux of our brand. And that, in a fashion world, is a complete oxymoron. We're an anti-fashion fashion company. And when I say "anti-fashion," it's not like we reject it. But the nature of our product is khakis. Khakis at their root don't change.

Once a man finds a great pair of khakis, all he really wants to do is go back and find them again. And go back and find them again. And pretty much have it that way for the rest of his life. And not have anyone move his cheese. He wants it just as it was the last time. That's not to say you don't need a little variety along the way. When it comes to a really good old pair of khakis, change is bad. [Smiles]

"We're an anti-fashion fashion company."

What about women and khakis?

We've dabbled in marketing to women, but not with a product specifically designed for women. All we've done is try to say, "Hey, some women wear Bills Khakis and [think] they're great." But it's more of a Katharine Hepburn sort of thing. It's a Saturday afternoon not Saturday night.

So, the nature of your product, what makes your product unique, is that it doesn't change essentially.

The essence doesn't change. Some of this is really captured on our Web site. We have a newsletter there, which is nothing more than just a place where we write about stuff that happens at Bills Khakis or things that are somehow pertinent to the essence of khakis.

(continued on next page)

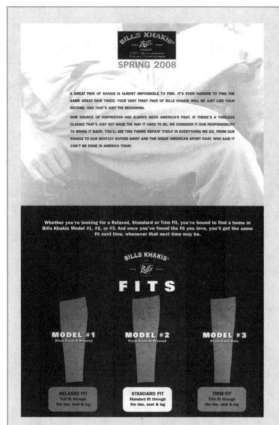

Creative descriptions of Bills Khakis products support and propel the distribution end of the business through a print catalog for sales reps.

When did you start the newsletter?

Seven or eight years ago. We call it the "Free Press" because we used to get a lot of free press. We still do. It was kind of a joke to ourselves. So anyway, if you go to our homepage, there's a button for "Free Press." Let me see if I can find it for you. Okay—"Khakis versus Blue Jeans." That really gets to the essence of khakis and, in the process, talks a lot about why khakis don't change.

Did you write that piece?

Yeah.

Do you write all of the newsletters?

Well, I'm basically in charge of getting them all together. Typically, I'd say I write about 75 percent of it.

On a regular basis?

Twice a year. We used to print it—and we may go back to printing it, but right now it's just online.

What about embellishments, hems, and sizes? Does any of that change at all?

Not at our core. We have two products, two portions of our product line, and one is our standard stock program. The other is what we call Limited Edition. Limited Edition is about our seasonal 25 percent of stuff that is off the beaten path. It's new. Now, it's critical that Limited Edition is consistent with the brand as we see it, as we determine it. It's not that we do things that we feel are out of our character to do. But I might have a hard time articulating to someone why a pair of kalamkari-print shorts—which are a tapestry-like material—would have anything to do with the essence of WWII khakis or a company that's based on or started from a WWII khaki. To me it makes sense. I see it very clearly.

I'd love to hear more. I know khaki goes back to India.

Well, it doesn't have to be that literal. But we look at our core customer, our target customer, and in our own minds we have a sense of "Who is this guy?" and we know that the guy's not always wearing khakis—I mean, he's a khaki guy, but yeah, he wants to break out a little bit, so he will want to wear a pair of madras shorts. It really goes back to more of a period of post war that existed from like post WWII till probably around the mid- to late 1960s. And that's the period of time that I think our brand, from a traditional mind-set, kind of captures.

How old is your target customer? What is the age range?

Really, it's anyone from 18 to 65, but it's probably more focused to 25 to 65. And I can whittle it down even more to say [age] 30 to 65 because the specialty stores [that we sell in] are very much geared toward servicing that customer. Our distribution services the customer who is not the 18-to-25 customer. That's not because it couldn't be our customer, but it's just because our distribution covers high-end men's specialty, so it naturally caters to someone who is 25 and up, more than 18 to 25.

That established, what kind of language are you using when you're addressing this customer, for instance when you're writing the newsletter, or you're putting together the Web site? The language seems as though it's written for someone who has a certain level of education or possesses a certain level of cultural advantage or knowledge.

Well, I think that there's a tonality, and the Bills Khakis brand, which I think all of us here can internally buy into, has a tonality and character to it that's a combination of a lot of things: It's simple. It's down to earth. It's humble. It doesn't take itself too seriously. But it's also authentic. It is values-based, values-driven. If I had to say what Bills Khakis represents, I'd say it is a nostalgic metaphor for America. It's an Americana brand. As soon as you say Americana, what's that? Well, that's a lot of things. That's a thick stew.

So, all of that sense of what Bills Khakis is goes into how you speak when you present the brand. Is it "smart"? Well, I like to think of Bills Khakis as a thinking-man's brand. We'd all like to think that. But we don't want to say that it's for a serious thinker— it's just someone who is thoughtful about things and

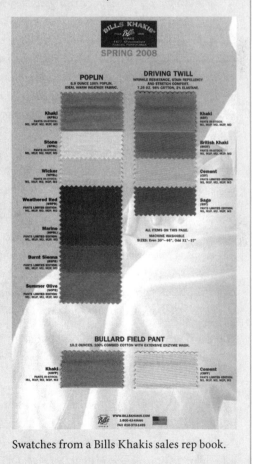

Swatches from a Bills Khakis sales rep book.

(continued on next page)

wants to connect. You know, someone who's looking for brands and things to connect with that represent something. I think consumers like connecting to things they find common value in or they identify with in some way, shape, or form.

The voice that Bills Khakis is—is a voice that is consistent with who we are. It's not really so much what message are we trying to put forth. We're just speaking in a voice of who we are. Are we trying to sell through that? Yes, but that's not our motivation. Our motivation is to present our brand, and then we hope other people identify with that. Now, as marketers we're doing that in an honest way. We're not doing that in a manipulative way. We're not doing the brand-was-invented-in-a-boardroom thing, like: "Okay, now, how do we want to make this brand sound? Well, we want to make it sound like this." A lot of companies do that. And they're big companies.

This company's authenticity is a grounding value, and it's authentic not because we want to try to be authentic. It's authentic because everything we do here pretty much comes from our heart. It's real and it's genuine, and in everything that we do. Not only in terms of the brand and what the product is, but [in] how the company is managed, how the stakeholders see us, and value the relationship that we've been able to develop with them, whether it's a supplier or a retailer. Because we really have two end customers. Well, we have one end customer and that's the consumer. But because 90 percent of our business is done wholesale through men's specialty stores, our customer is really also the retailer.

Since our distribution is through men's specialty stores, we spend an awful lot of time trying to help our wholesale customer be successful with our product and help them achieve their goals, which is making money and winning life-loyal customers. That's what it comes down to.

So, communication with the retailers is pretty critical?

Yes. We probably spend more of our time communicating with them than we do the end consumer. But we spend time communicating with both, and I think it's a very balanced approach. It [would] be hard to sit here and say we're focused on one more than the other. I think a lot of companies in the wholesale trade focus strongly on retail, with not as much consumer focus as we have, and our consumer focus is not analyzed, and studied, and focus-grouped, and all that kind of stuff. It's just what we feel.

You don't do much with focus groups?

No. We're not going into anything with a $20 million launch where we know we need to have the science to back us up to warrant the investment.

Getting back to how you write . . . you said the word "Americana." And you said a "thinking man."

[Hedging] That's aspirational on our part. That's part of a visionary statement for us. To connect with Bills Khakis it requires, I think, a couple [of] different levels. . . . If you connect on the surface level,

it's just, "Gimme a product that's good for not a lot of money. I don't care what it is. I want to wear it and move on and come back and not put much thought into it."

If you're the type of person that likes to buy things and say, "What's going on with this company? Or what's going on here? I want to know more about it." That's really more of a conscientious consumer, someone who wants to connect and identify with those products and the companies behind them. There are people out there that do that. I mean, I'm a little bit like that.

But the Americana reference, can't that be JCPenney? Your writing style is pretty different, I'd say, from Penney's.

Well, yeah. JCPenney has a target customer, and their target customer is more price-sensitive. Our target customer is 25 to 65, and someone we assume has a higher income to afford our product. Our product is more expensive for two reasons. One, we choose to strive to make the best. And second, we absolutely choose to make our product in America. So, those two basic fundamental facts or assumptions lend themselves to a more expensive product. A certain customer is able to afford our product. A lower-income person would not . . . And by the way, I shop at [local department store] BonTon, too. I drive a Chevy.

[Regarding copy writing for Bills:] When you're selling a Rolex, you're probably speaking a different language than if you were selling a Timex. Now a Rolex is an example of a pretty pretentious brand. They try to be. They're sponsoring equestrian events, and that's their target market. I think I'd be trying to do the same thing if I were them.

We, by nature, have to put ourselves in position, when we do market, to be seen by people who are our target audience. Otherwise, we're going to be paying for impressions or spending time and resources to get impressions for people who couldn't afford our products.

Are you a speaker and a "hearer" more than a reader?

No, I'm more a writer than I am a speaker.

I see a lot of catalogs here on the floor of your office. What do you look at most?

You know, catalog-wise, I get J. Crew, so I look at it. Brooks Brothers catalogs—I usually throw those away. I get this one from a company in San Francisco. It's really pushing the envelope for us. It's real fashion. The balance we have to strike in our product line is timeless and timely, at the same time. So, as I said, there's 25 percent of our line that has to stay fresh and new and different and—I don't want to say "hip" because that would really be a stretch—but you know we have to be timely because retailers, maybe even more so than consumers, pretty much thrive on that. They're in the fashion business. To a certain degree, we have to play in that arena in our own way, to remain relevant in their eyes, because they get tired of you. They just lose their focus on you. They get excited about other things—and they sell other things.

(continued on next page)

17

And so how do you keep up? What do you scan to keep up with things? Are you a museum-goer? Moviegoer? Is it travel that informs you? Is it looking at Scottish estate tweed? [Referring to an item within reach of Bill's desk]

Yeah, right. [Laughs]

So what do you do to keep up?

I think it's a combination of all the above. I think from a pure product standpoint it's a combination of what's going on in our heads and what's going on out there. "Out there" is not only other products within our distribution, but also, what are we hearing from our retailers? What are their needs? We can certainly take leads from that. What are we seeing outside of our distribution? You always keep your eye on what's going on there.

Do you read trade magazines? Which ones?

I do read trade magazines. DNR and MR are two [of them], but usually when we read something there, more often than not we've already heard about it. Our retailers are a really good source because they give us comments, suggestions. They communicate with us all the time. We have very good relationships.

How do you keep in such close touch?

On the phone, sometimes via e-mail, through our sales reps. We have independent sales reps who travel around the country. And they carry several other lines, but they'll speak to their sales reps and if the sales rep feels it's pertinent information, they'll communicate that back to us. So it can happen that way. It could happen through an e-mail directly to us or through our customer service. It could be face-to-face at a trade show. It could be while we're visiting the store—it involves an in-store visit with the rep.

Which trade shows do you go to? Do you have a select group?

Yeah, there's a fixed number of trade shows within the men's higher-end apparel. The biggest one is called MAGIC in Las Vegas. We attend that. The second one is called the Collective, and that's in New York and that has more of a high-end focus to it, it's not as big. And then there are more regionally focused shows. In Chicago, Dallas, Charlotte . . . and beyond that there are some even smaller regional shows.

When your sales reps communicate your line, they're taking along printed media with them?

Yes. The size of our line, in terms of the different products that we make, has increased from just pants to back-pocket jeans-style pants to sport coats and woven shirts and knit shirts, and that's happened in a very short period of time.

Are all these items still made in the United States?

Yes. Everything's made here. The most we'll do is import the fabric. So our tags will either read "Made in USA" or "Made in USA of Imported Fabric." And there's quite a bit of fabric that we have a hard time sourcing here. So, we can't even get some of it here.

Linens?

Linen, seersucker, corduroy . . .

These just aren't being made here?

No, or if it is made here, it's not being made to the quality that we need. More often than not, it's not being made here.

Who puts your interesting catalogs together?

Well, it's a combination of myself and our marketing team. We'll sit down. The whole product development process is a collaborative effort between a bunch of people.

Mary Jo, who is our director of sales and marketing, really spearheads putting this together. She manages getting this book together. This book's a team effort.

So there's communication going on there, too.

Yes, all the time. Meetings. We have a process laid out [for in-house communication].

Last question: Who does the naming, who thinks up these adjectives and color descriptions in your books? The "sun-drenched" and "the island" and "sand," "straw," "summer olive" references, for instance. Are they just refs to living the vacation life?

[Laughs] Honestly, it's what feels right for that fabric. And some of it is just baloney. It's a feel for what the fabric is, and there's a point where you could call it anything and if you don't have a good name for it, hey, "island twill," okay!

(continued from page 11)

Explore the terminology and any manufacturing documentation available (e.g., internal communication from the maker) pertaining to the garment in order to illustrate the underpinnings of an item that is created, marketed, and sold.

At the library, research the item to find out how, where, when, and why it developed. List key words that were used to describe or name the item and its characteristics. See Box 1.2 for a list of important tips on how to prevent **plagiarism.**

This presentation may be explored in an essay, PowerPoint, storyboards, poster, online, oral format, or a combination of them.

BOX 1.2

LEGAL BRIEF: PREVENTING PLAGIARISM

Plagiarism, intentionally or unintentionally using someone else's words or ideas (typically from a Web site, book, article, or other published materials) as if they are one's own, is a serious form of academic dishonesty. Outside of school, in the real world, the consequences of plagiarism include lawsuits, loss of reputation, significant monetary fines, ruined careers, and more. Take this mini-test to find out what you know.

TRUE or FALSE?

1. When a student summarizes an author's ideas, he or she sometimes begins by writing the phrase: "This article (book, etc.) discusses . . . "

2. Using one to four words taken directly from the author is not plagiarism. Technically speaking, plagiarism involves using five or more words of the author's original work.

3. Most colleges and other schools do not care about plagiarism too much. They know that students write essays using wording that has been cut and pasted from the Internet, and they have accepted the fact that plagiarism is common in today's society.

4. Placing quotation marks before and after words taken from a source is one way to avoid plagiarism.

(*continued on next page*)

Locate Your Wardrobe's Origins

Armed with a pad and pen, go through your closet and bureau (or shelves) and write down the label information from 20 to 50 items of clothing (not the laundering instructions—just the manufacturer's label). Bring the list to class. Within groups, or as a class, tally the results by country of origin. Which country's name appears the most often? Which country's name appears least frequently? Are there surprises? Discuss the results.

Start a Fabric and Embellishments Bank

This is a long-term project. Start setting aside samples of fabrics that you can label and return to as references, as well as embellishments (beads, buttons, etc.) that you can

---

BOX 1.2 (*continued*)

Answers:

1. True. As long as the student is summarizing the author *in the **student's** own words*—not slightly altering the author's sentences or word phrases—the student is giving credit to the source of information, and asserting that the information is not the student's own creation.

2. False. Plagiarism can be prosecuted with just one word, especially if the word was coined by the author. Always use quotation marks when picking up words, phrases, or sentences directly from a source.

3. False. Depending on the school, plagiarism may result in a failing grade and/or expulsion and a tarnished academic record. Plagiarism can follow you after school, too. Your professors may be unwilling to write recommendations for internships and job opportunities.

4. True. Properly quoting your sources takes some practice, but it does enable the writer to take especially good information and weave it into a paper, as long as the writer always gives credit and strictly observes copyright and intellectual property regulations.

Helpful resources: *MLA Handbook for Writers of Research Papers* is one of many good sources of information on avoiding plagiarism. Online sources are also available using "preventing plagiarism" as keywords.

---

categorize according to their material (glass, plastic, etc.). Adding their places of origin—where they are found or made—further enriches your personal resource bank of information.

Find a creative way to set up this personal resource bank by constructing a box or file system. Alternatively, set up a virtual information bank on a Web site database.

"What's It Made Of?" Challenge

If you have not taken a course in textile science, challenge yourself to learn more about common fabrics (see Box 1.3). You might explore the answers to questions like these:

- What is denim, and how did it get its name?
- Is seersucker a style or a fabric?
- What is the origin of cashmere? Why is cashmere so soft?
- How did panty hose originate?

BOX 1.3

WHAT'S THE DIFFERENCE
BETWEEN LINEN AND COTTON?

The well-rounded fashion communicator is never content with surface information. He or she always wants to know more. It is important to know the difference between descriptive words like "linen" and "cotton."

Among the many sources for accurate textile information are professional associations, books, nonprofit organizations, and commercial Web sites. Cotton Inc. *www.cottoninc.com*, an industry site, offers an interesting Q&A section on its sister site, The Fabric of Our Lives *www.thefabricofourlives.com*. There, a *"Did You Know?"* section gives easy-to-follow answers, including one for the cotton-linen question: "Natural fibers fall into two main groups: protein fibers, which come from animals, and vegetable fibers, which come from plants. The main ingredient in all vegetable fibers is cellulose, a carbohydrate found in all plant life. Both cotton and linen are vegetable fibers. Linen is made from the flax plant, cotton is made from the cotton plant."

- Were the first bathing suits made of wool?
- What is canvas?
- Is an "alligator" shoe really made of alligators?

Dissect Style

Ask someone, a roommate, classmate, friend, or family member, to describe what he or she is wearing, from head to toe. The instructions are: "Please tell me what you can about your outfit today. Just describe it for me, as best you can." Be prepared to write down (or record) what they say, word for word, offering no help, but simply interviewing the person, as a reporter would do.

Review all the words your interview subject used and analyze them. Did he or she discuss color? Shape? Silhouette? Materials? Fabrics? Zippers or other fastenings?

Next, check yourself. Without looking at labels, how well can you describe an outfit in your closet or what you are wearing? (See Box 1.4 for a range of descriptions.)

Option: Interview or consult one or more fashion professionals to dissect and analyze their styles.

BOX 1.4

WHERE A FASHION SEARCH MAY LEAD

Dissecting style can lead fashion communicators in a thousand different directions. The depth and breadth of descriptive details will vary according to the source. For example:

- A tie-dye T-shirt sporting a major, ready-to-wear label might have traveled through a wholesale tie-dye outfitter like ColorTone, which claims: to be "the largest tie-dye outfitter in the country" (United States), adding, "Our tie-dye work is seen all over North America in McDonald's, Gap Kids, Wal-Mart, K-Mart, Sears, Calvin Klein, Looney Tunes, Animal Kingdom, and NFL teams."

  Source: www.color-tone.com

- A handmade "drop" bag by Howling Ruth Productions may trace its origins to vintage tweed, with a label that reads: "Vintage fabric from 1950s dress witht he original detailing from the neckline accenting handle."

  Source: www.howlingruth.com

- The rhinestones glittering on eveningwear may be the sew-on variety provided by a Swarovski crystal dealer such as K. Gottfried, Inc., with a description that reads: "MC sew-on Cosmic Baguette #3255 Crystal Golden Shadow."

  Source: www.kgottfriedinc.com

- A pair of Gallante Uomo men's dress slacks made in Tuscany and offered online appears to be only a step or two away from the mills, according to the details in this description: "They are produced from luxurious butter-soft Super 110's Vitale Barberis Italian wool in a flat front with quarter-cut hip pockets. The legs are regular straight cut and the inside is lined to the knee."

  Source: www.VavraItaly.com

- A sleeveless red, white, and "dark navy" Betsey Johnson minidress trimmed with white ribboning at the shoulder straps and bodice, with dark lace at the hem, is characterized as a "Butterfly Kisses Charmeuse Tunic with Lace" in 100 percent silk on the designer's collections Web site.

  Source: www.betseyjohnson.com

(continued on next page)

BOX 1.4 (*continued*)

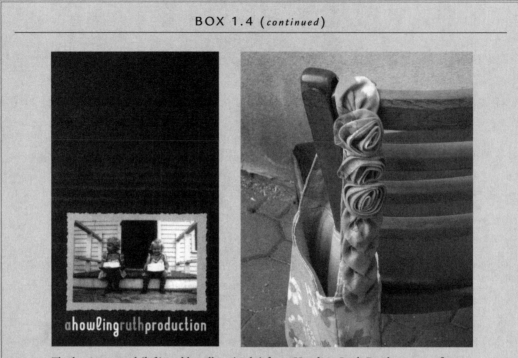

The business card (left) and handbag (right) from Howling Ruth Productions reflect the look and feel of the company.

KEY TERMS

bespoke

fashion classic

fashion communicator

haute couture

information revolution

plagiarism

prêt-a-porter

ready-to-wear

style dissection

U.S. Department of Labor

verbal description

CHAPTER TWO

Understanding Raw Materials

"Form follows function."

LOUIS SULLIVAN
American architect

CHAPTER OBJECTIVES

The information presented here is designed to help you understand:
- The effects of technology on fashion.
- Historical aspects that relate to textiles and clothing construction.
- How inventions influence the descriptions of garments and accessories.

Ideally, after reading this chapter, you will:
- Be familiar with key theories of clothing evolution.
- Recognize the importance of researching origins of fabrics and other raw materials underlying fashion.
- Be aware that a **holistic** view of fashion builds skills in fashion communications.

When MTV stars take the stage, fans eat up what the musicians wear. It's entertainment; it's cutting edge. Above all, it's fashion. With their sheer presence, musicians today communicate who they are and what their music represents, using clothing and accessories to visually support and supplement their sound. Dance and movement are an integral part of this storytelling process. But when the Pussycat Dolls sing, "Loosen up my buttons," anyone watching would find it literally impossible to locate a button on any member of the group. A button—defined as a "small knob or disk secured to clothing . . . and used as a fastener"—requires a buttonhole or loop for loosening to happen. As these high-energy entertainers skip around in heeled boots and swing their hips in the shortest of mini-shorts, it is apparent that they would not be able to cope with buttons or loops while putting on such a wild show (Figure 2.1).

Figure 2.1   Fashion in motion.

In fact, if these songstresses decided to dress in fashionable attire from their great-grand-mothers' days—even if just for fun—they would not even have the option of spandex synthetic fiber, as it was not invented until 1959. Spandex today is a textile that has become standard in most garments that are intended to cling *and* allow movement *and* stay in place on the body (to avoid a "wardrobe malfunction" in public arenas).

Considering how rock fashion has evolved, "loosen up my Lycra" or "un-Velcro me" might be a more accurate lyric. Nonetheless, the button analogy makes its point, and the song's invitation to love is not in question.

Becoming able to express fashion—to write and illustrate and showcase fashion—capably requires, to some extent, two activities:

1. Take a mental walk into the past.
2. **Deconstructing** how form follows function. (The famous phrase "form follows function" is a dictum attributed to architect Louis Sullivan in the late 1800s, and remains an important design concept to this day.)

ENTERTAINMENT AS THE BROTHER OF INVENTION

As an example of looking into the past with an eye on fashion's function, the connection between entertainers and fashion is worth examining. As twentieth-century pop stars and musicians discovered that audiences liked seeing them dance on stage (Elvis Presley, James Brown, Michael Jackson, and Madonna were some famous innovators), they started wearing costumes that incorporated elements of design, form, and construction derived from earlier inventions—inventions that can be traced to the world of acrobatics and dance. Dancers and performers (e.g., circus folk, ballerinas, modern dancers, and jazz dancers) were among the first performers to demand materials that enabled them to move freely without having their clothes come apart. It was the dancers who said, "This leotard invention is good!" And not long after, they said, "Okay, we like the leotards, but how about getting rid of that zipper?" Today, most people cannot imagine or remember that zippers or buttons ever existed on a leotard. Yet they did. In fact, the first leotard was more like a unitard—a full-body, flesh-colored suit that went from French acrobatic performer Jules Leotard's (Figure 2.2) ankles to his wrists.

Figure 2.2 The French acrobat Jules Leotard is forever immortalized in a name adoption that is still used to describe a type of closefitting activewear.

What distinguished the leotard from earlier acrobatic costumes, which lost their form fairly quickly, was its construction out of hand-knitted jersey made from cotton and closely stitched. With jersey, the right side of the fabric (worn outwardly) reveals vertical lines with a smooth sheen while the reverse (inside) part carries a horizontal grain. The technique and fabric together yielded a stretchy "give" along the grain, so that Leotard could show off his trapeze moves and his substantial muscles without worrying that the suit would get baggy during (or after) a performance. Leotard died without knowing that, by the mid-1880s, his name would be applied to a garment that evolved into a sporty, legless mainstay of dancers' and gymnasts' wardrobes and would ignite a race for fabrics that could provide a perfect combination of stretch, comfort, and durability.

According to Elizabeth Khuri, the petroleum-based fabrics that found their way into leotards included various versions of nylon (such as Helenka) and Milliskin, which incorporated Lycra (an elastic fiber, which is also an oil by-product). Today's high-tech leotards feature moisture wicking, a perk that Monsieur Leotard probably could not have even imagined (Khuri 2005).

Fashion evolved historically in ways that directly involved material goods and technological advances in physical materials. As textiles (e.g., wool, cotton, and polyester) and coverings (e.g., leather, animal skins, canvas, and plastics) were discovered and took form in clothing, they met a variety of human needs. These needs tended to match up with advances in civilization and changes in lifestyle. Accessibility to other countries through superior modes of transportation, more disposable income, and ownership of handheld computers—all these are factors that fed into a general expectation that newer, better, and ever-more-intriguing materials are always emerging for the fashion world to work and play with.

Nevertheless, some things always stay the same. Fashion, regardless of which materials it uses, must always function. Getting fashion to function is a challenge that will never disappear.

BLENDING FUNCTION WITH FORM

Marilyn Horn, writing in *The Second Skin* in 1968, sorted through research to conclude that there are basically five main theories of clothing evolution. Those are: **protection and utility**, **modesty** (and immodesty), **status**, **adornment** (how something is decorated), and **extension of self**. The latter two categories, Horn acknowledged, are similar and are sometimes grouped together. For simplicity, this book presents four main categories:

1. **Protection and utility**: Protection and utility (usefulness) are powerful motivating forces when it comes to people and clothing. This theory relates to weather and climate challenges, the need for practical, seasonal approaches to shield the body, so that humans can survive all sorts of conditions, from heat waves to rain and ice storms, as well as avoid harm and injury (Figure 2.3).

2. **Modesty:** The dictates of society have been, and still are, an influence on how humans decide to cover or expose parts of their bodies, adhering to modesty standards that relate to religion, gender roles, age, and more, within particular cultures.

3. **Status:** For centuries, wearing certain garments or assuming a distinctive style of attire and/or adornment has served as a way to set one person apart from another in terms of leadership, wealth, strength, and other measures of social standing.

4. **Adornment** and **extension of self:** This theory includes the concept of using fashion for the sake of aesthetics—sheer beauty—or decoration and adornment. Similarly, fashion may also be used as a way to express or extend the self, i.e., as a way to claim group identity, express individual identity, or show one's philosophical leanings (Horn, 1968).

By and large, the function of fashion may be assumed to fall into one or more of the above categories.

What relevance might these four categories have for fashion communicators? One of the goals of commercial fashion communications is to promote a successful brand, design, or product. To that end, figuring out how to describe, present, and sell a fashion product involves knowing what the potential consumer desires in his or her life. The building blocks of fashion, from raw materials to dress design to clothing construction and beyond, are always affected by function.

Writers and designers who create word and image combinations to convey fashion ask, "What is the main function?" to boost their comprehension of what they see. Taking aim simultaneously

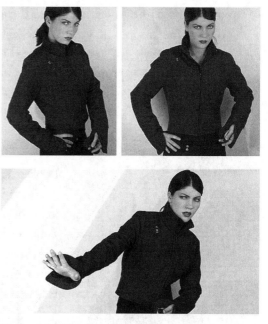

Figure 2.3   This "No-Contact Jacket" falls into the protective category of clothing theory.

at all four theories might be fun, but it usually results in confusion. The majority of people respond, at a gut level, to just one main, highly motivating force at a given time. This may seem like a sweeping statement because human psychology is a complex field of study, which involves exceptions to the rule. (Students yearning to understand human motivation and instinct more deeply can enrich their understanding of themselves and others by studying psychology, including such classics as Sigmund Freud's *Beyond the Pleasure Principle* and works by Erich Fromm—as well as anthropology, sociology, and philosophy.)

What forces are at work in the following scenario? When it starts raining in New York City, the Fifth Avenue sidewalks are soon flooded with designer slickers, eye-catching boots, and an explosion of color-coordinated umbrellas. Protection and adornment seem inextricably merged: Making a splashy appearance with colleagues at an upscale restaurant seems completely instinctual, and is just as important as staying dry. However, if a stylish slicker is not on hand, but an ugly black umbrella or a cheap, clear plastic poncho are available, a person who is heading out to lunch in the rain will likely use one of them. While unflattering, these accessories will still protect his/her clothing.

Using the "what if?" question is a valuable tool to help decide which forces are at work when it comes to covering and uncovering the body. To see how this works, four examples of fashion communications from the advertising world of the twentieth century are given below. They represent some of the last century's most famous **slogans**—or, to use a more contemporary term, **taglines.** These taglines each "speak" primarily to one of the four categories. Notice especially how the materials used to make each product unique are prominently displayed, referenced, and valued.

Figure 2.4   Calvin Klein jeans.

The Four-Theories Ad Challenge

Look over the ads that follow. Consider what the underlying need is in each situation. Then discuss the evolution of each item, brand, or fashion trend based on its raw materials, origins, form, and function. Use library resources to augment your discussion and provide historical context. Which of the four main theories seems to be the driving force behind the ad? Has that driving force changed or stayed the same over time?

"Nothing comes between me and my Calvins."

What does this famous tagline say? In what year did it make its debut? What impression does the Calvin Klein model (Brooke Shields) give to viewers? (See Figure 2.4.) Are jeans seen as protective wear? In the days before women started wearing blue jeans, how were jeans viewed? What does the word *dungaree* mean? How has the form and function of jeans changed over time? Pretend, just for the time being, that this slogan was something very different. What might an alternative tagline say?

"Just Do It."

What does this bossy Nike tagline suggest? When did it first appear in print? How does it differ from the Calvin Klein slogan? What is the feeling, or the impact, of these words and of this image? What materials are involved in the product? How has the athletic shoe evolved over time in terms of form and function? Pretend, just for the sake of stretching the mind, that this item was advertised for its decorative purposes only. (See Figure 2.5.) What other direction(s) could the fashion communications have taken?

Figure 2.5 The Nike swoosh.

"A diamond is forever."

With one of the most famous "it's a fact" taglines in ad history, the DeBeers jewelry brand makes a statement that refers to time, or—rather—timelessness. What does this image suggest to the viewer? When did it debut? Is it still used? How do the words affect the image? (See Figure 2.6.) What is the ring made of? What does science (i.e., physics, geology, paleontology, gemology, etc.) have to do with the raw materials? What does the buyer expect to gain from being seduced by this fashion promise?

Figure 2.6 Diamonds by DeBeers.

"Does she . . . or doesn't she? Hair color so natural only her hairdresser knows for sure!"

This hair-coloring slogan catapulted the Clairol name into fame and promoted a whole new fashion trend: going blond. Considered one of the longest of advertising's most famous taglines, the "here's a question, but we won't tell you the answer" approach hit home for women in the 1950s. Why was it so effective? Which is most prominent as an image, the product or the product result? What does the ad promise? (See Figure 2.7.) What if the same ad were written with a fresh tagline today? Have attitudes shifted with regard to hair dyes, and, if

Figure 2.7 The famous Clairol ad.

so, in what ways? Have home hair-coloring kits stayed the same, or have they evolved materially and technologically?

Analyze Your Approach

Turn to Box 2.1 for one possible interpretation and analysis of the four theories approach to these ad campaigns.

Understanding the roots of fashion in a holistic way, as a whole or complete system, gives fashion communicators an important breadth and depth of awareness that carries into their daily work. With genuine knowledge of a fashion subject, an insightful fashion communicator will be far more prepared for the career challenges that lie ahead.

NEW TWISTS ON OLD MATERIALS

Raccoon coats. Crocodile purses. Turtle fur. Which of these materials is most likely to show up in a winter collection?

BOX 2.1

FOUR ADS, WHICH THEORY?

One Possible Analysis of Form and Function

The Calvin Klein jeans are designed to be formfitting, revealing the body lines, with no hint of undies, thus focusing on sex appeal: modesty/immodesty.

Nike sneakers are designed in a snug, foot-fitting form, thus offering a sense of can-do ability, athleticism, and survival: protection/utility.

DeBeers diamonds are made of the world's hardest natural substance and are mounted on a ring or circular shape, thus suggesting no beginning and no end. A symbol of betrothal and marriage, they appear to promise longevity, enduring or endless love, and spiritual connectedness. They are costly: status.

Clairol hair is beautiful and lustrous while assuring that mum's the word about having hair that's not one's natural color. (This sort of personal secrecy was valued in the 1950s.) Today, hair coloring has become widely accepted and talked about as a way to appear more attractive and confident: adornment/extension of the self.

Answer: Probably turtle fur. A fabric that has nothing to do with the slow-moving reptile, this soft, strong, warm, man-made creation comes from 100 percent virgin acrylic. (See Figure 2.8.) The name Turtle Fur is absurd enough to be intriguing. Raccoon fur and crocodile skin raise eyebrows in a society that has evolved to a level where it can afford to design cozy hats without angering animal activists. See the Legal Brief in Box 2.2 for faux fur labeling problems that plague the fashion industry.

The reality of fashion in the twenty-first century is that political correctness is on everyone's minds. The state of the environment, recycling, and health consciousness are all at the forefront of the public mind. Ecologically sound textiles

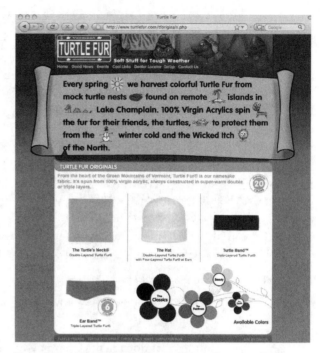

Figure 2.8 Turtle Fur features whimsical copy online at www.turtlefur.com.

will continue to evolve in this early part of the twenty-first century. Politically correct (PC) garments made with a guarantee of "No Sweatshops," ecofashions that boast of being in sync with the Earth (see Box 7.4), and suits that are embedded with peppermint aroma are all forms of PC apparel that are already being developed and covered in the press.

Profile 2.1 features an interview with a communications professional who works for a well-respected fur company. Fur has long been a commanding presence in luxury fashion. Today, the pros and cons of fur are regularly debated, and the use of fur will likely continue to be a controversial topic—more so in the United States, however, than in Europe and elsewhere.

PRACTICE: DIGGING UP THE FACTS OF FASHION

These exercises are largely investigative in nature. To find the most credible resources, check with a reference librarian or university information specialist for help. When researching online, conduct a series of Web site cross-references to see if data checks out across the dot-com, dot-org, and dot-edu spectrum (Box 2.3 on page 38).

BOX 2.2

LEGAL BRIEF: WHEN FAKE FUR ISN'T FAKE

In recent years, the Humane Society of the United States (HSUS) has been checking labels on coats and jackets and anything else that looks like fur. In a story that hit national news in late 2007, HSUS accused as many as six retailers (including Saks Fifth Avenue and Neiman Marcus) of displaying goods by Burberry and other name brands that read "faux" or "ecological fur" or even "polyester" on the label, but that were, in fact, rabbit or raccoon dog, sometimes known as Asiatic raccoon. See *www.hsus.org*. The retailers responded responsibly. This sort of publicity is not at all favorable.

The mislabeling of a fur product violates federal law, which states:

§ 301.49 Deception in general. No furs nor fur products shall be labeled, invoiced, or advertised in any manner which is false, misleading or deceptive in any respect. (Federal Trade Commission)

The entire set of documents regarding fur laws are available at the FTC Web site, and are an example of the rules manufacturers must follow to avoid lawsuits and fines. Measures to create more stringent labeling guidelines and penalties are in the works.

At companies like *mendels.com*, customers can buy faux fur and read a FAQ (frequently asked questions) that describes the source of its faux fur. The playful copy sounds like it is describing animals, but it refers to the patterns and textures of the garments instead. One product example reads: "Flat-Pile Leopard. This is an ultra-low loft, flat-pile fur. It is slick and fuzzy, but not fluffy. The pelting is a strip of fuzz going alternating ways (looks more real, you know!). The background on this changes from a warm tan to a chocolate brown and back again. A combination of nylon and polyester, this fur is machine washable and dryable." Now that's *true* faux.

Master Raw Materials and Inventions

Research the origin, invention, materials, and use of any of the following: rayon, acrylic, mink, sandals, panty hose, cashmere, brassiere, corset, Keds, stiletto heels, mascara, linen, etc.

For more ideas and for reference purposes, consult the *Fairchild Dictionary of Fashion* (2002). Also, see a relevant sample in Box 2.4 about the self-folding collar.

· Profile 2.1 ·

ON THE JOB AS A COMMUNICATIONS REP: AN E-INTERVIEW WITH CHARLES FERRO OF SAGA FURS

By Bernadette Sukley

Charles Ferro is the director of communications for Saga Furs in Copenhagen, Denmark. He communicates to fashion journalists, trade publications, and organizations, and he serves as the bridge between the fur and fashion industries. Nearly every designer from Cavalli to Versace comes to Saga's Design Center because Saga is an innovator in design and techniques, such as making a fur coat lighter than a wool one, using lasers to cut fur, and translating fur's functionality into fashion and home furnishings. The Saga label, says Ferro, assures that the fur is of the highest quality and was bred on farms that treat the animals ethically.

Charles Ferro of Saga Furs.

As his job title suggests, Ferro engages directly in exchanging information and maintaining interpersonal links that serve to support his company's standing in the global fashion industry.

What happens during your typical workday?

I usually catch up on trade publications and industry news. Check e-mails. Check the schedule to see if there will be a designer team interview. Not a week goes by when there aren't students or designers who are coming to see what's going on in the industry.

It all starts with an annual Saga event called FurVision. The event isn't so much a promotional affair as much as it is an opportunity to get an invitation to come to the Saga Design Center. At the center, guests can come in and work with the real thing. Some come with sketches. For example, they'll have a sketch for a coat and ask how the pockets can be trimmed, so they'll ask for Saga furriers and designers to come up with a technique. Others just come for the informative nature of the center. It's fascinating to see the interaction of people and fur. There's nothing like it. It's irresistible and people have to touch it.

My job is to interview the guests. I find out what their plans are for their designs, what they like and don't like, and what kinds of designs will appear in their lines. It's incredibly tough to get the major design houses to give any hints about the lines they are planning, but I try.

(continued on next page)

During the course of a day I usually handle internal calls for Saga, very few outside calls. I'll write trade press releases. Even though we are removed from consumers, the releases still need to be written in a manner that will garner attention from outside the industry. I primarily communicate the newsworthy issues to designers and breeders, and I receive news, too, so it goes both ways. There are very few [news feeds] from outside the organization, perhaps one or two a week. I'll generate, write, and edit articles for the Saga Web site. I also generate, write, and edit articles for the annual Saga magazine. I'll compile text for their lookbook. I make sure that any major designer (a team from Christian Lacroix was here in November) who is visiting or uses Saga furs gets interviewed. Events like fashion week (there are several each year—other than the one in New York) are heavily covered. I've never had a boring day.

What would you say is the best language to speak in order to communicate easily in the fashion business?

It's good to be a polyglot [a person who knows several languages], but English is the lingua franca of fashion. I will never downplay the importance of knowing the local language, so you can ask, "Where's the coffee machine?" And, I think it's helpful if you're in fashion to know a little French. It may sound like a cliché (and is), but fashion has gone global, has for some time, so you speak English, which is understood and spoken in most countries. English is a common denominator for fashion communication.

"Even with the current technology in information sharing, face-to-face is still absolutely critical."

If a student has to choose to major in either communications or journalism, which would be most helpful for a job like yours, one that involves interaction on a global scale?

It would need to be both. The journalism end, or at least communicative writing, is essential in getting the message effectively across. Communications overlaps, but knowing the channels of communication and how they function is very valuable, as is how a reporter thinks. You need to know how to write and to pitch press releases and stories, [to know] what will catch his or her eye. As an American, I'm fortunate enough to have an international perspective. Many people still think in terms of their own country or region, but many American expatriates have a sense of being global citizens.

However, the international angle draws in the question of cultural and/or business culture differences. To be sure, it's impossible to know about all of them, but the most important thing is to be aware of differences and ask questions before making certain moves. For example, you'd be amazed at the differences between Denmark and Sweden, and they're just two miles apart.

What's the best mode of information sharing today?

Even with all the current technology in information sharing, face-to-face is still absolutely critical. Cell phones that are Internet-capable are also extremely valuable for texting and e-mailing, and to check to see if a certain story went on a Web site. I usually use the text message feature. The Internet, as far as communication, is faster but you get so much junk that chews up time sifting through. Although our staff is spread throughout the world (Paris, London, Milan, New York, Moscow, and Beijing), time zones have never been a problem, thanks to the Internet you can be in contact with most everyone 24/7, though you may not always need to.

Who serves as your most helpful source of reference when evaluating fur and its market?

For a question of fashion, I'll usually ask Saga's creative director, Dorte Lenau Klint. She knows it in and out, studied in London, and has been all over the world. Plus, she speaks French, so she can also translate or sort out lingo problems. For technical topics, I go to our development manager, Per Reinkilde. He's great when it comes to questions about the nuts and bolts of fur. Local or general market questions [are directed at] either the market reps here or at other locations. For the real behind-the-scenes stuff I ask a friend who's been in the industry for 25 years. But you always need to make more connections within your organization or trade.

Challenge the Experts

Write a persuasive essay arguing for or against, or proving or disproving, an aspect of one of the concepts covered in this chapter. Use fashion examples to support your ideas. Some possible topics include:

1. "Form follows function."
2. Modesty/immodesty theory
3. Protection/utility theory
4. Status theory
5. Adornment/extension of the self theory
6. "Necessity is the mother of invention."
7. The future of fabric

BOX 2.3

ONLINE RESEARCH TIPS

When doing online research, keep in mind that while the popular Web site Wikipedia might be a helpful jumping-off point, it cannot be considered a reliable source of information. Many professors will not allow students to use it as source material. If you are not sure where to find solid information for your research, ask your librarian or professor for help locating credible, authoritative sources. Here are some basic techniques for locating accurate sources:

Ask: What is the Web site's purpose? If the Web site's purpose is to entertain, sell, persuade, make fun of, or complain, be suspicious about its overall accuracy. If the Web site's purpose appears to be educational and informative, it *may* be credible. However, some sites are set up to look informative, but they are written as hoaxes or to promulgate the ideas of non-professionals and non-experts.

To make a final determination, look for the Web site's "Site Map" at the bottom of the home page. Or check the "About" and "Contact" sections to see whose name, which institution, or which organization is connected to the information. Look for names and actual addresses and phone numbers, plus credentials such as Ph.D., M.A., M.D., Ed.D., and titles (director, etc.) that indicate the authors are well educated and expert in their fields.

Government sites are generally very reliable, as are many educational sites, since the information posted online is vetted (checked and updated frequently). Professional associations with a "dot-org" url (Web address) are often good sources, but not always.

Be sure to learn what some of the basic domain name endings refer to:

.edu	higher education
.gov	government agency
.org	organization or association (charitable or lobbying group, etc.)
.com	commercial (business, sales)
.net	Internet Service Provider

BOX 2.4

SOMEONE HAD TO INVENT
THE SELF-FOLDING COLLAR, RIGHT?

The excerpt below comes from the "History" section of the Phillips-Van Heusen (PVH) Web site *www.pvh.com* and was written as part of a larger corporate effort to encourage long-term customer trust and loyalty in the brand. Well-known names like Bass, Izod, and others emerge in the true story of how PVH came into being.

1876–1921

The foundation is laid for a modern, marketing-driven, world-class company.

In 1876, George Henry Bass purchases a share in E.P. Packard and Co., a shoe manufacturer in Maine, beginning his career as a shoemaker. Three years later, he becomes the sole owner, changing its name to G.H. Bass & Co.

In 1881, Moses Phillips and his wife, Endel, began sewing shirts by hand and selling them from pushcarts to local Pottsville, PA, coal miners. This grows into a shirt business in New York City that places one of the first ever shirt ads in the *Saturday Evening Post*.

In the early 1900s, Vin Draddy starts a men's apparel business and needs a strong name to associate with his quality merchandise. Vacationing in London, he encounters an elegant tailor shop in London, Jack IZOD's. Jack, a well-respected tailor who made custom shirts for King George VI and other royalty, is ready to retire and accepts Vin's offer to purchase the rights to his distinctive name.

In Holland, John M. Van Heusen creates a comfortable, self-folding collar. Traveling to the United States to find a partner, he meets Isaac Phillips, Moses' son. Together they form the Phillips-Van Heusen Corporation.

In 1919, a patent is granted for the collar. In 1921, the revolutionary new collar is introduced to the public with immediate and overwhelming success. *Source: www.pvh.com*

The history of mass-produced shirtmaking can be found on corporate Web sites such as pvh.com (Phillips-Van Heusen).

Note: Consider incorporating a researched item from the first exercise, *Master Raw Materials and Inventions.*

Deconstruct an Outfit

Using a photograph from a magazine, do your best to deconstruct an outfit. (Select *one* outfit on one model.) Use a spiderweb technique, drawing lines out from each detail and adding explanatory text, to work your way carefully, like a detective would, down to the raw materials and related inventions or embellishments that could have been involved in creating the ensemble.

Note: In a broad sense, this exercise is the reverse of what apparel makers do when they construct a **bill of materials** (BOM). The BOM is a listing of all the materials and quantities that are needed to manufacture a specific garment or accessory. It is used for production, projecting costs (or costing), and materials planning, and is an important part of record keeping. While these communiqués were once done on paper, today there are many apparel software programs available to streamline the BOM process.

Create a Compare and Contrast Presentation

Explore any instructor-approved topic for a compare and contrast presentation relating to garment construction, fashion advertising, marketing slogans, or textiles.

Possible topic: Present two jackets from two time periods (e.g., vintage vs. modern). Discuss the effects of form and function, materials, and cost.

Write a Short Definition-Style Essay (150—400 words)

Exploring the terms, history, and legalities of fashion broadens one's knowledge of both the past and the present. Research one of the following questions (or discuss a related topic of interest). Be sure to cite credible sources.

1. Why is "Lycra" capitalized, while "spandex" is not? How widespread is the use of spandex? What is another word for this material? How is it made?
2. Who came up with the name "cotton gin," and what effect did it have on the Civil War? What effect did the name cotton gin have on fashion?

3. What is the origin of silk? Who makes silk today? Which designers specialize in using silk in their collections today?

4. Can a company patent a new textile created in its labs? Give one or more concrete examples.

5. What is the origin of the word "compact" (as related to makeup)? When were compacts fashionable? Are compacts available at the cosmetics counter today?

6. What is polyester, and what impact has it made on fashion?

7. Explain what indigo is and how it is used.

8. What are the soles of athletic shoes made of?

9. Describe the ingredients of makeup and their earliest uses.

10. Describe a fabric failure, a fabric success, or an accidental discovery that affected fashion.

KEY TERMS

adornment	modesty
bill of materials	protection and utility
deconstructing	slogans
extension of self	status
holistic	taglines

CHAPTER THREE

Laboring for Fashion: Influences from the Industry

"With us, and especially among our women, regard for fashion is universal, and our servant-girls, instead of wearing a set dress of their own caste, as in Europe, spend more money upon fashionable dress, in proportion to their means, than do their mistresses."
"Fashion in America," *New York Times*, March 2, 1879

CHAPTER OBJECTIVES:

The information presented here is designed to help you:

- Become aware of the vast numbers of people who are involved in communicating fashion on a variety of levels.
- Learn about publications that influence business.
- Know more about the methods that the industry has historically used and currently uses to communicate.

Ideally, after reading this chapter, you will:

- Take an analytical approach to texts and illustrations in industry publications.
- Be ready to research labor trends, demographics, and work site safety issues, and possess an expanded knowledge of communication techniques.

Historically, the success of fashion in the United States cannot be divorced from its underpinnings: the rise of apparel manufacturing in industrial centers around the country and the story of the laborers who created ready-to-wear garments. New York City was one of those important centers. On March 25, 1911, the events that transpired in that city in one particular factory—the **Triangle Waist Company**—were to have a profound effect on American society with regard to workers' rights, factory regulations, emerging feminism, and much more.

THE TRIANGLE WAIST COMPANY FIRE

Figure 3.1   The Triangle Building in New York City, where blouses were made, was the site of a major fire in 1911.

The social history titled *Triangle: The Fire That Changed America*, by David Von Drehle, is a gripping account of a horrific fire that claimed the lives of 146 workers, most of them immigrant women, who were employed by the largest blouse factory in New York City ("waist" and "shirtwaist" were terms for blouse). Soon after a fire broke out that day "in a bin of scraps," writes Von Drehle, "fire horses charged into the streets with their engines rattling behind them. . . . Onlookers by the hundreds hurried toward the action, and the fastest among them arrived in time to see tangles of bodies, some trailing flames, tumbling from the ninth-floor windows. . . ." Von Drehle's account is hauntingly reminiscent of accounts from September 11, 2001. In fact, he points out, before 9/11, the Triangle fire "was for 90 years the deadliest workplace disaster in New York history—and the most important" (Figure 3.1).

Lessons from the Triangle Disaster

A book like *Triangle* constitutes an important resource for students of fashion communications because it provides:

1. **Awareness of history**. Fashion communications students must not only be aware of current events but they must also be informed about key events that shaped the garment industry in the past. Knowing fashion history makes a fashion communications career infinitely richer and deeper.

2. **Awareness of labor issues.** The attention currently paid to fair labor practices in relation to the fashion industry cannot be ignored. Every case of sweatshop labor and child labor that comes to light is a PR nightmare and a human moral dilemma for fashion. These dilemmas can, with prior awareness and sensitivity, be prevented completely. In *Triangle*, readers discover how this one fire led to women's true assumption of unified power through joining such groups as the International Ladies' Garment Workers' Union (ILGWU) and bringing about massive, long-overdue reforms and rules in workplace safety (see Box 3.1).

3. **Insight into a different sort of fashion communication**. Books on fashion run the gamut from biographies of famous designers to social histories. They serve to provide inspiration, education, and illumination to readers, and they provide support for student research efforts, professional magazine articles, managerial decision-making, and much more. The writing styles differ from other print media, and are worth examining for literary purposes as well.

The following excerpt from *Triangle* displays the highly personal, cinematic approach of its author:

More than a thousand blouses had taken shape in the seven working hours of March 25, one stitch at a time. The freshly cut pieces went in bales to the foremen, who distributed them to the wicker baskets on the floor by each operator's feet. . . . The operators fed the pieces through their humming, stuttering machines, and no matter how quickly the foremen cleared away the finished work, the tables always seemed to be heaped with garments. Piece by piece the blouses emerged. . . .

. . . A little after 4:30 P.M., Mary Laventhal, the pretty and popular ninth-floor bookkeeper, slipped down to the eighth floor for a bundle of cuffs so that a few more waists

Figure 3.2 Workers from the Triangle Waist Company tended to be female immigrants.

could be finished before closing time. She spoke briefly to a young admirer, and then headed back up the stairs. She and foreman Anna Gullo distributed the weekly pay envelopes. . . . Then at 4:45, Gullo rang the bell, and the power cut off abruptly, silencing the machines.

. . . Workers began making their way up the aisles between the sewing machine tables. Then, talking and laughing, they made for the dressing rooms along the west wall of the factory. It was spring and many of them had new clothes, new hats, new fiancés (Figure 3.2).

. . . Years later, a worker recalled that Rose Glantz struck up the popular tune: *Every little movement has a meaning all its own . . .*

Several of her seatmates chimed in.

. . . Someone noticed a muffled noise, much like screaming.

And outside the windows: smoke.

Then . . . *fire.* (Von Drehle 2003)

EVOLUTION OF THE U.S. FASHION INDUSTRY

In 1911, women were still making their own clothing, but change was in the air. In fact, once the ready-to-wear market took off, shoppers never looked back. The quote from the *New York Times* at the beginning of this chapter was an accurate assessment, and a good predictor, of the successful path fashion was to take in the United States. People of all social levels had ever-increasing access to fashion. Eventually, a federal system of standard sizing became established (see Box 3.2), and as fit improved, so did business profits.

Factory-made men's apparel had been developing from the time of the Civil War. Women's apparel was about to catch up as the **National Institute of Standards and Technology (NIST)** explains:

BOX 3.1

TALKING ABOUT LABOR

Fashion careers exist in all kinds of working environments. One person serves as a public relations (PR) representative for an apparel manufacturer, while another person writes and designs her own brochures to hand out at a trade show booth. No matter what the arena, health and safety issues are key considerations. They can make or break a business of any size.

Since the United States Congress passed the Occupational Safety and Health Act of 1970, employers have been required to provide workplaces free from dangerous conditions and health hazards and to comply with rules that help ensure worker safety. The Occupational Safety and Health Administration (OSHA) is the government agency created to oversee this effort. OSHA enforces regulations and provides resources and training assistance to all employers in the United States. Important occupational safety terms include:

- **Compliance**—obeying safety regulations. This includes posting safety posters and holding safety committee meetings.
- **Standards**—governing laws that spell out guidelines that companies and employees must meet.
- **Disclosure of information and materials**—concerning the proper and open way to communicate important data.
- **Ergonomics**—pertaining to people's bodies and the machines they work with, from looms to computer keyboards.

Learning, knowing, and actively using terms that form the foundation of a healthy, safe work environment are part of a communications professional's job. Two helpful online resources to access basic information about labor and safety and to become more familiar with communications issues pertaining to work include OSHA *www.osha.gov* and the National Safety Council *www.nsc.org*.

The mass production of women's clothing developed more slowly. Women's outfits generally continued to be custom-made well into the 1920s. In that decade, factors such as the development of industrial production techniques, the rise of the advertising industry, the growth of an urban professional class, and the development of national markets accessed through chain stores and mail order catalogues contributed to the success of the

BOX 3.2

TOWARD A MORE PERFECT FIT

When clothing shifted from handmade to mass-produced, it took a number of years before a set of sizing standards became available. That meant clothing often did not fit properly, and people often had to make alterations to ready-to-wear items. In 1901, the National Bureau of Standards was founded, to "promote U.S. innovation and industrial competitiveness by advancing measurement science, standards, and technology in ways that enhance economic security and improve our quality of life." Today, the organization is called the National Institute of Standards and Technology (NIST). It sets up measuring standards for everything from ATM machines to mammography equipment.

The NIST describes how early sizes were developed, explaining what it meant to be a woman whose dress size was 14T- ("fourteen T-minus"):

During 1939 and 1940, about 15,000 American women participated in a national survey conducted by the National Bureau of Home Economics of the U.S. Department of Agriculture. It was the first large-scale scientific study of women's body measurements ever recorded. A technician took 59 measurements of each volunteer, who was dressed only in underwear. Volunteers were paid a small fee for participating. The results of the study were published in 1941 in USDA Miscellaneous Publication 454, Women's Measurements for Garment and Pattern Construction. The purpose of the survey was to discover key measurements of the female body—that is the important measurements from which other measurements could best be predicted—and then to propose a sizing system based on this discovery.

In the mid-1940s, the Mail-Order Association of America, a trade group representing catalog businesses such as Sears Roebuck and Spiegel, asked the Commodity Standards Division of the National Bureau of Standards (NBS, now NIST) to conduct research to provide a reliable basis for industry sizing standards. NBS agreed, and punch cards holding the USDA survey results were transferred to NBS at its request for reanalysis. (While the women's apparel sizing standard is the focus of this exhibit, NBS also reanalyzed USDA data for teenage girls and children, resulting in other standards.) The USDA data was augmented by data received from the Research and Development Branch of the Army Quartermasters Corps during World War II when measurements were taken of 6,510 WAC personnel.

(continued on next page)

BOX 3.2 (*continued*)

From January 1949 until April 1952, the NBS Statistical Engineering Division made analyses for the Commodity Standards Division. NBS statistical engineers conducted frequency and correlation analyses with the body measurement data so that they could devise the shortest possible, useful size notations for garments, which would accommodate the greatest number of female consumers without alterations. The resulting commercial standard was distributed by NBS to the industry for comment in 1953, formally accepted by the industry in 1957, and published as Commercial Standard (CS) 215-58 in 1958.

The sizing designations recommended in the published standard combined a bust size number (in even sizes from 8 to 38) with one of three letters—tall (T), regular (R), or short (S)—indicating height, and with a symbol to indicate hip girth: either slender (-), average (no symbol), or full (+). For example, a tall woman with a size 14 bust who was slender in the hips would be considered size 14T-. This combination of signifiers would place the consumer into one of four trade classifications: either misses', women's, half-sizes (shorter women), or juniors'. (NIST, 2004.)

---

women's ready-made apparel industry. Ready-made articles of clothing were portrayed as modern and fashionable during a time when the new consumer industries were rapidly redefining the way Americans viewed mass-manufactured goods. Instead of seeing the purchase of mass-produced clothing as entailing a loss of individuality, American women began to accept the pieces of ready-made merchandise as convenient, affordable, and up-to-date fashion items that could be replaced easily as styles changed. (www.nist. gov 2004)

Big Business

Today, some $250 billion is spent annually on fashion and accessories in the United States, generating revenues of $20 billion. New York City still has the largest concentration of showrooms, 5,000 of them, but many large cities across the country are strong in fashion as well, including Los Angeles, San Francisco, Miami, and Dallas.

The fashion industry accounts for an estimated $750 billion in global revenues. Milan, London, and Paris continue to be trendsetting centers for high fashion, but other centers where runway shows are held cannot be discounted, including Tokyo, Rio de Janeiro, and Berlin. CBS News recently listed Hong Kong, New Delhi, Moscow, Beirut, and Seoul as possible "**emerging fashion centers**."

COMMUNICATING WITHIN THE INDUSTRY

Considering the ever-widening scope of apparel, shoes, and accessories, it is to be expected that the **flow of information** would expand to reflect what the market demands. **Trade reports** that serve the fashion industry are written and produced daily, feeding news items and images about fashion and the fashion industry to viewers and readers via every conceivable media, electronic and printed, beamed and broadcast, and sent over smartphones and MP3 players. Such industry-specific information is crucially important to apparel manufacturers, investors, fashion designers, buyers, government overseers, and labor representatives. They all have their own reasons for accessing these information sources.

Some well-known, general **business news publications** that cover aspects of fashion include the *Wall Street Journal* and the *Economist*, among others, most of which are targeted to people who possess an interest in the economy.

Business-to-business publications (also called **B2B**) exist with a *specific* mission of serving other businesses and are not geared toward the general population.

Still other media outlets are used by **industry associations** (like the cotton growers or manmade-fiber makers) to lobby for political advantage.

Coverage of issues relating to the **fashion workforce** appears in numerous other venues, from in-house newsletters to Web sites. Some of the topics include labor trends, fair labor practices, work site safety issues, union matters, advertising issues, and lawsuits (see Box 3.3).

How can we tell the difference between the different types of information sources?

First, look at the **masthead** of any magazine, newsletter, or newspaper (see Box 3.4), or the "About this site" section of an online source. If there are names, phone numbers, and addresses listed, then a degree of validity may be presumed. However, always ask this follow-up question: What is the purpose of this media outlet (publication, video, CD, or e-newsletter)? Is it to inform or is it to *convince* the reader? The line between informing and convincing is often a fine one. It is always wise to examine the sources of your information deeply. Another important question to ask is: Who is paying the salaries of the writers and illustrators in this information source?

Consider this hypothetical example: A writer is assigned to produce, plan, write, and photograph an article covering the bikini collections in an upcoming Sydney, Australia,

BOX 3.3

LEGAL BRIEF: WORKER WATCH

In the late 1990s and into the new millennium, Americans found themselves reading headlines that charged several brand-name designers with producing their gorgeous fashions through sweatshop practices. Calvin Klein, Donna Karan, Levi-Strauss, and numerous others suddenly found themselves under the harsh light of labor and ethics scrutiny. In 1999, the Chinese Staff and Workers Union (CSWU) took action against exploitation occurring in New York City, citing working conditions that included seven-day workweeks with 12-hour days, bathrooms that were padlocked, and denial of time off (even to take care of sick children). There were even allegations that workers were being forced to sign two separate sets of time sheets, one showing hours that met Department of Labor requirements, the other for the actual hours worked.

In recent years, many manufacturers have moved operations overseas, where labor is less expensive, and working conditions are more difficult to monitor. Over time, designers salvaged their reputations as best they could. Below are three excerpts regarding breaches of labor law.

Breach Example 1

From "Lawsuit Accuses Fashion House of Running Sweatshops," the *New York Times*, June 8, 2000:

> A class-action lawsuit filed yesterday accuses one of New York's best-known fashion houses, Donna Karan, of running sweatshops that cheated workers out of millions of dollars in overtime pay.
>
> The lawsuit, filed by the Asian American Legal Defense and Education Fund, contends that Donna Karan and several factories that make or made its clothing systematically break the law by not paying time and a half to employees who are forced to work seven days a week, usually putting in nearly 75 hours each week. (Greenhouse 2000)

Breach Example 2

From "Asian-American Garment Workers: Low Wages, Excessive Hours, and Crippling Injuries," published c. 2000 (online at UNC School of Law Web site):

(continued on next page)

BOX 3.3 (*continued*)

Los Angeles's garment industry still accounts for $28 billion dollars of the region's economy. Los Angeles's lucrative garment profits are made off the backs of Latina and Asian women—94 percent of whom are immigrant, 75 percent Latinas, and about 15 percent Asian (Chinese and Vietnamese) women. The vast majority are non-English speakers. Work is assigned on the basis of gender. Higher-paying cutting and heavy pressing jobs are almost exclusively performed by men while the sewing operations are almost exclusively performed by women. Over half of Los Angeles's Latino garment workers are undocumented, most arriving within the last 15 years. Immigrant workers are employed by contractors who are also immigrants. Production is concentrated in downtown Los Angeles's garment district but in the last 10 years has spread to the immigrant communities of El Monte, East Los Angeles, Orange County, and San Fernando Valley as contractors look for cheaper labor and better space.

Given the large numbers of undocumented workers, Los Angeles's workforce is especially vulnerable to exploitation . . . (UNC, 2000)

Breach Example 3

From "Saipan Sweatshop Lawsuit Ends with Important Gains for Workers and Lessons for Activists," published January 8, 2004, online at *www.cleanclothes.org*:

This month, the last of three lawsuits over sweatshop conditions on the U.S. island of Saipan came to a close. Saipan garment workers voluntarily dismissed their class action suits against Levi-Strauss and Company, the only retailer to refuse to contribute to a settlement fund for the workers. Recognizing that they had already won a landmark $20 million settlement with 26 other U.S. retailers and 23 Saipan garment factories, the workers and labor advocates declared victory. (Bas et al. 2004.)

---

runway show. How would that individual cover the event if he or she were writing a fashion column for a travel magazine? An e-zine for swimwear buyers? A feature for *Style.com*? What if this fashion writer was covering the show for one of the bikini designers? How objective would the writing be?

When it comes to pursuing a career in fashion communications, there are as many scenarios as the mind is capable of imagining. Some people have no desire whatsoever to cover the trade. They like to write about fashion, photograph it, or comment about it, but please

---

BOX 3.4

WHAT'S A MASTHEAD?
(OR, WHO'S SAILING THIS SHIP?)

Sailors think of a masthead as the top of the vertical pole on a sailboat that serves to support the sails. (It's also a method of rigging the vessel.) When journalists refer to the masthead, they mean that all-important list in magazines and newspapers that gives the publication's contact information and identifies the publisher, executive editor, art director, and other staff members. It usually is located on the editorial page in newspapers, and in the front pages of magazines (after the table of contents).

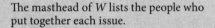

The masthead of *W* lists the people who put together each issue.

A masthead can also refer to a banner in publishing, as well as the top of a Web site page where the company logo and accompanying elements are displayed for identification.

Fashion communicators who wish to keep up with who's who in the magazine world can quickly see who is doing what by looking at the masthead. In recent years, a Web site called *Mastheads.org* has emerged to make it easy to find the most current names on mastheads in hundreds of periodicals.

---

don't make them say anything nice about a designer or style that they dislike. Conversely, there are those who love the retail and sales aspects so dearly, they could not even envision writing a purely journalistic story. Their main joy in life is finding fresh ways to gush over the exciting new trends they see.

WORDSMITHING IN THE FASHION TRADE PUBLICATIONS

Every day, industry writers and editors are called on to put together compelling pieces that explain all the behind-the-scenes aspects of the fashion industry. Without these business writers and their collaborators, including photographers, assistant editors, fact-checkers, art directors, photo editors, and copy editors, the fashion industry would not run like the well-oiled machine that it has become today. The glossy magazines that the average person thinks of when hearing the phrase "fashion magazine," *Vogue, Glamour, Harper's Bazaar, GQ, Elle,* etc., thrive alongside *Women's Wear Daily, Footwear News,* and other **trade publications**. The fashion communicators who report on business and industry topics occupy a special niche, providing in-depth informational angles on specifics and trends, company finances and trades, serving as a cohesive link in the long chain of fashion information. The articles they write can have a significant impact on the survival of designer goods, the ready-to-wear market, fabric usage, color, and even the staffing within corporations.

Information content seen in trade publications, whether in e-news, newsletters, newspapers, or magazines, is likely to include **statistics**, **interviews**, **descriptive details**, and **projections** (often in the form of quotes) for the future. Also, **critical analyses** of the overall scene are often given in some form or other, with **conclusions** drawn by the reporter or someone whom the reporter is quoting. It is important to note that the business environment has a built-in slant that varies widely. Reporters who write those articles are much more likely to project a positive bias toward the industry, reporting on shifts in power (such as promotions and retirements), new products, location changes, and acquisitions. A **fashion news journalist** who writes for a newspaper such as the *Chicago Sun-Times* or the *Wall Street Journal* approaches his or her story in a radically different way, using hard-nosed fact-finding techniques that aim to serve the public without cozying up to business. This type of fashion news journalism is discussed more thoroughly in later chapters (see especially Box 9.3 about the *Washington Post* editor Robin Givhan). However, Madelyn Shaw's excerpt in Profile 3.1 discusses the fact that, historically, sticky problems have long existed when it comes to heavy-handed influences in fashion communications.

Since their work is a crucial contribution to the daily ins and outs of fashion, industry journalists involved in this arena typically operate at a fast pace. Their workday is often more exciting, more challenging, and more deadline-driven than most people might think. **Networking**—keeping up with contacts via e-mail and phone, lunching with people in-the-know, and generally building and maintaining personal relationships on various professional levels—is part of the job. Traveling to shows and meeting interview subjects are also requirements for the job. Securing and keeping track of images and captions that illustrate stories is a must for many trade journalists, for pairing a strong illustration with an intriguing headline is what draws readers' attention.

• *Profile 3.1* •

FASHION IN PRINT: A QUESTION OF POWER

"Anna and Laura Tirocchi maintained a small, personalized dress business in Providence for over 30 years . . . " These are the opening words to *American Fashion: The Tirocchi Sisters in Context,* an important essay written by Madelyn Shaw that accompanies a research project and exhibit about two sisters who made fashionable dresses in Providence, Rhode Island, from 1915 to 1947.

Shaw was an associate curator of costume and textiles at the Museum of Art of the world-famous Rhode Island School of Design (RISD), when this work was first published. Shaw now works at the New Bedford Whaling Museum, where she continues to present exhibitions related to textiles in American history. *American Fashion: The Tirocchi Sisters in Context* and the exhibit it accompanied offer an intimate, well-researched look into the past that educates the public about fashion history. One portion of the essay is particularly relevant to students of fashion communications. In the section excerpted below, Shaw describes how business interests get mixed up with emerging fashion journalism:

Anna (above) and Laura Tirocchi (below).

Some publications, such as *Elite Styles, Le Costume Royal,* and *Le Bon Ton* were specifically aimed at professional dressmakers. (12) The Elite Styles Company even held fashion shows at its New York headquarters to acquaint out-of-town dressmakers with the latest models. The Woman's Institute of Domestic Arts and Sciences in Scranton, Pennsylvania, published *Inspiration,* beginning in 1916, for its dressmaking students, and the *Fashion Service,* which illustrated for subscribers both Paris adaptations and patterns from American sources such as *Pictorial Review, Butterick, Ladies' Home Journal,* and *McCall's.* (13) Examples of some of the titles mentioned are found in the Tirocchi Archive.

(continued on next page)

During the 1920s and 1930s, *Vogue* magazine asked readers to send in for names of shops where the merchandise featured in its pages could be purchased.

Newspapers, of course, also had fashion information, usually in the "women's pages," which also carried reports on club activities and society doings. Sunday photogravure sections of the paper also included the latest in dress. In the 1920s and 1930s, the *Providence Sunday Journal*'s fashion editor, Madeliene [*sic*] Corey, attended the Paris openings and later put together articles describing the new styles, illustrated with photos or sketches of models available locally. No Providence shops or dressmakers were mentioned in the text, although the Paris designers often were. Readers had to call or write for a list of local purveyors. (14) *Vogue,* during the same decades, also asked readers to send in for the names of shops where merchandise mentioned in features or sections such as "Seen in the Shops" or "Fashions for Limited Incomes" could be purchased.

The *Providence Journal* was not the only newspaper with a fashion editor, and some, such as Eugenia Sheppard of the *New York Herald Tribune,* wielded real power in the fashion industry. Syndicated columnists, most notably Tobé (Mrs. Tobé Coller Davis), were also extremely important in spreading a uniform fashion gospel throughout the nation. Edna Woolman Chase noted that in addition to her column, Tobé advised "more than a thousand stores on fashion trends, compiling, printing, and mailing weekly a 50-page report telling her clients how and where to buy the clothes customers will shortly be demanding." Tobé didn't invent dirndl skirts, sweater blouses, slim pants, and years ago, Bramley dresses, but she foresaw their immense popularity and by advising the nation's stores accordingly made these clothes great fashion Fords . . . (15)

"Syndicated columnists were also extremely important in spreading a uniform fashion gospel."

The Tirocchi sisters could never have imagined that they and their Providence, RI, shop would be made famous thanks to a museum exhibit at the Rhode Island School of Design. Many of the ideas for their designs came from magazines.

Fashion critics noted that the relationship between fashion makers and fashion writers entailed a conflict of interest between journalistic integrity and advertising revenue. Designers, manufacturers, or retailers who advertised in a publication often expected favorable editorial treatment over those who bought little or no ad space, and advertising departments were often reluctant to offend an advertiser through editorial coverage of a competitor. Efforts to preserve advertising revenues often meant that local makers or retailers remained anonymous except to those few who wrote in for the information. Edna Woolman Chase detailed her efforts to keep *Vogue*'s fashion features free from the tyranny of advertisers during this period. She explained to one manufacturer that in order to maintain the prestige of *Vogue*, the major attraction for advertisers, she could not use his product: "But how do you suppose we have won that prestige? . . . It is because we insist on quality in the merchandise we show . . . You may get into *Vogue* through the

(*continued on next page*)

advertising pages, but to come in the editorial door you must give me material we can be proud to use." This assessment of the relationship between advertising and editorial space in the magazine was not always accepted by other observers, who claimed to see a direct correlation between the amount of advertising space a company paid for and the number of times its products were featured editorially (16). (Shaw, n.d.)

The following paragraphs come from well-respected trade publications that are available online as well as in printed media formats. A person who is reading these articles should be able to identify such informational elements as statistics, interview quotes, descriptive details, projections, trend analysis, and general conclusions (Figure 3.3). It should also be relatively easy to see with whom the reporter is networking. The opening lines of an article comprise the **lede** (or **lead**), in journalistic terms, since they lead into the main body of the text.

Figure 3.3 *Footwear News*, serving the shoe trade, uses a combination of images and reporting.

Writing Sample 1

The following excerpt from the story "Shoes Shine on Runway," by Lindsay E. Sammon, appeared in the October 15, 2007 issue of *Footwear News*:

NEW YORK—Footwear took center stage on the Milan and Paris runways, with color and height emerging as top trends.

"The footwear really stood out on all the runways more than ever," said Jeffrey Kalinsky, founder of Jeffrey New York and Jeffrey Atlanta, as well as the director of designer merchandising for Nordstrom. "[Shorter garments] allowed you to really see the shoes. The shoe is more important than ever, and when the shoes get a lot of attention at the runway shows, it creates a sense of demand by the consumer."

Retailers also said that, for the first time, shoes are becoming seasonless, as spring styles are crossing over from fall with unique updates. "What's really interesting is that each shoe is looking [like an] individual," explained Barbara Atkin, VP of fashion direction at Holt Renfrew. "There is so much novelty."

Varied skins and bold color dominated footwear at the most trend-setting shows including Fendi, Balenciaga and Prada, said buyers.

"It is such an exciting spring '08 season, probably one of the hottest shoe seasons we've had because of all the color, the patchwork and mixed media of fabrication," added Atkin. "I saw velvet and exotic skins at Prada—who did the most incredible shoes—and multi-exotic skins in bright colors at Dolce & Gabbana. [D&G] has really turned their shoes around."

Atkin also praised the color-block patent leather details at Marni, along with innovative heel shapes from various designers. "We're seeing a cone heel, very architectural and beautifully sculpted, with a 3-D feel," said Atkin. "Ferragamo did an ombre lucite heel, and there were carved heels at Fendi."

Hand-carved florals at Prada, teacup and scepter heels at Miu Miu, and misplaced heels at Marc Jacobs were highlights for Michael Fink, VP and women's fashion director at Saks Fifth Avenue. "This idea really adds novelty to the shoe wardrobe, especially for a more light-hearted spring season," he said.

Styles with height also seem to be gaining traction. Platforms in low and high wedges were a standout runway trend for Sandra Wilson, accessories fashion director at Neiman Marcus. Wilson also said that ankle straps, as well as T-strap and thong sandals with embellishments, were important, as were neutral tones, such as pearl gray, followed by strong bursts of color.

"Color will be the major trend in footwear for spring," said Debbie King, VP and DMM of women's shoes at Bloomingdale's.

Gladiator-style sandals also continued to shine on the runways, with Balenciaga's take on the silhouette generating high praise. "Those are going to be heirloom museum shoes one day," said Atkin of the knee-high, strappy style.

Writing Sample 2

The following excerpt from the story "Street Cleaning," by Jessica Pallay, appeared in the June 11, 2007 issue of *DNR*:

While many segments of the denim market have maintained their seemingly unending momentum, in the past year the young men's market has played the role of nonconforming teenager, bucking the bullish blue-jean trend. According to The NPD Group, men in the 18-to-24 age range spent nearly 10 percent less on denim in the 12 months ending in March 2007, just $992.9 million versus $1.1 billion during the year prior.

The dip in denim sales points out an obvious disconnect between the fast-moving young consumer and the brands that service him. He's already bought all the over-embellished, overpriced denim that he can stand, and is instead moving towards subtler, more toned-down versions. This fact is not lost on his favorite streetwear labels, which, for spring '08, must compete with the denim basic that seems to have taken the young men's urban market by storm: Levi's. (Pallay, 2007.)

Writing Sample 3

The following excerpt from the story "Givenchy Zeros In on Lipstick With Rouge Interdit," by Julie Naughton, appeared in the November 17, 2006 issue of *Women's Wear Daily:*

Givenchy plans to pay its color cosmetics business more than lip service by launching its new lipstick line, Rouge Interdit [Figure 3.4], in March.

The line heralds "a return to serious lipstick," said Nicolas Degennes, artistic director of makeup and colors for Givenchy.

"Rouge Interdit is a full-coverage, deeply colored formula," said Linda Maiocco, vice president of marketing in the United States for Guerlain and Parfums Givenchy. "Liquid crystals are the breakthrough feature that allow for maximum light reflection. While classic lipstick pigments rely on mother-of-pearl, which only reflect one color and can look opaque, liquid crystals reflect every shade of the light spectrum, from yellow to red to blue. The result is luminous color and satiny gloss in a lightweight, comfortable finish." (Naughton, 2006.)

Creative Copy Definitely Counts

Generally speaking, the businesspersons, retail storeowners, fashion-lovers, style editors, and others who read articles like "Shoes Shine on Runway" and "Street Cleaning" are aware that there is a certain cleverness that captures their attention as readers. Readers often respond first to a catchy title and image, and then begin focusing on the presentation of facts and impressions. Rarely, though, is the reader aware while reading that he or she is being subtly seduced to keep on reading by the same creative writing techniques that are used in fiction (novels, plays, scripts, etc.) and creative nonfiction (feature articles in newspapers, magazines, Web sites, travelogues, etc.).

Givenchy Zeros In on Lipstick With Rouge Interdit

GIVENCHY PLANS TO PAY ITS COLOR COSMETICS BUSINESS MORE THAN lip service by launching its new lipstick line, Rouge Interdit, in March.

The line heralds "a return to serious lipstick," said Nicolas Degennes, artistic director of makeup and colors for Givenchy.

"Rouge Interdit is a full-coverage, deeply colored formula," said Linda Maiocco, vice president of marketing in the U.S. for Guerlain and Parfums Givenchy. "Liquid crystals are the breakthrough feature that allow for maximum light reflection. While classic lipstick pigments rely on mother-of-pearl, which only reflect one color and can look opaque, liquid crystals reflect every shade of the light spectrum, from yellow to red to blue. The result is luminous color and satiny gloss in a lightweight, comfortable finish."

The formula also includes poppy extract oil for hydration, ricin oil to aid in shine and beeswax and candellia wax for a spreadable texture, she added.

The lipstick has another distinction: Degennes created Rouge Interdit's colors without looking at the current Givenchy palette of lip colors. "I wanted to do something completely new and different and not be influenced by anything we are currently doing," said Degennes, who winnowed the line's 24 shades down from a spectrum of 100. The colors, which range from pale pinks to dark reds, will each retail for $26.

While the formula is intended to be the star of this product, the packaging is an apt understudy. Created by two designers trained at London's Central St. Martin's School, the lipstick case is a sleek square black with the Givenchy name in silver. Inside, the lipstick bullet is housed in a silver-toned tube embossed with the brand's signature Gs. The lipstick tube has a black ribbon pull at its base, which the user employs to remove the bullet from the outer casing.

In the U.S., distribution for Rouge Interdit is very targeted, said Maiocco: It will be available in five Saks Fifth Avenue doors and nine Sephora doors. It will be sampled in-store via cards with several color samples and a mini lip brush. Direct mail is also planned.

While neither of the executives would comment on projected sales, industry sources estimated that the lipstick would do about $1 million at retail in the U.S. in its first year on counter.

Elsewhere, the brand will launch a host of limited-edition fragrance flankers next spring, including Very Irrésistible Givenchy Summer Sun, due in March; Very Irrésistible Givenchy for Men Fresh Attitude, in May, and Ange Ou Démon Silky Drop in April. Three other flankers that make up the Harvest Collection — Amarige Ylang Ylang 2006 Eau de Toilette, Organza Fleur D'Oranger 2006 Eau de Parfum and Very Irrésistible Givenchy Rose Centifolia 2006 Eau de Parfum — will launch in mid-April.

— J.N.

Rouge Interdit

Figure 3.4   A product, Rouge Interdit lipstick, is covered in *Women's Wear Daily* (*WWD*) on November 17, 2006.

The title "Shoes Shine . . . " begins with a same-same sound, or **alliteration**. The author or headline writer deliberately selected "shoes" to pair with "shine" because they sound better together and grab attention, as opposed to two perfectly accurate alternatives: "Footwear Shine . . ." or "Heels Shine . . . ." The words "Center stage" have a similarly alliterative impact, as does the cliché of "top trend." (See Box 3.5 for sources to learn more about using alliteration and other creative elements.)

The first quote used in the story contains a **double entendre**, which is French for "has a double (or second) meaning." The writer quotes Jeffrey Kalinsky as saying, "The footwear really stood out on all the runways more than ever," which seems innocuous, even straightforward, as a quoted comment. However, a closer examination reveals that it means two things at once: (1) the footwear are unusually different and/or exciting to the degree that people focused their attention on models' feet as they walked, and (2) the models' shoes almost "stood" by themselves, an activity that people do in shoes, they stand in them. Here, two more literary terms come to mind: **connotation**, an idea that is suggested by a word or thing, and **anthropomorphizing**, which is attributing human form or personality to an inanimate object.

The writer also varied her **pacing**, another element that keeps readers' attention. Pacing refers to speed, rhythm, and sentence lengths—and mixing those up in just the right way to keep the reader going; it is exactly like pacing in a sports event such as running, tennis, or basketball, where mixing moves up perfectly brings success for the athlete. The writer

BOX 3.5

AVOIDING ALLITERATION ANGST

Using alliteration and other literary techniques can make writing come to life, but understanding and properly executing these when creating copy can sometimes be a challenge. Two good sources of knowledge are discussed below.

The Internet is one place to explore writers' perspectives on **wordsmithing**. Writer Tonia Jordan digs deep into the subtle differences between alliteration, assonance, and consonance in an online article at: *http://ezinearticles.com/?Alliteration,-Assonance-and-Consonance&id=675686*. On this Web site, she also offers other valuable articles found under the category "Writing-and-Speaking."

The Copywriter's Handbook, by Robert Bly, is a 400-page paperback packed with tips for punchy PR, ad, and Web writing. Bly also includes advice on copywriting and direct mail packaging at www.bly.com.

and editor learn ways to keep details exciting but not too exciting, placing all the necessary points in the piece without ever dragging. In this case, the writer achieved proper pacing by peppering the article with short, tight, direct quotes in seven out of the nine paragraphs.

Other elements of literary crafting are evident as well, upon a close reading of nearly any article in top-notch trade publications. It is worth taking the time to read and reread such articles, and identify word-and-image techniques that lead to the communicator's fondest hope: that the business audience (and anyone else perusing the piece) will say, "Well, that was worth reading."

PRACTICE: SCANNING THE RANGE OF RESOURCES

Fashion communicators of all sorts—whether they are working for a daily trade newsletter, e-zine, news service, or glossy magazine—hate to waste time spinning their wheels chasing down information that is inaccurate or simply not helpful. These exercises are designed to help students develop a body of knowledge about various Web sites and news sources to stay current, while always assessing the validity of the information presented for consumption. Don't be afraid to contact an expert directly with specific questions (see Box 3.6).

BOX 3.6

DOING RESEARCH USING E-MAIL QUERIES

When seeking facts and figures, start by communicating directly with other communicators. Government entities (Web sites ending with ".gov"), trade associations (usually ".org" but sometimes a ".com"), and companies (".com") all have employees whose job it is to share information with the public. Whether their titles are "information specialist" or "assistant director of corporate communications," these individuals are ready to steer writers in the direction of helpful information.

A Query Example

Hello,

I am looking for the latest statistics on how many apparel companies are in the United States and how many of them actually manufacture their goods here. Any and all links to this sort of information are greatly appreciated.

Thank you.

Danielle Molsen

Brightways College student

Response Example

Ms. Molsen,

Census Bureau industry data are based on the North American Industry Classification System (NAICS) codes. For example, NAICS 4481 is Clothing Stores. *http://www.census.gov/epcd/naics02/def/NDEF448.HTM#N4481*

Our Statistics of U.S. Businesses (SUSB) program provides aggregate statistics for the U.S. and NAICS detail. View SUSB data at *http://www.census.gov/csd/susb/susb.htm*

You may also want to contact our Manufacturing Division at *http://www.census.gov/mcd/* for more detailed information.

Please feel free to contact us with any additional questions or data requests.

Thank you,

Lara Smith

Company Statistics Division

(555) 763-3321

Subscribe to Trade Publications

Become a subscriber to *WWD* or another trade periodical, or follow a source of fashion trade information online. After a period of about four weeks, map out what types of stories are most common and what kinds of stories are least common, in terms of topical coverage. Or compare and contrast:

- One trade magazine with another; or
- A trade magazine and its cyber-counterpart (online version)

Visit Unfamiliar Web Sites

Below is a list of Web sites and/or names of organizations online to explore and report on, either individually or in pairs or small groups. Review a chosen site thoroughly, allotting at least 30 minutes to click through and read each part of the menu, including the Site Map, generally found at the bottom of the homepage. Or, find other Web sites that relate to the underpinnings of the fashion industry and explore them.

Exit the site. (This is important to do, since the temptation to borrow wording from the site itself is great.)

Then summarize the site in your own words, writing an in-depth description of the look and feel of the site. Figure out what circumstance might prompt a visit back to the site.

Later, go back to the site and find the section (or sections) that you found most interesting or valuable. Print out that section and attach it to the essay. Share what you learned with the whole class.

The following is a suggested list of Web sites to explore:

- United Nations Global Compact www.unglobalcompact.org/ParticipantsAndStakeholders/labour.html
- International Labor Organization www.ilo.org
- U.S. State Department http://usinfo.state.gov/gi/global_issues/human_trafficking.html
- Organic Consumers Association www.organicconsumers.org
- Folio www.foliomag.com

- Pantone www.pantone.com
- Fashion.Infomat http://www.infomat.com
- The Textile Institute http://www.texi.org

Do Some Fieldwork

Take a field trip to an apparel factory, garment distributor, atelier (designer's studio), textile association headquarters, Chamber of Commerce, trade publisher, product photography studio, or other location that supports the fashion industry. For ideas, check the phone book, read the local newspaper, or go online to see what businesses exist in nearby towns or cities.

Going as a class may be a possibility. If not, take the time to make a visit outside of class. The goal is to make connections up close, perhaps even interviewing an owner, manager, or worker, to see firsthand how the members of a community contribute toward the larger industry picture.

Tip: Always ask permission to use a camera or record video images. Do not be surprised if you are denied permission. Some businesses have strict policies about photography and video recording.

Options for observation: Write an essay, take notes, journal, or simply discuss what new insights arose from the experience. Some questions for evaluation might include: What was most impressive? Least impressive? Most surprising?

Look into Labor

If making fashion a fairer environment for workers appeals to you as a subject of journalistic interest, spend time researching the situation of garment workers today and in the past (see Box 3.7). A wide range of publications and other media is available for doing such investigation. *The Industrial Workers of the World: Its First 100 Years* by Fred W. Thompson and Jon Bekken has a concise section on textile workers that leads the reader to numerous additional sources.

Comparing past conditions and issues to those of today inevitably involves looking at the fashion industry in the global context and exploring how information and technology sharing fit into the larger labor picture. The role of news outlets in effecting change by bringing labor violations to light is also worthy of study.

BOX 3.7

WORKING CONDITIONS:
THE APPAREL INDUSTRY

The excerpt below comes from a government report in the U.S. Department of Labor's *Occupational Outlook Handbook, 2006–07 Edition*:

Most people in textile, apparel, and furnishings occupations work a standard 5-day, 35- to 40-hour week. Working on evenings and weekends is common for shoe and leather workers, laundry and dry-cleaning workers, and tailors, dressmakers, and sewers employed in retail stores. Many textile and fiber mills often use rotating schedules of shifts so that employees do not continuously work nights or days. But these rotating shifts sometimes cause workers to have sleep disorders and stress-related problems.

Although much of the work in apparel manufacturing still is based on a piecework system that allows for little interpersonal contact, some apparel firms are placing more emphasis on teamwork and cooperation. Under this new system, individuals work closely with one another, and each team or module often governs itself, increasing the overall responsibility of each operator.

Working conditions vary by establishment and by occupation. In manufacturing, machinery in textile mills often is noisy, as are areas in which sewing and pressing are performed in apparel factories; patternmaking and spreading areas tend to be much quieter. Many older factories are cluttered, hot, and poorly lit and ventilated, but more modern facilities usually have more workspace and are well lit and ventilated. Textile machinery operators use protective glasses and masks that cover their noses and mouths to protect against airborne materials. Many machines operate at high speeds, and textile machinery workers must be careful not to wear clothing or jewelry that could get caught in moving parts. In addition, extruding and forming machine operators wear protective shoes and clothing when working with certain chemical compounds.

Work in apparel production can be physically demanding. Some workers sit for long periods, and others spend many hours on their feet, leaning over tables and operating machinery. Operators must be attentive while running sewing machines, pressers, automated cutters, and the like. A few workers wear protective devices such as gloves. In some instances, new machinery and production techniques have decreased the physical demands on workers. For example, newer pressing machines are controlled by foot pedals or by computer and do not require much strength to operate (U.S. Dept. of Labor 2006–2007).

KEY TERMS

alliteration

anthropomorphizing

business-to-business
   publications (B2B)

business news publications

compliance

conclusions

connotation

critical analyses

descriptive details

disclosure of information
   and materials

double entendre

emerging fashion centers

ergonomics

fashion news journalist

fashion workforce

flow of information

industry associations

interviews

lede or lead

masthead

networking

National Institute of Standards and
   Technology (NIST)

pacing

projections

standards

statistics

trade publications

trade reports

Triangle Waist Company

wordsmithing

part ii

FASHION COMMUNICATIONS— THE BUSINESS END

HOW DOES FASHION GET "OUT THERE"? HOW DO STYLES GET LABELED "fashionable" in the first place? The answers to these questions involve a complex mix of aesthetics, persuasion, desire, access, and, most important, communications savvy. Whether a look is promoted in advertisements or sold directly to buyers at trade shows, a successful fashion owes its success to the millions of people who distribute, brand, display, order, and sell products to the public. The business end of fashion communications is frequently overshadowed by fashion in print media; however, the two are interdependent.

Chapter 4, *Details, Details*, discusses the necessity of information sharing in business by taking a close look at the retail environment, including the crucial chain of communications on the path to placing merchandise on the racks. A general manager chats about her work in a trendy store of a designer brand powerhouse, divulging her own set of day-to-day communication techniques that keep profit levels high.

Chapter 5, *Becoming Fashion*, focuses on the complexities of how fashion becomes fashion, looking at historical origins (e.g., the role of royalty, dolls, early print media photography, etc.). The maxim of "it must be seen to become fashion" still applies, but the technologies available to today's society allow for immediate and near-immediate display online, in film, and on TV, with decidedly positive results for businesses.

Chapter 6, *Out There for All to See*, walks directly into the broad-view basics of marketing, branding, advertising, sales, and public relations—some of the separate but interconnected tasks behind one common goal: to present merchandise so as to attract buyers and their dollars.

CHAPTER FOUR

Details, Details

"Retail is detail."
Adage

CHAPTER OBJECTIVES:

The information presented here is designed to help you understand:
- The daily nature and importance of constant communication in the wholesale and retail environments.
- That employers value appropriate and necessary information sharing.
- The marketing strategy of living in the future and how communicating well smooths the path.

Ideally, after reading this chapter, you will:
- Demonstrate detail consciousness.
- Be equipped with tools to avoid making mistakes and maximize positive results when writing business e-mails.
- Have gained practical knowledge about interview protocol by following the text example and by practicing interviewing skills.

When it comes to wholesaling and retailing the hard goods of fashion, the industry has its own unique set of communications needs. The business of fashion involves a diverse range of tasks, which include:

- placing orders (e.g., buying fabrics, embellishments, finished goods)
- converting (making samples from sketches)
- distribution and inventory
- exhibiting and attending trade shows
- buying
- visual merchandising (store displays)
- interacting with advertising and marketing firms for branding
- hiring and training sales associates and other personnel
- providing customer service
- interfacing with media for public relations

In every case, **attention to detail** is one of the most important aspects of a job in fashion. Even non-supervisory positions, such as stocking inventory or working as a retail sales associate, require attention to details. Those details must be communicated between workers and managers, and/or workers and the public. In addition, workers often are required to enter detailed information into a computer, which then communicates and shares that information with other divisions of the company.

Consider the following qualifications for retail workers in general, according to the U.S. Department of Labor (see also Box 4.1):

Employers look for people who enjoy working with others and who have the **tact** and **patience** to deal with difficult customers. Among other desirable characteristics are an interest in sales work, a neat appearance, and the ability to communicate clearly and effectively. The ability to speak more than one language may be helpful for employment in communities where people from various cultures live and shop. Before hiring a salesperson, some employers may conduct a background check, especially for a job selling high-priced items. . . . Opportunities for advancement vary. In some small establishments, advancement is limited because one person—often the owner—does most of the managerial work. In others, some salespersons are promoted to assistant manager. Large retail businesses usually prefer to hire college graduates as management trainees, making a college education increasingly important. The

---

BOX 4.1

THE FUTURE OF RETAIL IN AMERICA: WHAT THE GOVERNMENT'S CRYSTAL BALL SAYS

The federal government is a useful source for industry information, which can be valuable for managerial communications, fashion journalism, and business writing. In addition to publishing data that show what has been going on, government analysts also publish forecasts for future trends in the industry. The retail employment forecast is given here:

Predictions for Employment: Employment is expected to grow by 12 percent over the 2006–16 decade, which is about as fast as the average for all occupations. In fact, due to the size of this occupation, retail salespersons will have one of the largest numbers of new jobs arise, about 557,000. . . . This growth reflects rising retail sales stemming from a growing population. Many retail establishments will continue to expand in size and number, leading to new retail sales positions. Since retail salespeople must be available to assist customers in person, this is not an occupation that will suffer negative effects from advancements in technology. To the contrary, software that integrates purchase transactions, inventory management, and purchasing has greatly changed retailing, but retail salespersons continue to be essential in dealing with customers. (U.S. Department of Labor 2008–2009).

---

worker who takes the time to communicate efficiently and well—no matter what the job title—is often the worker who is retained and promoted, etc. (U.S. Department of Labor 2008–2009).

The worker who takes the time to communicate efficiently and well, no matter what the job title, is usually the worker who is retained and promoted. Those staff members who inaccurately communicate the very details that make the store or office run smoothly incur costly, time-consuming damage to sales and reputation. Making a few mistakes is human, and forgivable. Making chronic errors in business communications can result in job termination. (See Profile 4.1 for expert advice on crafting **business e-mails**.)

THE INS AND OUTS OF E-MAIL
By Claudia J. Strauss

E-mail probably feels as natural to you as pulling on your clothes. And you probably think less about it than what you are going to wear. E-mail is something you do, not something you plan. E-mailing in your professional life, though, is not something you should do on autopilot.

Why is that? Because e-mail, like all communication, has a purpose, as well as an impact on the people who receive it. What's important is that the impact serves your purpose.

In business, e-mail has two primary functions: getting the job done and building relationships. Sometimes it's more the first, sometimes more the second, but it's always about both. Anything that gets in the way of that will make your e-mail less effective. And when your e-mail is less effective, sad to say, *you, too*, will be less effective. And sadder still, you may be *perceived* as less effective.

Some of the ways to ensure effectiveness form the bedrock of all good communication: know your purpose, know your audience, stay focused, be organized, be clear. E-mail has some extra wrinkles. If you want your audience to do something as a result of your e-mail, they shouldn't have to work hard to figure out what that something is. If you are asking something of someone who does not work *for* you, you need to think about why that person might want to fulfill your request, and provide a context or a reason or a benefit in that e-mail. If you are not clear in your own mind about what you want from this e-mail, don't send it.

Why E-mail?
Because it's fast, efficient, and direct. What you choose to say, how you say it, how much you include, and whether you send it at all, should all be viewed through those filters: fast, efficient, and direct. If it's not those things, or not supposed to be, you have decisions to make.

Why *Not* E-mail?
First, decide whether your message is necessary. Everyone has a lot of pressure to complete any number of tasks, an e-mail inbox tends to fill up with all sorts of clutter, and no one ever has enough time to do, to read, and to respond. People resent it if you waste their time; they respect people who have a track record of not doing that.

Second, decide whether e-mail is the right medium. Maybe the subject is *sensitive*, and things can be worked out on the phone or face-to-face. That minimizes the possibility of misinterpreting someone's meaning or someone's tone of voice. Then everything that's been resolved, and any follow-up questions, can be summarized in an e-mail. Maybe the issue is *complex*, or involves a lot of details that need to be agreed upon. A phone conversation can be much more efficient, avoiding many e-mails going back and forth. Afterwards, a single e-mail can be a record of everything that's been decided. Maybe the subject is *confidential* or the information is *proprietary*. Depending on an organization's electronic security and its internal policies, relying on hard copy can maximize the safety and privacy of the communication. If speed is of the essence, there are overnight delivery services, messenger services, and faxes. And maybe the subject carries a lot of *emotional freight*. Handwritten notes show care and thoughtfulness and our appreciation of the importance of a life event. They are the best response to a death, a birth, a wedding, and to occasions when someone has gone out of their way to be a gracious host.

Third, consider the oops factor. Never say anything in an e-mail you wouldn't want the whole world to see. That you wouldn't want forwarded to the wrong person. Or posted on a bulletin board. Or reported in a newspaper.

"Consider the oops factor."

Your Slip Is Showing

Fashions change; sometimes showing bits of lace and underwear is in, sometimes not. Whatever the fashion, some wardrobe malfunctions stay constant. And that can cover a lot of territory when it comes to e-mail. It applies to inappropriate topics, opinions, grammar, spelling, choice of words, tone of voice, and emotions. Never send an e-mail in anger, disappointment, or when you're bursting about some honor you've received. Wait until you've cooled down. And extend the same courtesy to others. Don't forward someone else's e-mail without permission. Don't reply to everyone when your message is meant for only one person.

Basting Your Words

We think nothing of basting our seams preparatory to the final product. It allows for roughing out, for getting a feel, for making adjustments. E-mails work better when we treat them the same way. Piece your thoughts together; check for fit, check for flow, check for style;

(*continued on next page*)

check for purpose, check for clarity, check for tone. Did you say so much that the reader will miss the main point? Did you say too little so the reader won't be sure what you want or how you want it done?

Then pretend someone sent your e-mail to you. How does it make you feel? Do you want to work with the person who sent it? Do you understand what you are to do? Do you feel respected and appreciated?

Stitching It Together

We measure clothes by how they feel, how they look, their presentation, their drape. E-mails should flow, be easy to follow, appear finished. Keep them simple. Keep them conversational. Proofread carefully. All of these show respect for the other person.

Mirroring

Follow the other person's lead when crafting your e-mail. This is important in how you open the letter: Dear, Hi, Hello; first name or last name; using colon, comma, or dash; as well as how you close the letter: Sincerely, Best, Take care, or just your name.

Pay attention to changes in the other person's responses. Style will evolve based on how well you know each other, how frequently you write in general, how close together in time you are e-mailing on a particular topic.

If someone signs a response to you with just a first name, open your next e-mail that way. As someone relaxes the formality of their closing, or increases the level of warmth, mirror that in your response.

As e-mails go back and forth on a particular topic, they can become briefer and even dispense with openings and closings. Doing this too early, though, can cause confusion, sound abrupt, feel cold, or seem disrespectful. Let the other person set the pace.

If someone becomes more distant, more formal rather than less, it's a subtle sign that something might be wrong. Don't ignore what might be an early warning signal. Maybe you didn't do something you said you'd do; maybe you got too personal in your last e-mail; maybe something you said was misinterpreted. Don't try to fix whatever it is via another e-mail; pick up the phone or drop by to see if the other person thinks everything is on track. Give the other person a chance to see your sincerity, to volunteer what might need to be addressed.

Getting a Response

This cuts both ways. When we make requests, we want people to let us know whether they will be able to deliver or not. One way to maximize the probability of a response is to end your e-mail with a question. "Does this work for you?" "What else do you need from me?"

"How soon do you think you'll be able to get to this?" "Would you have time to meet on Thursday?"

Keep in mind that just as you would like, and often *need*, a timely response, so do the people who are writing to you. You may not be able to answer their questions, gather information, or perform some other request right away, but you can let them know that you'll "get back to them on it" or that you've started working on it or that you've already contacted the people who will help you respond. Let them know what to expect and when to expect it, as this will help them to do *their* jobs.

Cutting away Material

Cutting away is like sculpting. It not only forms the shape of a garment, it reveals and highlights its important elements. Before sending an e-mail, cut away whatever is unnecessary and obscures your message. Consider putting supplementary information, documentation, evidence, and full reports in attachments. If you're not sure the recipient needs that information, don't send the attachments. Attachments take up space, take time to download, take time to read. Instead, add a sentence saying they are available and you'd be happy to send them.

Designing for the Occasion

Some things come down to what your audience prefers. Some people want only as much information as they need to know. They prefer you not send the entire sequence of past e-mails when you respond, that they not get copied on e-mails to other people unless strictly necessary. Some people do not like opening attachments and prefer you paste what they need to know within the e-mail itself. Others like to see the whole picture; find it saves time to get the whole thread of past e-mails so they can review the history; appreciate the convenience of supporting documentation in attachments. What's important is to find out what people's preferences are . . . and to honor them.

Making a Statement

E-mail can be a wonderful thing and it can be a terrible thing. It's great for creating a paper trail—a record of who did what when and who asked for what where and how everything was handled and how everything turned out. Some words, though, are better *not* preserved. They can come back to haunt you, your company, and other people. They can become statements to the press you never intended to make, statements in court that are entered as evidence.

And e-mail can be too easy. Too easy to send, too easy to broadcast, too easy to dash off without careful thought. Anything you send can take on a life of its own.

(*continued on next page*)

Communicating online has become a mainstay of the fashion business. This Hewlett Packard ad features a paisley-patterned designer look.

Working with Mixed Media

The communication tools available to us keep getting more sophisticated, and every year there are additional choices. It's important not only to target your audience but to tailor the communication tools you use to that audience, the situation, your purpose, and your company culture.

And it's important to remember the oldest forms of communication—in person, face-to-face, with eye contact, body language, and your voice. There are times when only a meeting or a phone conversation will do. "Interfacing" is both a business term and a staple of the rag trade. It serves similar functions in both arenas: giving body, sustaining shape, and strengthening. It is people who make the business of fashion work, people working together—within organizations, across organizations, between organizations. Sometimes a meeting of the minds is enhanced by a meeting of the humans that house those minds. Relationships are built on trust; old-fashioned interfacing adds dimension to that trust. We get a lot of information from eyes, stance, handshakes, tone, pitch, and intensity. When all our senses get involved, a stronger connection is possible.

The more tools in your arsenal, the more effective you can be.

EIGHT KEY TIPS TO CREATING SUCCESSFUL E-MAILS

Dos and Don'ts to Remember

Don't Waste People's Time
- Keep it brief.
- Be clear.
- Stay on point.

Decide Why You Are Writing
- To get information
- To provide information
- To set up a meeting

- To get a go-ahead
- To give reassurance
- To clarify a situation
- To create a record
- To keep a project on schedule
- To protect yourself
- To build rapport

Keep Things Simple

1. Stick to one purpose per e-mail in order to:
   - minimize confusion
   - maximize results
   - avoid things getting lost between the cracks
2. Specify a topic in the subject line in order to:
   - ensure the message will be read
   - make life easier for the recipient
   - speed the response
3. Help the recipient stay on track by:
   - putting lengthy material in attachments
   - using a cover note to list attachments/highlight purpose
   - sending a "heads-up" e-mail to alert the recipient that a separate e-mail on other subjects will be coming

Know Your Audience

- What matters to them
- What style they prefer
- How they use e-mail
- When they prefer another medium

Stay Out Of Trouble

- Don't hit the send button right away
- Think twice before forwarding
- Make sure "reply all" is really necessary
- Keep company e-mail for company business
- Don't complain, vent, or attack
- Avoid cute remarks and emotions

(*continued on next page*)

- Stay away from humor and irony (too easy for a reader to misread the tone, miss the joke, or take it literally)
- Never skip the checklist basics (see below)

Review a Checklist of Basic Questions

- Is this subject suitable for e-mail?
- Am I sending it to the right person?
- Have I listened to the tone?
- Are all the mechanics correct (grammar, spelling, punctuation, etc.)?
- Is the message clear and easy to read?
- Will the recipient know what to do . . . and want to do it?
- Would it be all right for anyone besides the recipient to see this? (If no, and it has to do with how the e-mail was written, revise it. If it has to do with the subject matter, don't use e-mail.)
- Should anyone else receive it? Make sure cc/bcc are appropriate.
- Is this important/sensitive enough to run by someone else before sending?

Observe Proper Etiquette

- Respond right away to acknowledge a request.
- Promise to respond more fully later when you don't have time to respond right away.
- Alert people early when you anticipate problems or delays.
- Say thank you immediately.
- Don't check e-mail or cell messages when in meetings (even when that meeting is one-on-one).
- Create an instant reply message if you will be away from e-mail for more than a day; include when you are likely to be checking and responding to e-mails again and a person to contact in case of something urgent.

Remember an Employer's Expectations

- Employees are to conduct company business on company time, and personal business on personal time. Hardware, software, network, Internet, databases, phone lines, IS, tech support are ongoing costs, in addition to the costs of salaries and benefits.
- Employees sign a handbook stipulating their understanding of how electronic media are to be used (and not used).
- Employees acknowledge that their electronic activity will be monitored.
- Employees recognize that inappropriate use has consequences.

ABOUT THIS AUTHOR

Claudia J. Strauss (left), an award-winning communication consultant, teaches business communication and public speaking at Albright College, coaches executives in effective communication approaches, and consults with businesses on strategic communication issues. The author of a series of books on health communication (*Talking to Alzheimer's, Talking to Depression, Talking to Anxiety*), and coauthor of a fourth book in that series (*Talking to Eating Disorders*), she has appeared on TV and radio shows across the country, and her books, translated into five languages, reach people across the globe.

Claudia J. Strauss is an award-winning communications strategist.

FASHION COMMUNICATIONS ON THE JOB

Whether you're a supervisor or sales associate, having a good memory and communicating information sensitively and effectively is a valuable asset. Paying attention to detail and caring deeply about detail are part and parcel of the fashion business, whether dealing with **inventory management** and personnel issues, or overseas markets and the wording in **trade agreements**. (See Box 4.2.)

The following interviews reveal the real lives of five individuals who work or have worked in positions related to fashion retail. In gathering responses, standard **interviewing protocol** involved: (1) devising a set of questions; (2) using a tape recorder or e-mail trail to ensure accuracy; and (3) presenting the final transcripts in a logical order.

- In "The Outreacher," a communications specialist shares tips and trends gleaned from her recent position as coordinator for PR and special events at a large, fashion-forward department store chain.
- A visual merchandising specialist talks about using technology to keep in touch both on the road and back home in "Road Warrior."
- A salesperson's viewpoint is represented in "Follow That Script!"

BOX 4.2

LEGAL BRIEF:
KEEPING CURRENT WITH TRADE LAWS

Trade agreements with other countries are among the many types of legislation enacted on the national level. Since such laws directly affect the flow of goods between countries, fashion communicators must stay apprised of changes that may have an impact on goods in the future. The *DNR* article below, delivered through an e-mail subscription, is typical of such announcements.

House Passes Andean Trade Extension

BY KRISTI ELLIS
Feb. 28, 2008

WASHINGTON—The House passed a 10-month extension of trade benefits for Colombia, Peru, Bolivia, and Ecuador on Wednesday, giving some relief to apparel importers and textile producers who benefit from the trade program. The bill passed by voice vote on the House suspension calendar, a procedural step for noncontroversial bills that limits debate and requires a two-thirds majority for passage.

Although the House passed the bill, the preference program, which gives duty-free status to apparel made in the four Andean countries and exported to the U.S., could still lapse if the Senate does not act quickly and the president is not able to sign it before it expires on Feb. 29.

That has many apparel importers and textile producers nervous about the loss of duty-free benefits and could lead to a drop in orders in the region.

U.S. apparel importers shipped $1.23 billion worth of apparel made in the Andean region to the U.S. in 2007.

Apparel imports from the region fell 14.26 percent on a volume basis in 2007, primarily due to the uncertainty associated with short-term extensions of the program, according to importers.

Domestic textile producers also benefit from the program because the rules of the trade preference program require that U.S. importers largely use U.S. fibers, fabrics and yarns in the apparel they make in the four Andean countries.

(*continued on next page*)

BOX 4.2 (*continued*)

But textile companies have been hurt by the decrease in apparel imports from the region. U.S. textile manufacturers exported $190 million in yarns and fabrics to the Andean region last year, down from $207 million in 2006, according to the National Council of Textile Organizations.

Top House Democratic and Republican lawmakers on trade reached a compromise on the legislation, which originally would have extended the benefits for two years, and scaled back the length of the extension to 10 months, through Dec. 31.

Although business groups had pressed for a longer extension, most apparel and textile companies supported the short-term extension to avoid a lapse in the program's benefits.

"Everyone would have preferred a longer extension but 10 months is probably enough to give companies the comfort they need," said Julia Hughes, senior vice president of international trade at the U.S. Association of Importers of Textiles and Apparel. "A lot of production that comes out of the region is cotton knits and we are right at the place where companies are starting to get deliveries for late spring and summer production, which is why it is pretty important to get this completed quickly."

Cass Johnson, president of NCTO, said, "There is already a business risk with these short-term extensions, which causes importers to shy away from placing more orders in the region and U.S. textile producers to lose business." (Ellis 2008)

- An assistant planner in jewelry shares the importance of paying attention to numbers as well as appearance in "The Planner."
- "From Actor to Super" reveals how a high-level manager's career path was set in motion at a young age and how education bolstered her communication skills.

The Outreacher

Position: Corporate PR and Special Events Coordinator

At the stores' corporate offices, how much of your day did you devote to e-mail, Internet, talking on the phone, talking face-to-face, etc.?

I would spend at least a couple of hours responding to e-mail communications from the media, customers, buyers, local nonprofits, and our stores' public relations managers.

About an hour each day was spent thinking of ideas and writing content for our store's blog. I would usually follow up e-mails with a phone call and would also be on the phone a lot during the planning/brainstorming step of a new project.

Picking up the phone and talking to someone is much more effective for me unless the subject matter is simple—cut and dry. If it requires any amount of conversation I would prefer to talk on the phone over an e-mail. People do not always read their e-mails carefully and I don't want my message to get lost in translation. I would spend most of my time talking to our stores' public relations managers on the phone or via e-mail; there was very little face-to-face contact other than when we had a special event and I would travel to a particular store.

Figure 4.1   Much communication is based through e-mail and over the phone.

The same is true with many of the other contacts that I had. Much of the communication was based solely on e-mail and phone (Figure 4.1). That said, there is no substitute for meeting someone face-to-face. Even if the majority of a relationship will be based on e-mail and phone communication, you should try to meet face-to-face at least once.

What kinds of interactions did you have with the press?

Interactions with the press varied greatly depending on what was going on at the time. During holiday shopping season and other big retail times they would call for information regarding products and sales. With the downturn of the economy, there were many inquiries regarding sales forecasts and how we were handling the situation. When we had special events, especially those involving a nonprofit organization, we would get calls for more information about our philanthropic efforts. We also always tried to produce a press release for these events.

What's the timeline (advance time) for event planning—and related communications?

In January we would set event dates for the entire year. We would begin confirming participation in these events immediately. The actual event details would be planned and then communicated to the public relations managers about two months in advance of the actual event date.

Our fashion shows featured merchandise that was in the store during the time of the show. Usually, that meant that you were showing fashions for the upcoming season. For example, a July show is featuring fall fashions.

When reaching out to the press, what works? What doesn't?

When reaching out to the press you must establish a relationship before you need something. Be proactive about the relationship and it will be easy for them to feature you where appropriate. You should definitely leverage your advertising with additional publicity. If you spend money with them, a part of the negotiation process should be additional features, community events, and other out-of-the-box opportunities to partner with one another.

Does the company engage in outreach with the community? In what way or ways?

It does an enormous amount of outreach in the community. . . . Whenever an organization asked us to do a speaking engagement or fashion show we always tried to participate. Not only did we have a lot of information to enhance their event but the grassroots marketing and being active in the community is extremely important.

Have you seen changes in the methods people use to communicate with each other?

I think that while people rely on e-mail and phone communication for their day-to-day tasks, it is becoming apparent that there is no substitute for face-to-face contact. More people are starting to realize this and are reverting back to making time for face-to-face meetings.

Is it a good idea to have an in-house newsletter?

A newsletter is a very good tool to use in addition to e-mail. People are so bombarded by e-mail messages that many times they will read or skim an e-mail without fully grasping the entire message. A newsletter that is well written and has relevant content is a useful way to break through the never-ending e-mails.

Any tips you could share regarding your experience?

One thing that I would recommend to anyone who is in public relations and communications is to take notes when you are talking to someone, not just on the business-related issues but about personal issues as well. When you speak with many people every day it is hard to remember the small details that came up during your small talk. The next time you speak with them it will mean a lot if you remember to ask them how their ailing mother is, or how their child's birthday party went . . . or whatever it was that you spoke about last. It shows that you care, and sometimes that is more appreciated than anything else.

Road Warrior

Interviewee: Visual merchandiser and marketer

Can you describe the duties of overseeing in-store presentations of your apparel supplier's new fashions?

First of all, the job involves a lot of mobility—and writing and recording details. I'm transitioning to a different position now, but when I was most active working for Alpha-Beth Sportswear*, I traveled to stores located on the East Coast to merchandise them with the A-B product. I wrote Store Visit Reports for each store I visited and End-of-Month Reports for all of my accounts. I collected all Store Visit Reports from A-B merchandisers who visited the department stores and organized the information into an End-of-Month Report and a Visual Merchandising Review. The reports included photographs that I took of the store before and after each visit, the quantity of product, feedback from employees and customers, a rating that I gave to the store, areas the store excelled in and areas they could improve in, a piece count, a section where I could request an order, and fixture feedback. Talk about details!

Sounds busy! What was an average day on the job? Or is there no such thing as an average day?

Hmmm . . . an average day? Well, the job did require traveling, so some weeks I would leave on Sundays; other weeks I would leave on Mondays; and other weeks I would be able to leave later on. I tried to schedule my store visit when a manager was available, so that was hard because I had to match up my schedule with theirs and quite often that required me to work different hours. Sometimes my day started at 7 A.M., and other times I wouldn't have to be at a store until 1 P.M.—it all depended on when a manager was available.

Typically, a store visit should be completed between the hours of 8 and 5, just like a normal workday. Some days I would set up new stores, and other days I would merchandise existing stores, and other days I would be working with the store's visual department to produce a section that would be seen by VPs and CEOs later on in the day. I would get to the designated store, meet my contact, and then they would show me where they keep their shipment and other various A-B "stuff" such as fixtures and accessories. Once I became familiar with the area, I would take pictures of the store pre-visit. I would then count the merchandise that was already on the floor. From there I would merchandise the section, meaning bringing more merchandise onto the floor and basically making it look "pretty." I would have to make it visually attractive to customers, meaning I would have to make it

---

Not the actual company name

so they can eye up the space and see their options, but also make it comfortable and roomy enough for them to walk in between the fixtures.

I also had to merchandise mannequins and put outfits together to communicate to customers ideas for what they could do with what is right in front of them. After I would rearrange and stock the store, I put accessories [props] out, such as water bottles on top of fixtures and sneakers at the base of mannequins, all A-B merchandise, of course. Then I would take a piece count of every item for A-B and I would get a percentage from before and compare it to after, because A-B likes to see their space packed full! I would also change fixtures and posters to make them more up-to-date with the seasons.

Then I would take "after" pictures and spend time talking to employees and customers about the product. I also had to go around and collect information about competitors. I would take pictures of their merchandise and record what their fixtures looked like and how they were setting up their space. That was a typical day.

Gathering and writing down information is a big part of the job, then?

Fridays were usually office days, spent writing reports. Since I was also a major department store's "Key Account Lead" person, that meant that I was in control of all of *those* store reports. I collected reports from everyone in the U.S. and compiled averages to send both to A-B and to the department stores' corporate centers.

Did you socialize or meet with colleagues after hours, or establish some face time to catch up with each other in person?

The truth? Traveling was very depressing because I traveled alone, which meant I went out to restaurants and had to eat alone, I went shopping alone, I worked out alone—this job did not build relationships. One time I was traveling from Maryland to somewhere past Pennsylvania and it was snowing and I did not know where I was going, and I did not arrive until 1 A.M.—and I still had to complete a report. There were also good days, like the ones when Alpha-Beth would call up and say that your allowance was available; that usually happens twice per year and you get clothing from A-B for free because they expect you to wear their merchandise.

There were also days that were not typical, such as flying to the West Coast for meetings, usually during the autumn to see the upcoming spring merchandise and then during May to see the winter merchandise (Figure 4.2).

What role does communication maintenance play overall, would you say?

Good communication was key in this job because you are working alone and you are talking to a boss who is across the country or in another country. A person has to

Figure 4.2   It's important to arrange face-to-face meetings, even if it means flying to meet a client.

stay up-to-date on their e-mail, but more importantly stay in touch with each and everyone via cell phone, which is provided by the company, while on the road. Good communication is essential because you need to be on top of dates for meetings, deadlines for reports, deadlines to submit expenses, what promotions are coming up. Every Friday morning all of the larger-region merchandisers had a conference call that lasted about an hour to an hour and a half. We discussed what we did in the stores that week and what was going on in the upcoming weeks. We were made aware of "goodies" we might be getting in the mail to give to stores, such as hats or lip gloss for the store employees or new signage that needed to be in place right away. If you are not on top of communications, then you don't know what's going on, and that doesn't look good on a report going out to the CEO.

Getting back to the communications methods you employ in such a position: How useful are tools like e-mail compared to the phone and printed texts?

Technology came into play every day of my life. Since I had a laptop, every time I would hear my e-mail going off, I would pull it up right away so as not to miss anything, but it also took away from my "free time." E-mail was very important because that is how everyone sent their reports, either to me, or me sending my reports to someone else in the company. The Internet was important [as a way] to stay up-to-date with competitors. I was able to check out their prices and their merchandise and if I saw something that I thought was a good idea, I could write that on my report to let someone higher up know about that.

Talking on the phone was very important especially since my one boss lived in the South, my other boss lived in the Midwest, and my regional manager lived six hours away from me. It was important getting in immediate contact with these ladies if there were any problems at a store—they had to know immediately.

Printed hard-copy forms were not very important since everything we did was over e-mail. I sent reports that were attached to e-mails and I also downloaded reports to CDs and would send them via snail mail when it was necessary, such as if some files were too big and if my boss needed a backup copy.

Assuming that visuals play a part in nonverbal communications, what about your physical appearance on the job? Are there do's and don'ts?

The physical appearance of A-B employees must portray what A-B sells. When I would go into stores, I would wear A-B merchandise from head to toe because if a customer saw what I was wearing and liked it, then she was more likely to buy it.

You are not allowed to wear jeans, and you are not allowed to wear anything with open toes because since you are working with fixtures, they don't want something to fall and break your toes. If you must meet with the executives at the department store, like I had to do, then A-B does have some merchandise that is dressier than others.

One should always look professional going into a meeting. Also, when I interviewed for this job, even though I knew that the job was for A-B and their fashion is more casual, it was still very important to wear a business suit. The lady that interviewed me was dressed very casually, but it is a MUST to wear a business suit and look professional, because it is still a professional company and they need to see that you are serious about the position you are interviewing for.

Does the adage "retail is detail" match up with your experience?

Absolutely. Retail is detail because you have critics all around you. You have employees looking at what you are doing, there are customers eyeing up what you are doing, there are competitors that are watching what you are doing—so everything you do must be detail-orientated to the highest degree. If you miss one small thing, the person next to you will do that one thing and then *they* will get the credit for it and then maybe they will sell more of their product, when you could have done the same exact thing.

On the selling floor, pay attention to everything you can capitalize on, such as accessorizing. Don't just put a shirt and shorts on that mannequin, but get a jacket and drape it over the mannequin's shoulders, put some socks and sneakers at the base of the mannequin. Because if you don't put those socks at the bottom, a customer may not know that you sell that particular object and they might buy it from a competitor when all along you had what they wanted—they just didn't know that. So, every chance you have to put more detail into one project, do it—pack it full of detail (to a pleasing extent) so you give the potential buyer ideas and then they will buy from you and not go somewhere else to get it.

In your experience, what is a good system for ensuring teamwork? What role does communications play in this?

At A-B, in my position, there was not much teamwork just, "Here ya go—here is everyone's report and here is the due date." In my current position, we do have a lot of teamwork to achieve our sales goals. We ensure teamwork by having contests. I am in charge of the marketing and to achieve our goals, we try to make it fun by having contests and giving out prizes. For example, if we get great results this week as a team, we will get breakfast. Showing employees appreciation is a good way of getting the job done and it promotes teamwork. Plus there isn't much pressure on any one person.

Are in-house newsletters and training sessions helpful when it comes to good communications on the job?

In-house newsletters are a big thing to keep the employees on top of current situations, and are helpful because you can highlight important things and hang them up in your office if you need to.

Training sessions are helpful when it comes to good communications on the job. When I had my first job, I was overloaded with e-mails. I took an organization class and it really helped me get organized with communicating over e-mail. I learned that you should designate a specific time to read e-mail; otherwise you won't get much accomplished because you are constantly trying to catch up on e-mails. Also, prioritize your day with a list of what is most important to least important. If your boss wants to see how your day is going, communicating your prioritization list through e-mail is a good way. Then they can also make suggestions on what else needs to be on the list or what they would move around to get done first.

Training sessions are also helpful because they teach appropriate ways to communicate, how to communicate in a professional way if something is bothering you.

Did you ever face a tough issue where miscommunication was at the bottom of the problem?

Before the days of **instantaneous communication** [e.g., handheld devices], during my first week at A-B, I was coming home from traveling late Thursday night. I knew Friday was an office day, but because I got in so late I did not check my e-mail. I figured I would catch up on my e-mail the next day. Well, I was awakened on Friday morning by my boss wanting to know why I wasn't on the conference call yet. She'd sent me the e-mail about a *regional* conference call on Thursday while I was traveling.

Embarrassed, I quickly got on the call. After the call, my Midwest boss and I spoke, and she said she usually sends out **mass e-mail** about conference calls days ahead of time. She understood about my traveling and not getting the e-mail—and I understood that no matter how late it is, it is vital to check your e-mail.

What do employers look for when hiring someone in fashion retail? What qualities would you look for if you were the one doing the hiring?

Well, of course, someone who started off by taking fashion classes in college is a plus. Internships are great. Students should do as many of those as you can. Fashion employers look for people who are motivated and are willing to learn new and different ways of doing the same thing.

If I were hiring, I would look for someone who is a good communicator, enthusiastic, energetic, and someone who is *not* content to stop learning, because the fashion industry constantly changes and you must stay on top of it.

"Follow That Script!"

Interviewee: Retail sales associate

In your experience on the floor, how much does a salesperson's visual presentation count? Let's say there's a scale of 1 to 10, with 10 being "critically important."

In retail, personal appearance is probably the most important communicator in general! More often than not, the salesperson does not have the chance to speak with a customer extensively. Most shoppers shy away from conversation with store staff—they want an uninterrupted shopping experience. Often, customers won't even ask a salesperson for help for fear of being pushed into something. For this reason, sellers must present themselves as professional, available for service, well put together, and appropriately dressed for the store's targeted audience/consumers. *How* a seller wears his or her clothes is even more important than *what* he or she wears—everything down to the makeup is important. If a salesperson looks sloppy, customers will shop sloppily. They won't get the idea that the product is worth much because the staff doesn't present themselves as though it is.

Details like accessories are extremely important—not only do they exponentially enhance an outfit, they subliminally project an image that says, "I care, therefore *we* the seller care." They also increase the amount of merchandise you can sell through bodily display!

Dressing appropriately also shows the employer that the employee cares about selling well, which leads to mobility in a position.

Figure 4.3   Giving accurate information to a customer helps to make a sale.

Do you have to act and look just like the designer image you're selling?

Especially in high-end retail, it is essential to represent the brand aesthetically—and to look like even *you* shop there. Even if you are not required to wear the brand's clothes, you have to wear clothes that speak to the brand's targeted consumers. If the store features a lot of clean lines and pressed fabrics, wear clean lines and pressed fabrics.

Do you ever practice word for word what to say to a customer?

Yes, especially when I changed companies. Each store/brand has a different protocol and lingo. I learned this through emulation, and through asking my general manager how to handle certain situations. However, I also developed a style of my own that was a cross between professional and neighborly. I think people like to be spoken to on a level of familiarity that does not cross professional boundaries.

I have practiced very specific phrases before, such as how to ask a customer for their contact information, which can be a very touchy exchange! I had to develop a persuasive defense as to why we asked for it.

If a customer asks you a baffling question, how do you respond?

Be honest. Tell them that you are not confident that you will give them the most accurate answer, but that you will find someone who will. Then go find them! (See Figure 4.3.)

What sort of access to communication technology is there? Or is that restricted?

Cell phones have always been restricted on the selling floor, in my experience, as have been other personal communication devices like laptops, e-mail, and smartphones. There has always been a landline phone for interdepartmental use, and for dialing out to other brand locations. There has also been a computer with intranet, which allows salespeople to check stock inventories in-store and at other brand locations. Perhaps wireless handheld devices are the interdepartmental and interstore communication tools of the future!

What is the single best way to establish a good relationship with a customer?

Be available and informative—not pushy.

Is it reasonable to assume you've met some difficult customers? And is dealing with them—even using a memorized sentence response or script—a potential topic for a weekly or monthly staff meeting?

Yes to both. My last retail manager was incredibly supportive, motivating, and helpful on this score. She held daily meetings—pump-up sessions—prior to setting foot on the floor that sales day. We would go over the quota and store news, etc., but the most innovative things she orchestrated were her skit sessions. We would practice dialogue between customer and seller. We practiced exchanges between the seller and various character portrayals of the customer: irate customer, happy customer, inappropriate customer, confused customer, stealing customer, and inquisitive customer who wanted to know everything about cut, fabric, weave, color, and pairings. Obviously, you can never predict everything, but these skits helped us feel more confident about communicating under pressure. Retail is very much about improv [theater], but it's the preparation that makes you a better improviser.

If you could fix one thing to make on-the-job communications flow more smoothly, what would it be?

In general, better managers—like my last boss. She really knew how to get her employees not only excited about the brand, but knowledgeable and articulate about what we were selling, down to its very fibers. We were a very successful store because of her. We had many regulars. In retail, if the people above you are not motivating, the brand suffers.

The Planner

Interviewee: Assistant planner (jewelry) and former retail sales employee

In your experience in fashion retail and as an assistant planner, how important is your personal appearance as a nonverbal communicator? In other words, on a scale of 1 to 10, with 10 being "critically important," how much does a person's visual presentation count?

In my experience, personal appearance would rank a 10. In spite of the more casual dress codes in the workplace today, a professional appearance still makes a positive statement to clients. Putting thought into how you go to work in the morning shows your customers and coworkers that you are serious about your job. This provides a level of comfort for the customers in that they can feel confident in purchasing from you. Looking professional and acting like a professional come hand in hand. Putting your best foot forward in order to be taken seriously is crucial when dealing with others in my work setting.

What does the word "detail" mean to you?

As an assistant planner, I work with numbers on a daily basis. I run several reports on our computer system that include sales trends based on cost and retail, gross margins, percent changes, merchandise on hand, etc. One of my jobs is to translate these numbers, break them down by season, month, and week, and then input them into various recaps. I also input several formulas into each recap. For example, when comparing sales from January 2009 to January 2008, I would input a percent change formula to tell me how much sales went up or down from the previous year. Accuracy is critical when dealing with these reports. If one number is off, the entire report will be off as well and I would ultimately be reading a false report.

Sometimes I help with assistant buying so I deal with creating **SKUs** [stock-keeping units] for individual merchandise. Being detail-oriented is extremely important during this process. The first step is to create an abbreviated detailed description of the jewelry. For example, the description of a white gold ruby and diamond ring would look like: "10K 6MMRuby .18CTTW DIA RNG W/G." This means that the gold carat is 10, the size of the Ruby is 6 millimeters, the carat total weight (CTTW) of the diamond is .18, and the ring is white gold. Precision is key when writing the description because this is what the department store employees use to identify the merchandise.

What sort of access to communication technology do you have on the job?

While on the job I have access to an office phone, a computer, and e-mail. These are to be used for work purposes only. Personal use is prohibited.

I assume you received training in using those tools?

Yes, I was given a handbook as well as a few days' worth of training.

Do you ever practice what to say to a customer?

Yes! I often prepare myself with several different greetings and open-ended questions before the workday begins. I find that I can better assist my customers when asking open-ended questions as opposed to those that only require a one-word answer. It's also important to be prepared with more than one phrase or question.

If a customer asks you a question that you can't answer, what do you do?

Rather than give my customer false information, I am always honest whenever I am unsure of an answer. I tell my customer that I can't answer that question at the moment, but I will do my best to find out and get back to them as soon as possible. This benefits me as well as my customer in that they get the correct information they need and I get to learn something new.

What do you think is the best way to establish a good relationship with other staff?

Figure 4.4   Regular staff meetings lead to good communication.

Being friendly to every staff member is a great way to start. I like to gain the respect of my coworkers by showing them that I am a hard worker and a team player.

How about approaching customers—what communication techniques do you use to establish rapport?

I try to be mindful of my body language by keeping it positive. A smile and a warm greeting, as well as maintaining eye contact, never fail.

Are there difficult customers?

There are always difficult customers. The key is to be prepared and know the right things to say or actions to take. I think it is beneficial for everyone involved (employer, employee, and customer) to have a **monthly meeting** for staff regarding ways to handle difficult customers on a professional level (Figure 4.4). This prevents unnecessary aggravation and will hopefully limit the degree of the issue by keeping everyone happy.

How would you make on-the-job communications flow more smoothly?

I would ensure that all communications coming to the employees from the main organization are geared toward helping employees support the end-user (the customer). When employees are provided with enough information to answer specific questions and make informed decisions that will ultimately help the customer, they become more competent and confident, which in turn enables them to deal more effectively with their customers.

Transparency within a company ensures that everyone is on the same page as often as possible, and would lessen any confusion or misinformation. Effective communication is vital to make sure that happens.

From Actor to Super

Interviewee: Supervisor at a high-end store

About your career path—from childhood on forward. Can you share your first experience with fashion?

It started at a really young age. In my family I was always known for changing my outfits, like, six times a day. And my mom and my dad would get really mad at me because I would put on an outfit and then throw it in with the dirty clothes—and it wasn't even dirty. So I would say at five or six, I was starting out putting my own outfits together, and asking my parents to buy things . . . like—"I want that!"

But my dad—he was really involved in fashion. He always wore [designer shoes] . . . So I was always a preppy kid, wore the penny loafers with the pennies in them. So really, at an early age, I was exposed to high fashion.

When did you know fashion retail management was something you wanted to do as a profession?

What happened was, when I was in high school, I wanted to be a theater arts major, because I was doing acting, singing, and dancing all throughout my career as a child—up until I was 18. Then, when I was a senior, I was thinking that being an actress is probably not going to pay my bills; and I'm the type of person that just really needs stability, always wanted to know where my next paycheck was coming from. And I just kind of tied my passion for clothes into what it was that I wanted to do. When I was a senior, that's when I got the ball rolling with fashion merchandising—looked at FIT, looked at Marist College as a program, and Johnson and Wales University.

How did your educational experience beyond high school enhance communication skills?

I had a great education. I started off at Johnson and Wales University in Providence, RI. People think that it's a culinary school—and it is—but it was actually founded by two women, and it started off as a business school. So they have a large business school there that had fashion merchandising. When I went to go look at the FIT campus, I was like, "I can't deal with New York yet!" I was too young. I felt really uncomfortable. Everybody looked really focused on what they were doing, and I just wanted to experience what college really had to offer, so I got my associate's from Johnson and Wales—you know, did internships through the school, and was really involved with the school. I did all sorts of college-esque things—was in a leadership program, was a resident assistant, all that stuff . . . sorority . . . all that stuff. That was my plan—two years there, and then get my bachelor's from FIT. So then I went to FIT and still majored in fashion merchandising management, and graduated in 2002.

About your experience as an actress and a singer: Has that part of your life come into play in your profession now? Have those skills helped you?

Absolutely! I would never take back those experiences that I had as a young adult, because they taught me how to be professional, taught me how to talk to people, how to engage people. They also taught me how to kind of leave myself at the door, so to speak. If I was having a bad day, I really knew how to cover that up and be that person that other people needed me to be. But definitely, I gained poise, confidence, self-esteem; was very articulate for a young person; always knew what I wanted to do; and that sort of thing. Definitely. I always encourage young people that are kind of dabbling [in theater] to do that, because it makes you very aware of who you are and it really does provide a lot of self-esteem and confidence for a young person or any person in general. It was a great experience.

Last question, just out of curiosity: How practical is it to learn a foreign language for a fashion career?

I have used my knowledge of Spanish often, but I wish I had learned Japanese, Chinese, French, and Italian. . . . I think a working knowledge of Japanese, Chinese, French, and Italian would come in handy. (See Box 4.3 for more on intercultural communications.)

PRACTICE: COMMUNICATING THE DETAILS

Not everyone is naturally detail-minded, but everyone probably has the potential to develop an eye for detail. The exercises here all revolve around the importance of caring about details in fashion communications.

Create a "Detail Quiz" (Group Task)

Devise a test with a group of fellow students (four to five is ideal) called "How Detail-Minded Are You?" Create the same kind of self-testing quiz that fashion magazines typically feature for their readers. Questions for a "yes/no" quiz might include something such as: "Do you know the color of your best friend's eyes?" or "Does it bother you when you see a man wearing an out-of-date tie?"

BOX 4.3

DOING BUSINESS ABROAD: INTERCULTURAL COMMUNICATION

Traveling overseas? If so, it is crucial to be aware of communication do's and don'ts. This is important not only for speaking and writing purposes but also for mastering tricky nonverbal communication like body language and fashion choices. Communications gaffes can make or break your entire trip. Consider just a few examples from Terri Morrison and Wayne Conaway's book *Kiss, Bow, or Shake Hands: The Bestselling Guide to Doing Business in More than 60 Countries:*

- In England, talking while keeping your hands in your pockets is impolite. It is wiser to wear a solid tie with your suit, as "the British 'regimentals' are striped, and yours may look like an imitation."
- When visiting Pakistan, women should avoid winking, should wear tops that cover their arms, and should choose a pantsuit instead of any dress that is not full-length. Jeans and shorts should remain at home. Be careful with names: "Some Pakistani names make sense only in context, relating a first name to a second name. For example, the name Ghulam Hussein means 'slave of (the Islamic martyr) Hussein.' To call him simply Ghulam is to address him as slave."

(continued on next page)

Allowing at least 7 to 14 days to discuss the assignment, write out your questions, figure out a scale and/or a scoring system, and do the wordsmithing and fine-tuning together. A good target number is 20 questions, with multiple-choice answers. Do not forget to include the scoring system in a box as well, preferably with lively **copy**, or wording.

Option

Consider using graphic elements, such as photographs or drawings as well.

Follow-through

To see if the quiz really works, give the quiz to classmates as a test—perhaps designate a class period during which everyone swaps tests. Then make final adjustments, if needed.

BOX 4.3 (*continued*)

- In Israel, women are generally advised *not* to wear pantsuits, but wear modest, fairly concealing dresses with "hemlines . . . well below the knee, if not ankle-length." As for wearing yarmulkes, don't do it if you are not Jewish, unless inside a synagogue.
- In Greece, meeting in public for coffee is not just a social break—so do not let down your guard, assuming that business communication will happen later in the office: "Business is usually done over a cup of coffee—often in a coffeehouse or taverna." Don't worry if you tend to fidget after sitting for a while: foot-tapping and fidgeting are acceptable practices.
- In China, when visiting a factory where the workers have assembled to applaud your arrival, applaud them in return. Keep in mind, though, that the Chinese are pretty sensitive about hand gestures in general—a reality that could derail smooth communications. For example, Morrison and Conaway advise, "Use an open hand rather than one finger to point," and, "Avoid making exaggerated gestures or using dramatic facial expressions."
- In Japan, seek help when dressing in traditional kimono: "Wrap it left over right! Only corpses wear them wrapped right over left." (Morrison and Conaway, 2006)

Examine a Press Kit/Create a Press Kit

Choose a wholesale or retail company to study with relation to their public face. Select a company that has a press kit or media kit they can send out (via the mail) or that can be downloaded from their Web site.

Review the entire kit carefully, noting the writing style and frequency of their press releases, as well as the types of information and illustrations included in the press kit. Compare various press kits in class and discuss differences and similarities.

Creative Challenge

Invent a personal boutique or other fashion business, or a fashion item, and use Photoshop or other software to draw up a mock press kit to "sell" it. Include images if possible. Part of the process will include establishing a goal and an audience, since these are two functional factors in press kit design. Example:

Goal: Selling a new line of hand-painted scarves to retailers.

Audience: Trendy boutiques in college towns in a 200-mile radius.

Take cues from the format of other press kits. Strive for ways to establish brand identity via every element in the press kit.

Conduct an Interview (Individual Assignment)

Interview someone who is directly involved in the fashion business—i.e., from a clothing store, shoe store, jewelry boutique, fashion wholesaler, etc. The focus of the interview should be on the role of communications in business. Here are some tips:

- Decide on a set of questions before conducting the interview. For example, "What do fashion communications mean to the success of this company/store?" "Does e-mail play a role?" "How important are details?" "Are verbal communications important?" "What is your target market?" Always include a challenging question as well, such as "How do you deal with communication breakdowns?" or even "What is an ideal day for you?"
- Decide on where and how the interview will be conducted. Which works best— phone, in person, via e-mail? Defer to the interviewee's preference, if possible, and send a reminder e-mail (or call) the day before. In person is almost always the best mode of interviewing.
- Always share the purpose of the assignment. (If it is just for a class assignment, say so. If the piece may end up printed in a school newspaper or online, communicate that information.)
- Always ask permission to record the interview if possible. Handheld machines with sensitive microphones are fairly inexpensive and can augment notes taken during the interview. Tell the interviewee that during the course of the interview, if something they say is "off the record," they should directly state that request.
- Quote accurately. Not only is this a journalistic mandate but it is the main way to ensure any future interviews with the same person.
- Follow up with a thank you.
- When transcribing the results of the interview, always include: date and time, circumstances (on site, via phone, etc.), the interviewee's name, affiliation (company), title/position, and contact information.

KEY TERMS

attention to detail

business e-mails

copy

instantaneous communication

interviewing protocol

inventory management

mass e-mail

monthly meeting

patience

SKUs

tact

trade agreements

CHAPTER FIVE

Becoming Fashion

> *"Nothing will stop her until she owns what I own. Wears what I wear.*
> *She is frighteningly clever. . . . She follows every clue, badgers every salesperson. . . .*
> *She's my fashion stalker."*
>
> MARIA BELL
> *New York Times Style* magazine, Spring 2005

CHAPTER OBJECTIVES

The information presented in this chapter is designed to help you understand:
- Influences that contribute to fashion as a phenomenon.
- The importance of public exposure through a variety of media.
- The practical value of trendspotting.

Ideally, after reading this chapter, you will:
- Understand patterns of fashion adoption.
- Appreciate historical events and media that propel fashion.
- Be motivated to investigate concepts surrounding fashion persuasion.

Figure 5.1   Before photography took over, dolls and paper dolls served as fashion models.

Fashion becomes fashion only after it is seen, or viewed by the public. Someone, somewhere, creates a style; the style is worn; then the style is seen. If the style is appealing, it is eventually imitated and adopted by the public. Voilà. Fashion is born.

This is, of course, a simplistic explanation of how fashion becomes fashion. In reality, the process is vastly more complex. A certain style or look could merely be described verbally in letters or conversation from Mrs. X to Mrs. Y, and Mrs. Y might then attempt to mimic the style in her own way. The style might not have even been worn by a human being. In eras past, especially in the 1800s, **fashion dolls** (Figure 5.1) wearing the latest Parisian and English styles were regularly transported by ships to American harbors (New York, Philadelphia, etc.) and were then used to tip off American dressmakers about the latest fashion trends in Europe. It seems likely that the phrase "all dolled up," which appeared first around 1906, has its origin in this phenomenon.

The **fashion plate**, a term that is still used today to describe someone stylish, refers to a highly detailed fashion illustration produced for early ladies' magazines. For many viewers, it was a first look at a fashion-forward direction. Historical and sociological complexities aside, it remains important to understand that a style, look, or wearable item must first make a public appearance or appear in a display or exhibit before it can even hope to become fashion. After that, all the other elements of human nature come into play, including the psychology of how people become convinced to see a look as fashion.

FOLLOW THE LEADER

Fashion is something like a game of follow the leader. In fashion lingo, being a **trendsetter** refers to someone who qualifies as a leader, to a certain degree, or to something that leads the way for others to follow. Diana, Princess of Wales (1961–1997), was unarguably a trendsetter in many aspects, including fashion. Princess Diana wore her hair in such a way that her shy but engaging eyes perfectly peered out through strands of hair falling on her forehead (Figure 5.2). (In the United States, we refer to this hair as "bangs," while in Britain it is called "fringe.") Hairdressers across several continents were exhorted by their clientele to cut and arrange their hair similarly, and the Lady Di hair trend was set in motion.

One can look back to examine how the influence of one beautiful member of the British royal family gave rise to an original way of wearing hair. First, the media ran photographic images of Diana, focusing on her face, her facial features, and her hair. Admiring Diana's look, **early adopters** (those with a fashion-forward sense or daring) of the hairstyle showed the world what this hair looked like on someone other than the princess. Scholars have termed this pattern **top-down adoption**. This imitative action influenced others, who then felt compelled to adopt the hairstyle. As numbers of women wearing the Diana style grew, the phenomenon shifted solidly from rare sightings into mass fashion.

Trendsetting in the Information Age

Today, fashion trends can be set in motion literally overnight, or even sooner. Styles popularized by movies are a prime example of this (see Box 5.1). The information age has forever changed how styles, looks, and accessories get seen through rapid advances in information technology, from TV to the Internet, to cell phone cameras. A Webcam set up on a trendy street corner in Tokyo provides instant access to anyone around the world who's seeking to explore the latest looks in that part of Asia. Adopting a trend seen on the street is the opposite of following what the royals do. It is referred to as **bottom-up adoption**. In addition, it is evident that people themselves, especially youth and those living in industrialized,

Figure 5.2 Lady Diana's hairstyle and clothing, shown to millions through print media and TV, were evidence that the top-down effect—a theory of fashion adoption that says fashion starts at the top of the social ladder and is imitated by the masses—can still be a formidable force.

information-savvy countries, have accelerated their own rate of changeability, exhibiting that they are ready to adopt and explore new ways of presenting themselves within shorter periods of time. The **side-to-side adoption** pattern is more of a peer-based pattern, whereby the primary fashion influencers and fashion adopters are mutually important to one another.

In recent years, it has become harder to say with authority exactly how fashion trends are diffused, or spread, especially in an increasingly globalized world. In her article "Diffusion Models and Fashion: A Reassessment," sociologist Diana Crane writes:

> Changes in the relationships between fashion organizations and their publics have affected what is diffused, how it is diffused, and to whom. Originally, fashion design was centered in Paris; designers created clothes for local clients, but styles were diffused to many other countries. This highly centralized system has been replaced by a system in which fashion designers in several countries create designs for small publics in global markets, but their organizations make profits from luxury products other than clothing. Trends are set by fashion forecasters, fashion editors, and department store buyers. Industrial manufacturers are consumer driven, and market trends originate in many types of social groups, including adolescent urban subcultures. Consequently, fashion emanates from many sources and diffuses in various ways to different publics. (Crane 1999)

With globalization, the pace of fashion has become relentless, to the point where manufacturers struggle to compete with one another in terms of being able to provide the right kinds of machinery, automation, and labor necessary to keep up with shifting styles and textile trends. For example, a factory that once handled all the woolen knitting for a sweater designer may find it impossible to gear up quickly enough when that same designer creates a new line of tops made from a newer, thermally innovative fabric. In short, going from looms designed for woolen thread from sheep to a fabric made as a byproduct of oil requires more time and money than the manufacturer can afford. The high level of flexibility required for today's fashion world has effects on all levels.

Trendspotting

Tracing origins and keeping on top of fashion influences is a critical practice in the field of fashion communications. At the end of this chapter are suggested topics to explore for

---

BOX 5.1

BLOGGING ABOUT SHOES

As this blogger indicates, a celebrity wearing a shoe in just one movie can launch massive sales—and establish a classic.

Saturday, June 03, 2006

Shoes in movies

I saw yesterday two fragments of two radically different movies. First, *Aeon Flux*, which was so undescribably bad we could only survive through 20 minutes of it. The only thing that sort of stuck with me: wedge shoes whose heels serve as storage containers for your run-of-the-mill assassin kit. Just think of the possibilities! In a well-constructed wedge, you could hold a basic makeup kit, for example, tissues, mints, floss, pepper-spray, and whatever else a busy girl on the go requires, bag optional. Now that's what I call multitasking!

"Assassin-kit" shoes worn by Charlize Theron in the film *Aeon Flux*.

Seriously, though: Charlize Theron is gorgeous as usual, but what we saw of the movie was egregious.

On a completely different note, I turned the TV on and Luis Bunuel's *Belle de Jour* (1967) happened to be on. I had never seen the movie from one end to the other, so I decided to watch the last hour or so of it. Oh boy, was Catherine Deneuve just the classiest, most stylish movie starlet EVER. Icy cold, sure, kind of frosty, but still jaw-droppingly beautiful. Naturally, I admired her fashion and her shoes. From an interesting newly discovered site I've found out the following: Roger Vivier designed Catherine Deneuve's

(*continued on next page*)

BOX 5.1 (*continued*)

---

classic Pilgrim flat shoes for the movie *Belle de Jour* in 1967. Over 120,000 pairs of this shoe have been sold, and the Pilgrim-style silver buckle pump has become the most copied shoe. Known today as the *"Belle Vivier,"* the shoe is a timeless classic.

This only served to fuel my hankering for a pair of Pilgrim flats, of the kind still sold in Roger Vivier stores (none of which is located in the US, I'm afraid . . .). Now, if I only had a fraction of Catherine Deneuve's style and grace to go along . . .

Posted by Scarpediem @ 11:59 PM

---

essays, PowerPoint presentations, and other projects. These projects will yield real-life research practice for future fashion communicators to strengthen their **trendspotting** and trendsetting skills. Included in that list is the **personal interview** (see Profile 5.1 for an in-depth interview with CEO Chris Lindland of Cordarounds).

As an investigative practice, seeking anecdotes about personal fashion awareness from friends and acquaintances is one of the most important ways to educate oneself on this vast subject. It is precisely this type of original research that makes the most significant contributions to the fashion communicator's comprehension of how fashion becomes fashion. For example, the true story of the six-year-old girl who cut off the fingertips of her gloves just before leaving the house for church is not just a silly childhood scenario. It turns out she wanted to mimic the style that pop singer Michael Jackson exhibited in a music video in the 1980s. Revealing this influence helps to uncover the origins of a certain musician's influence on fashion during the 1980s, which can then be compared to current musical influences on fashion, and assessed accordingly. Today, a designer who wants his or her tuxedo line to be seen by millions will probably not wait to create an advertisement. Instead, he or she will try to dress a musician who is headed for the Grammy Awards. Such public relations avenues can generate enormous amounts of business for a designer. Many people will buy an item of clothing just because they have seen a favorite celebrity wear the item. (See Box 5.2 to find out about a time-traveling method of getting publicity.)

· *Profile 5.1* ·

THESE CORDS GET AROUND

or

THE CORDS THAT LOVE THEMSELVES

By Arthur Henning

"I'm driving to see my dad," said a calm voice, "and I have about 30 minutes to talk." Thus began a cell phone interview with an American original, Chris Lindland, owner of *Cordarounds. com*, and the irreverently wacky brain behind a fashion-with-a-following: the corduroy pants with a horizontal wale.

Here are some of the burning questions I had for him:

Chris Lindland of Lindland's Cordarounds.

- Do you have a patent on this fabric design?
- How viable is your company at this point?
- Are you planning to continue, or expand, or just have fun?
- Are you making profits—enough to keep happy, that is?
- Can you talk about the creativity factor? How do you stay so . . . juiced?

Why should anybody care about Lindland's Cordarounds? After all, these garments are not sold in stores, never appear in slick magazine ads, and don't appear on a Milan or New York runway. They are only found online. The Web site, *www.Cordarounds.com*, is no flashy, über-preppy cinematic wonder. It's straightforward in presentation, and it has all the traditional aspects an online shopper would expect, including a shopping cart and shipping information.

While the sales of pants and jackets and other clothes might be the logical, ostensible, central focus and main reason to visit the Web site, the dedicated fans of *Cordarounds.com* probably spend much more time reading and laughing than they do making purchases.

(*continued on next page*)

The blogging is addictive, and the site itself is regularly updated with contests and travel pictures (a visit to Antarctica, for instance) and even a Customer Hall of Fame. There are plenty of new styles as well. The "Black Sheep Sweaters" photo gallery shows off how these cozy garments can be worn by fashionable men and women, and it displays some lovely images of black sheep interspersed between the models' shots, as if to say these attractive sweaters are simply not the only important fashion to notice. Sheep coats are just as attractive, suggests Lindland's Cordarounds.

The infectious nature of this site, this catchy product name, and this owner's unique writing style and marketing ability are all reasons why a tiny fashion company has consistently found itself garnering the kinds of publicity other companies would kill for. Lindland's Cordarounds has been reported in the *Wall Street Journal, Newsweek,* the *New York Times Sunday Styles,* and many other newspapers and media outlets. Millions of people have been exposed to the concept of a corduroy fabric that makes rings instead of long lines.

How does Lindland do it? Could it be as simple as the fact that he is targeting fashion and business writers who are looking for a story that's edgy and fun?

And does he really write all this stuff?

"Yes, I do," confesses Lindland, as he's cruising up the northern California coast. "Well, I do, but I should say I collaborate with my old friend from college, Anthony Jaffe. We've been cracking each other up since college." College was the University of North Carolina, Chapel Hill.

The company has only been around for a short while. "We launched in January 2005," says Lindland. The bare truth is that this entrepreneur has no background in fashion, and claims to have "no interest really" in high fashion. The notion of producing clothing in horizontal corduroy was "a silly idea I had," he explains, one that he kept talking about until finally, "I had a friend I knew in PR who introduced me to an atelier. He (the PR guy, Enrique) said, 'I know someone who can make clothing,' so I had it made so I could rid it—talking about horizontal cords, that is—from my small talk vocabulary."

It wasn't easy to explain to the atelier what he was seeking. "It was incredibly difficult to communicate that I wanted [the pants] made a certain way . . . the construction aspects," admits Lindland. But once he got his first pair of pants made, a minor miracle happened: He had mojo . . . instant chick-magnetism: "My pants became this item where women would touch my leg and say 'ohh . . . horizontal corduroy.' And it became the top come-on of all time," he says, laughing.

"I came up with the name myself," he says, and with this, a small-scale marketing legacy began.

"I figured out how to make more pants—we were approaching the holidays of 2004—and the timing was good, I thought, to put them in stores or on the market. But the stores were quick to say, 'Hey, we buy in April.' They already had all the Christmas stock they needed, of course. I knew that for a chance to survive, we'd have to bite the bullet and manufacture 200 pairs of pants—fast." He was determined to place his pants on other people's legs.

Embracing Oddness

"This animator I had worked with offered me a $5,000 Web site for $500. Truly, I was a rank amateur at fashion, but we put the company online, and right away the *New York Times Sunday Style* magazine thought it was funny and covered it," Lindland recounts happily. "We'd only sold about 15 pairs of pants—it took a few thousand dollars to start the business—and everything was projected heavily in image only. After the article came out, we had 190 sales the first day."

Lindland's Cordaround pants.

As often happens with such scenarios, sales then dropped drastically. The next step Lindland took made all the difference: He started communicating directly with his customers. "Because I think about Cordarounds literally all the time, I'd send an e-mail each week to all the people who bought them. I thought, I'll give them good stories and jokes to tell, so they'll wear their pants to dinner and maybe we [Cordarounds] will take over the dinner conversation."

The plan worked.

"At this point, *Newsweek,* the *Wall Street Journal* . . . just about every major media outlet has written about us. All the major newspapers, too, except *USA Today*." He adds, "I'm sure that's coming."

With a sixth sense for what others like in terms of entertainment and personal service, Lindland asserts that his basic approach to communication is focused on one goal: to create notoriety as a brand. "Most companies attend the trade shows, invest time finding more and more places to show the product, and spend more time in sales than anything

(*continued on next page*)

else. I thought to myself, I don't know if I have an interest in being a full-time salesperson. My thought was you can create more awareness if you start first online and sell only online." Lindland also believes that it's more than the pants that are selling points: "What gets attention is that we are this inherent oddity. We have exclusivity [because the clothes are only available online], and we have plenty of oddness. So, technical editors, business journalists, and reporters in general find us interesting—and amusing."

"After the article came out, we had 190 sales on the first day."

Lindland's sensibility for marketing strategy comes partly from former experience in a previous career. He says, "I'd seen the work of PR firms—actually, I was a cofounder of 'idrive,' and my background is writing. I know that PR firms across the board have good writers, but they all have the same press releases [and] they all sound the same. It's a formula. You know, 'Hot for Fall!' 'Hot for Fall!' I just put myself in the journalists' shoes. I mean, how many 'Hot for Fall' press releases can you *see*? So every time I sent out an e-mail to my customers—the humorous stories I'd create—I'd also collect the names of journalists and send mass e-mails, and I'd check to see who actually clicked on the link immediately. Then I'd contact that journalist, because obviously they might be more interested in interviewing me, or whatever."

"What's the Story?"

In a recent *Wall Street Journal* article, a journalist added a blurb about Cordarounds in a piece on preppy clothes for fall. That sort of coveted placement happens "once you send a journalist some e-mails they enjoy reading," says Lindland. Good writing has always been his best "in" with the press. "You need to establish a personal relationship with the journalist, if possible," he says. "Now, this particular article talked about us—not a lot—but with big names like Lily Pulitzer and Polo, companies with 60 people or 1,000 people working for them, and we're capable of fitting in. We've earned the right to be discussed. We deliver in design and the all-around experience. It's always entertaining. When it comes to business, I ask myself all the time, 'What can I do to get press?' Then, whenever we're in the press, it always creates spikes in our business, so I'm often thinking about the next funny story for the customers and the press."

Readers who like Lindland definitely react well. He points out, "An average of 40 percent of people who see my e-mails open them. That's an enormous percentage." Why does he think they like it? "Okay," he says, ready to share The Big Secret. "Here's the mantra about *Cordarounds.com*: 'We're 99 percent fiction, 1 percent fashion.'" The writing is critically important, with a tone described as "self-reverential." (See Box 3.4.)

"Check out the babyrounds," says Lindland enthusiastically. "You'll see that all the stories build on each other, there are like 30 stories that relate to the babyrounds. If you go on the blog, you'll see how far back this storytelling goes. . . . [Go to *www.cordarounds.com/babybaby.html*]. You'll see all the cross-references."

That's just one example of what Lindland means by "self-reverential." Reverencing the product and the site itself is one way the brand builds loyalty. "I have one stupid experiment a month, either trafficking or video-blogging, or whatever. Right now, my friend who's a video-blogger—he does stuff on YouTube—is doing something where we put him in a dollar-for-dollar challenge involving Google. I am going to lose money for sure, but not with Google: The sheer fact that I'm losing money is newsworthy." Lindland literally turns whatever happens into positive press and profit, using humor as his main tool.

Clearly, an attractive product counts, but in this case, it's the *Cordarounds.com* experience and the relationship that buyers crave. And for now, Lindland is having fun, concentrating on profile. "I just need to build this enormous portfolio. . . . Maybe someday later a big company will be looking around, looking to acquire . . . " he says, dreaming out loud.

What about Lindland's attitude toward success? Is he a bit more traditional than his Web site suggests?

"Am I going to succeed? It's the operating principle!" he says without a second's hesitation.

Finally, it's time for the last of the burning questions: Is there a patent for his curiously round-the-leg pants? What are the legal issues?

"You can't patent it. We weren't the first to do it," Lindland states. Maybe back in the seventies Levi's or somebody else made horizontal cords. "But," says Lindland, "nobody ever acted like it was the greatest invention since sliced bread. That's what I'm really proud of as a marketer."

TROUBLESHOOTING

"The only difficulties we have are with the hazards of the Internet. They—customers—can't try on the clothes. The only other problem is if people start writing back to us, if we make this truly interactive, sometimes spammers are writing. This is a reality, a problem.

(*continued on next page*)

I have to maintain the site myself, but I am going to try to outsource the spamming problem to a guest editor."

Chris Lindland's Preferred Media

"I go for the instant click-through capability form of communication. Of the three big communications media, I'd rank them as:

1. online
2. newspapers and magazines, etc.
3. TV and radio, they're last."

THE MAGAZINE MAKES FASHION

Figure 5.3 "Behold! The Emerging Ear" from *American Woman* is illustrated with a photograph of a woman whose earrings were considered daring at the time.

Magazines occupy a coveted place in fashion communications. Since the early part of the twentieth century, they have been the primary outlet for fashion communications and have dominated for a variety of historical and cultural reasons.

To be fair, newspapers count, too, and may, in fact, be enjoying an even bigger impact than in earlier centuries. In the TV/Internet-instant-news age, more newspaper coverage manifests in sweeping, in-depth features as well as fashion commentaries.

At one point in time, women were not encouraged to read newspapers; news content was not considered "genteel." Eventually, though, magazines designated as "fit for ladies" became the primary venue for fashion expression—exhibiting both men's and women's fashions (although women comprised the readership). Sometimes these expressions took the form of whole articles. Appearing in the January 1923 issue of the *American Woman* was an article titled "The Emerging Ear" by Nanette Hancock, illustrated by two photographs (Figure 5.3). The story's lede stated:

BOX 5.2

LEGAL BRIEF: PRODUCT PLACEMENT DEALS: INTO THE FUTURE

Behind those product names and designer bags seen in everyday sitcoms are legal contracts that require time, money, and foresight for all concerned. Fashion writer Michelle Lee points out an interesting phenomenon in her 2003 book *Fashion Victim*. According to Lee, television is a rich stage for influencing the public, and as designer labels continue to arrange deals for celebrities to wear their clothing on popular shows, a new twist has emerged:

> Now placements don't end when the director says, "Cut." . . . The next frontier of product placements? Reruns. In 2001, New Jersey–based Princeton Video Image was negotiating a 10-year deal to embed computer-generated logos and ads into reruns of *Law and Order* when it aired twice a night on TNT. For example, a Kenneth Cole billboard could be added to the background of an outdoor shot, or a logo could be prominently added to a shirt.
>
> The possibilities are scary to think about. One day we could be watching a rerun of *ER* with George Clooney wearing a logo that wasn't originally there or repeats of *Miami Vice* with Don Johnson walking in front of billboards for companies that didn't even exist back then (Lee 2003).

"With legs and ankles beginning to be concealed from public view, as our dresses grow longer, it seems as if women must counterbalance this by some other sort of revealment, so behold the emerging ear!"

This article typifies the elaborately wordy style of fashion journalism that was characteristic of early women's magazines. Flowery and excitable, with no compunction to avoid exclamation marks, Hancock's piece discussed not only new earring styles but an **evergreen** topic, the **shifting erogenous zone**. (In journalism, the term "evergreen" refers to article topics that are always relevant and regularly cycle their way into magazine lineups.)

For centuries, sexually or sensually appealing areas of the body, erogenous zones, have gone in and out of fashion, particularly in the West, and clothing and accessories reflect these movements in social life. When legs are in, hemlines are up. When necklines plunge, busts are the focus. In other areas of the world, zones shift depending on cultures and their acceptance of outside influences. In Japan, for instance, a woman's ankles and the nape of her neck are considered erogenous zones. The traditional kimono, still worn for many formal occasions (including weddings) is linked to these established zones. Despite such firm traditions, newly established trends in erogenous zones have become fashionable in Japan and elsewhere in Asia, due to Western exposure, magazines, TV, the Internet, and to globalization in general.

Short stories, essays, fashion layouts, mass production of patterns, and stage reviews all found expression in the fast-growing magazine market and contributed to propel fashion into public view and mass consciousness. Figures 5.4 and 5.5, from *Ladies Home Journal* in the 1940s and 1950s, illustrate approaches to teen fashion, seasonal wardrobes, and make-overs (where the reader is asked, "Still wearing your hair as you wore it pre-war?"). Advertisements were also present, of course, as the bread and butter for early magazines (see the nylon ad in Figure 5.6), and they remain valuable fashion influences today. Drawings and paintings were increasingly replaced by photographs. Models then entered the fashion-influencer scene in greater force.

Figure 5.4   The makeover has always been a strong selling angle for communicating change. This *Ladies Home Journal* exhorts women to consider a new, post-war hairstyle.

In Chapter Eight, the dominant role of magazines in promoting fashion is explored more fully. When it comes to the art of becoming fashion, achieving visibility in a major magazine (whether in an ad or via editorial coverage) was, and still is, near synonymous with a healthy measure of fashion success.

PRACTICE: FASHIONING FASHION

These research assignments focus on different aspects of fashion communications in action, and the role of individuals and media in fashion adoption.

Uncover the Influence of Historical People

What is the role of royalty in fashion? What part did Napoleon play? Louis XIV? Queen Victoria? Chinese royalty? Modern-day royalty? Why do certain people have more influence on fashion than others? Which U.S. first ladies and presidents had little fash-

Figure 5.5 Teen fashion found expression in a popular women's magazine, *Ladies Home Journal*, in August 1946. Today, teen fashion is considered a large, growing market, and has many more venues for expression.

ion influence, and which had the most (Figure 5.7)? What proof is there? What are implications for future politicians in communicating, affecting, or promoting fashion?

Activity: Explore and compare one or more historical fashion figures.

Discover the Influence of Materials (Objects and Fabrics)

When new fabrics and objects appear on the fashion scene, the runway is not always involved. What happened when the zipper was invented? Who first wore velvet? Who is wearing it today? Can a bra be made of velvet? How did patent leather first appear? Who adopted it, in what form, and why? How has the baseball cap evolved?

Activity: Choose a fabric or an object and explore its relationship to fashion. One helpful resource is the American Textile History Museum, located online at *www.athm.org/ educational_programs.htm*

Figure 5.6   Nylon stocking ad.

Find Out Underlying Motivations for Fashion Adoption

Why do people dress the way they do? Why do they shop where they shop? What sorts of fashions do they admire? How do strong fashion statements like Chanel suits, painter's pants (1960s), and smoking jackets become famous, or infamous?

Activity: Research a particular fashion trend or look that occurred in the past 100 years. Attempt to follow its initial exposure and history of adoption.

Option: Conduct one or more personal interviews (preferably in person) to discover a person's underlying reasons for style adoption. Interview questions may include: What memories do you have of what fashion is? Did magazines play a role? Catalogs? TV? Parents? Siblings? Blogging? YouTube? Which media carries the most weight? Why? How?

Figure 5.7   President John F. Kennedy and First Lady Jacqueline Kennedy found themselves at the forefront of setting new looks.

Examine Fashion in Print over the Decades

Which newspaper(s) have influenced fashion adoption the most over time? How have catalogs and other print media from various decades presented fashion in words and images?

Activity: Choose a specific magazine, newspaper, or catalog to explore and compare with a similar publication, or select a model, actress, or sports figure to study with respect to his or her ability to influence fashion. Provide concrete examples.

Conduct a Comparative Analysis of a Fashion Item with a Focus on Fashion Communication

Comparing and contrasting how two fashions were communicated in the past or in today's world is a helpful way to assess the value of specific communications techniques and/or expression.

Activity: Select at least two items, trends, or fashion expressions and compare them. The items or trends can be similar or very different. The main focus of this project should be to describe the various ways in which each fashion emerged as a communications phenomenon. The text on tennis bloomers in Box 5.3 provides an example of this sort of comparative analysis.

BOX 5.3

COMMUNICATING THE "BLOOMER"

Female tennis players have all but forgotten where their bloomers came from. According to most sources, bloomers first appeared in 1850, when Amelia Jenks Bloomer daringly wore a pair of loose-fitting pants under her skirt. This look was popularized by British actress Fanny Kemble. Today, the tennis bloomers worn under women's tennis skirts have evolved technologically. New designs even feature special pockets to hold balls that are not in play. (Men just use their shorts pockets.)

Gussy Moran made tennis bloomers famous.

In between the first bloomers and these high-utility bloomers was a famously shocking fashion episode that occurred on the staid grass courts of England, in 1950. *Sports Illustrated* reported the events: "When Wimbledon officials denied Gertrude 'Gussy' Moran's request to wear colors in 1950 she didn't get mad, she got even. Designer Ted Tinling created an outfit that shocked the championships: lace-trimmed panties for 'Gorgeous Gussy.' The undergarment was front-page news worldwide, as well as the subject of debate in the British Parliament."

BOX 5.4

"SOUTHERN GENTLEMEN TESTED: APPROVED!"

A Web page from one of Cordarounds' summer fashion products opened with these words:

Southern Gentleman Tested: APPROVED! A team of scientists from Cordarounds Labs traveled to the famed leisure proving grounds of Worthington P. Chesterfield's wide and gracious front porch to put our horizontal seersucker pants to the test—the Southern Gentleman test. Under rigorous analysis, Summerounds scored high marks in all manner of Southern Gentlemanly arts . . . And why shouldn't they? After all, these pants were sewn in San Francisco's South of Market district by ladies who hail from southern China. And you can acquire a pair for well south of $100. It doesn't get much more Southern than that, does it? Until our pants scientists figure out how to fabricate them out of sweet tea, we don't think so. . . .

KEY TERMS

bottom-up adoption
early adopters
evergreen
fashion dolls
fashion plate
personal interview

shifting erogenous zone
side-to-side adoption
top-down adoption
trendsetter
trendspotting

CHAPTER SIX

Out There for All to See

"A single word can make the difference between success and failure."

JOHN PHILIP JONES

author of *Fables, Fashions, and Facts about Advertising*

CHAPTER OBJECTIVES

The information presented in this chapter is designed to help you understand:
- The basics of marketing, advertising, sales, PR (public relations), promotions, and branding.
- The importance of communicating brand as a powerful force for corporate unity.
- Goal setting and its effects on fashion presentation in print and other media.

Ideally, after reading this chapter, you will:
- Know basic terms used in advertising and promotions.
- Be able to analyze advertisements, press releases, branding, and other facets relating to public exposure.
- Conceive fashion publicity as a team effort requiring multiple skill sets that contribute to a common goal.

People who love fashion agree there is nothing quite as delicious as a gorgeously fat fall or spring issue of their favorite fashion magazine. The cover that shouts "50+ Pages of the Best Fall Clothes!" (*GQ*, September 2007) or proclaims lavishly "Our Biggest Issue Ever! 840 Pages of Fearless Fashion" (*Vogue*, September 2007) is like a long-lusted-for dessert. All earlier editions of that same magazine are either forgotten or maybe even discarded. All thoughts of school and work are tossed aside—momentarily, at least. Some people rip right into reading the thick book. Others delay turning back the heavy cover, opting to wait until they can sit down without distraction to savor each glossy page. The promise of new colors, new fabrics, new shapes, and new creations is literally at one's fingertips. At the back of the hungry mind of every fashion lover exists the most enticing morsel of all: the potential to adorn and drape one's own body anew, to cast aside an old self, and to find fresh ways to express an established personal style.

The **allure of fashion** depends upon a system of seasons and cycles that are exemplified by fashion magazines. This allure feeds on freshness, newness, originality, and the unique sort of creative competition that is played out in an array of photographs, drawings, symbols, and words (Figure 6.1). From the moment a designer displays new work, for example at seasonal runway shows held at staggered **fashion weeks** around the world, the clock starts ticking. A highly select audience of invited buyers, critics, editors, celebrities, socialites, and image makers begin reacting to what they see. In years past, there was a long wait to see what was new in the world of fashion. Word traveled slowly, and the clock was quite slow. Words and images appear instantly today. Reaction is even faster than ever. Writers post their criticism and praise on online **blogs** (journals),

Figure 6.1   *Style.com* covers major fashion trends, the main catwalks, designer news, post-runway parties, and other state-of-the-art news.

a word that originally comes from the expression "Web log," so that the latest fashions are available before print newspapers can report them.

Placing fashion in the eyes of the world involves many professionals whose job is to communicate fashion within their respective fields. It is important for fashion communicators to be able to distinguish between those fields.

THE MANY FIELDS OF FASHION

Creative professionals are constantly coming up with innovative approaches to communicate fashion, but most careers fall into one or a combination of the following disciplines: marketing, sales, advertising, public relations, promotions, and branding.

Marketing

Marketing concerns itself with figuring out who will buy what thing in what city, zip code, or nation, and targeting particular groups as buyers of particular goods. Marketing professionals use **surveys**, **focus groups**, **demographic charts**, and other instruments to try to find out which groups of people are most likely to buy which item. They work closely with everyone in fashion, but most important, they work with salespeople. Special words or sets of words, **terminology,** pertaining to marketing are listed in Box 6.1. Be sure to familiarize yourself with these terms.

Sales

Sales are exactly that: the receiving of monies in exchange for fashionable goods. Sales professionals are interested in how, when, where, and what fashions will sell and are selling. Before a sale, many factors must be in place. For example, in the front windows and on the floor of a store, **visual merchandising** is a key consideration. Is clothing placed or displayed in such a way as to catch the eye and entice buyers? Is the signage (i.e., words, visuals, and presentation) going to enhance sales? Are shoppers treated in a certain way as to maximize the potential for buying? As a shopper purchases an item, is she or he encouraged by a **retail salesperson** to also consider a **complementary fashion item,** to boost the total number of dollars gained in that shopping session? In online sales, the goals are generally the same: to secure the most money possible each and every time a shopper starts browsing. People who are involved in the sales end of fashion

BOX 6.1

TERMINOLOGY TO REMEMBER

The worlds of marketing, advertising, public relations, promotions, and publicity refer constantly to a wealth of special terms. Before interviewing an expert, or before applying for a job as a copywriter, be sure to master as many terms as you can, including:

focus group—a research methodology where a small number of consumers are led through a series of questions by a professional facilitator in order to gather information about public opinions and attitudes, buying habits, and market-worthiness.

target audience—those persons (potential buyers) whom a company or service is trying to woo or gain the attention of.

demographics—statistical information about a population, often divided according to age, cultural identity or race, income, etc.

primary research—research that collects information that does not already exist, through surveys and other instruments.

secondary research—the summation of information from existing research (e.g., books, articles, and data otherwise made public), often used as a starting point for primary research in sales, marketing, or promotions.

tagline—carefully chosen words (usually short in length) used in consumer advertising to sum up the selling point of a brand, product, or service.

slogan—often used interchangeably with *tagline*, those words used in consumer advertising to sell something but sometimes perceived of as being longer in word length (even a full sentence) than a tagline.

positioning—ensuring that a product, brand, or service finds a place and visibility in the most desirable niche and/or display arena within the market.

product placement—attempts to gain visibility for the brand by putting a product in easy reach or vision. Designer bags displayed on a TV sitcom is one example.

brand equity—the value attributed to a particular product's character and marketing potential (as established by its name and sales attributes).

promotional theme—a coherent, agreed-upon focal point defining the activities (other than advertising) that serve to encourage a customer to buy.

(continued on next page)

BOX 6.1 (*continued*)

cross-promotion—pairing (or joining) of products to encourage buying of those brands. A car company linked to a fashion show is one example of cross-promotion.

loyalty programs—sales promotion efforts characterized by tangible rewards, designed to encourage repeat customers and secure faithful purchases of the brand.

copy platform—a statement that defines the creative strategy behind an advertising or promotions plan.

B2B—business to business, both the seller and the buyer are business entities and not private consumers.

point of purchase—a display for a product placed where the buyer can immediately buy the product or service (also called *point of sale*).

sponsorship—the financial backing of a product or promotion by a company, individual, or group.

layout—a physical representation of how a final page might look.

campaign—a program where promotion and advertising are coordinated.

copy—the text of a promotion or advertisement.

testimonial—the personal story of a customer who describes the value of a brand, product, or service.

direct mail—printed materials that come to potential consumers via the mail.

---

include cashiers, store managers, accountants, secretaries, data entry workers, banking personnel, stock traders, Web site owners, and consultants. Their main interest is in the exchange of goods for monetary gain. They are interested in, and often responsible for, the bottom line, which includes how many items are sold, how many items are projected to be sold, how much money is being made, whether or not the store has enough items to sell, and the numbers of buyers in particular locations.

Sales personnel engage in a variety of communication methods. Speech is needed for meeting customers, answering phones, ordering goods, and communicating effectively in staff meetings. Writing is a crucial skill and ranges from filling out forms to writing sales reports and providing clear data analysis for corporate annual reports. Additional information pertaining to sales forecasts and earnings, as well as the ups and downs of the marketplace, invariably involves sales experts and journalists who are capable of covering these aspects of the fashion industry. Hundreds of thousands of people rely on reading articles in *WWD*, the *Wall Street Journal*, and business-to-business publications in order to make sound judgments and business decisions, which affect millions of laborers and consumers.

Advertising

Advertising has traditionally referred to the art and practice of putting a product in the public's eye. Before the advent of television in the 1950s, advertising was limited to certain spheres. An advertisement before the age of television might have been a small, boxed grouping of words and images (i.e., it had tooling lines around its words or images) in the classified section of a newspaper or magazine. It might have been a one-quarter page, one-half page, or even a full-page advertisement. If a peddler was traveling from town to town, bringing a trunk full of new fashions for the local people to try, advertisement for these fashions might have occurred only by word of mouth: "Did you hear? I heard Mrs. So-and-so say that some of the newest colors will be displayed!"

In remote parts of the world, fashion advertising might still be conveyed by word of mouth. The **trunk show**, however, is a different story. It has not gone out of style, although the advertising around it has definitely changed from word of mouth to **direct mail**, display ads in publications, and e-mail notifications (the kind that begin with "Dear Preferred Buyer . . . ").

Today, advertising finds expression in a variety of forms. The large, glossy photographs of models wearing designer clothes in such consumer magazines as *Elle, Esquire, Lucky,* and *W* are obviously some of the purest forms of advertising that exist. Inserts, those often-colorful sheets promoting clothes, accessories, jewelry, and shoes that are tucked into Sunday newspapers, are also examples of straightforward advertising. Television commercials, shopping channels, direct mail (including credit-card bill inserts), and department store signage are all vehicles for advertising fashion. They are just the tip of the iceberg. With the international proliferation of the World Wide Web—a term coined in 1990—advertising has moved in creative new directions. Pop-ups, podcasts, targeted e-mail, online music videos, and handheld communication devices are all potential and potent outlets for fashion advertising.

Creative Gurus

When it comes to communicating ideas, images, and words associated with fashion, advertising professionals play a vital role. Advertising professionals must become comfortable and proficient with a variety of communications avenues. They must possess a natural curiosity in order to build a broad base of knowledge across seemingly unrelated subject areas, and they must be able to visualize artwork, color, models, and their clients' goals. Like marketing and sales experts, they must be budget conscious. A top-notch advertising professional engages in daily communications that typically involve speaking (articulating well in conversation as well as giving instructions to staff and others), writing, drawing, photographing, accessing images, and doing computer-aided design. Above all, advertising professionals have to be creative. Throughout history, advertising professionals have been credited with developing some of the world's best-recognized, wealth-producing taglines (slogans). Brevity is the key, says self-dubbed tagline guru Eric Swartz of San Mateo, California. Witness such powerful words as "Just do it" (Nike) or "lifts and separates" (Playtex bras). "Anything less than seven words is good," Swartz said in a recent news piece. "These days, they tend to be two, three, four."

Choosing the best design **layout** is as important as words and images used in the advertisement (Figures 6.2 and 6.3). Three of the most basic ad layout formats are: column(s); grid (also called Mondrian, or geometric); and field-of-tension (chaotic) in which the designer uses expert alignment to tie together various elements.

Public Relations

Public relations (often called by its abbreviation, **PR**) is frequently confused with advertising. An easy way to remember is to memorize the two words: "public" and "relations." It almost seems too simple, but consider that, literally speaking, the public is anyone outside one's self. Home, family, and close friends represent a private, inner circle. How well one gets along with family members is referred to as the quality of relationship. For example, you might hear someone ask, "What kind of relationship do you have with your sister?" The answer might be "Great! We can tell each other anything, and she's always there for me." Or, it might be the opposite: "We always seem to fight. But we are working on making our relationship better."

Public refers to everyone outside one's immediate close circle, or the people in society and the world at large. In the business sense, *relations* refers to the quality of communication and the connection or status (standing) that exists between a business entity and the larger public. Public relations professionals concern themselves with how positively or negatively a company (fashion designer, particular fashion item, or brand) is perceived by the buying public.

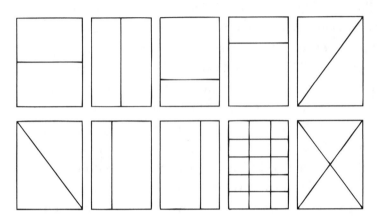

Figure 6.2   Examples of various ad layouts.

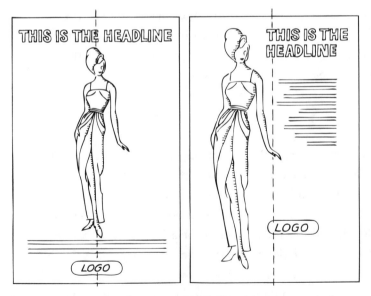

Figure 6.3   Examples of a symmetrical (left) and an asymmetrical (right) ad layout.

Public relations expertise is needed in order for a business entity to succeed over the short term as well as over the long term. A single mistake in public relations can pull a company's profits into a downward spiral and cause permanent damage.

Public relations involves communications as its primary focus, especially since it deals with human beings and how the public comes to think about a particular company, person, or thing. Recognizing that images and words play key roles in the scheme of human perception, PR professionals are often knowledgeable in the areas of psychology, sociology, political science, and language. They typically exhibit mastery of all the basic communication arts such as public speaking, writing, and personal image projection. Most public relations professionals are experts at networking.

(continued on page 132)

BOX 6.2

PROMOTIONAL WRITING FOR TRADE SHOWS

Trade shows are a vital part of the fashion industry. To communicate their intent, and to promote their big events, trade shows must display a variety of tightly written promotional materials that sound compelling, comprehensive, and enticing. The two samples here are by MAGIC International, a company that presents semi-annual events held in Las Vegas, attended by more than 100,000 people in the fashion business. Notice the heavy use of superlative adjectives, such as *premier, largest, ultimate, unbeatable, key,* and *newest.*

Sample 1: Media Fact Sheet (Fabric-related)

Sourcing at MAGIC is the premier trade event in North America for the production/supply side of the apparel industry. Co-located in the MAGIC Marketplace, the largest and most comprehensive fashion industry trade event in the world, Sourcing at MAGIC provides exhibitors direct access to the largest concentration of buying power in the United States. Here product development, merchandising and design teams have direct access to the largest gathering of apparel manufacturers, fabric and component suppliers in North America—900+ companies from over 35 countries—in ultimate efficiency to shorten research, travel, and merchandising time and increase speed-to-market.

Sample 2: FAQs about MAGIC (Excerpted from a 2008 press release)

What is MAGIC?
The MAGIC Marketplace is the premier fashion trade show event in the international apparel industry, hosting global buyers and sellers of men's, women's and children's apparel, merchandising apparel alongside footwear, accessories, and sourcing. As an incubator of fashion, MAGIC is where new trends surface and develop into what will be seen on the consumer. The show's goal is to connect and inspire the fashion community, fuse diverse trends, while offering unbeatable service to its customers. . . .

How many exhibitors feature their collections at MAGIC?
More than 4,000 companies, 5,000 brands, and 20,000 product lines are featured at the MAGIC Marketplace each show.

(continued on next page)

BOX 6.2 (*continued*)

What makes MAGIC different from the other fashion trade events?
The MAGIC Marketplace is the only show that brings together key industry segments under one roof, vertically connecting the industry from sourcing to runway to retail. At each show, buyers can find the newest trends and resources in men's, women's, and children's apparel, as well as in footwear, accessories, outerwear, swimwear and lingerie . . . Manufacturers, on the other hand, can also come to find original prints, fabrics, and other sourcing resources. But what makes MAGIC Marketplace *truly* different is the fact that it draws the largest retail audience in the world. . . .

BOX 6.3

HOW TO WRITE A PRESS RELEASE THAT REALLY GETS NOTICED: SIX TIPS FROM THE TOP

By Rosemary Brutico, CEO, Quintessence Communication

Although public relations has evolved into a sophisticated, high-tech industry with the emergence of electronic communications, the traditional press release is still considered the bedrock of the public relations profession. That said, the quality of your press release (often referred to as a news release) can be the bane or boon of your PR efforts. By adhering to these six tips, you'll not only ensure that your release will be picked up, read, and distributed by the media but you'll also ensure the success of your campaign to get your company's news out to the public and raise your organization's visibility in the marketplace. Of course, these tips apply only after you've determined that your "news" is indeed newsworthy.

Tip 1: Know Your Audience and Tailor Your Message to Them

Before you put pen to paper, take the time up front to define your audience. Ask yourself: "Who is my primary audience?" "What do I want to tell them?" "What kind of action do I want them to take?"

(continued on next page)

BOX 6.3 (*continued*)

Tip 2: Make Sure Your Headline Says It All and Says It Well

You have just a split second to capture the interest of the media whose job it is to sift through an avalanche of press releases at breakneck speed to determine what's news and what's not. The only thing that will save your release from being DOA (dead on arrival) is the quality of your headline. The sign of a "killer" headline is one that distills the essence of your news. But that's not enough. Your headline needs to sound fresh, pithy, even clever (hackneyed headlines will doom your release). Ask yourself: "Is my headline an attention-grabber?" You'll know if it is.

Tip 3: Structure Your Release Using the Inverted Pyramid

This may sound like Journalism 101, but the formula is tried and true. The first paragraph should contain the broadest information—the main point—with subsequent paragraphs containing information in descending order of importance. Essentially, the first two or three paragraphs should answer the five W's (who, what, where, when, and why) and sometimes "how."

Tip 4: Use Third-Party Endorsements Effectively

Nothing lends credibility to your product or service better than a testimonial from a satisfied customer or a company spokesperson (such as a celebrity or a CEO). The purpose of an endorsement is to describe the benefits of a product or service in a way that spurs your audience to action. Therein lies the challenge. A well-crafted quote should sound enthusiastic (without sounding over the top) and be believable (without getting bogged down in minor details) at the same time.

Tip 5: Banish Jargon, Hyperbole, Typos, and Grammatical Errors

The quickest way to lose your audience's interest, as well as your credibility, is to litter your copy with superlatives, gobbledygook, and glaring errors, which in effect shows sloppy thinking, careless writing, and disrespect for your audience.

(*continued on next page*)

BOX 6.3 (*continued*)

Tip 6: Keep It Short—500 Words Max

Time is what the media has too little of, so don't waste it. Think of your press release as a haiku where less is more.

Rosemary Brutico of Quintessence Communication in Boston.

ABOUT THIS AUTHOR

Rosemary Brutico founded the public relations firm Quintessence Communication (*www.quintcomm.com*) in 2000 to provide strategic and tactical public relations counsel to growing organizations in the public and private sectors. She has held executive positions in the publishing and corporate communications professions, and is a member of the Greater Boston Chamber of Commerce, Public Relations Society of America (PRSA), and Women in Technology International (WITI).

(*continued from page 128*)

Depending on the job order, public relations professionals may need to be quite creative. When a creative opportunity presents itself, they almost always work in conjunction with other people, so **teamwork** is especially valued. In one assignment, a public relations team might have to come up with creative approaches to meet ongoing PR needs. For example, their job might be to put together and keep current a **media kit** or press kit. A media kit is a packet of materials (either printed matter or online materials) that is made available to members of the media or other businesses. A media kit may contain information about the company, the designer, new designs, new lines of clothing, and a press release about the item, or items, being introduced. A public relations team might be asked to stage **promotional events**, such as a holiday party, a get-together during fashion week, or photo opportunities during trade shows (see Box 6.2). Writing press releases to publicize such events is one of many ways to introduce a fashion item or trend to the public (see Box 6.3 for expert tips on press release writing).

Public relations people are also called upon to solve existing, newly identified, and potential problems. **Publicity** is within their purview, so they concern themselves with the quality of their clients' public image. For example, negative publicity may assail a designer whose clothing is discovered in production in a factory (or country) with questionable labor practices. Public opinion regarding a particular fashion could also start diving quickly when celebrities are used to advertise or **promote** a line or product—such as when a sports celebrity breaks the law prior to launching a line of athletic shoes or when a famous model behaves badly enough to warrant disapproval. Because of the "P" in PR, whatever is done in view of a camera or within earshot or view of the public eye, relations can be affected for good or bad.

Good PR responds to the spirit of the times, also called **zeitgeist**. Ideally, it anticipates expressions of zeitgeist. As with dynamic advertising, the best public relations strategy sets the course for others to follow.

One important trend in the fashion industry is the association of fashion with causes. As the world grows smaller, by virtue of global communications expanding, social and political problems too upsetting for people of conscience to ignore have grabbed the spotlight. Thus, fashion is increasingly used to symbolize social consciousness, whether it is to use a pink ribbon motif to symbolize breast cancer awareness (Figure 6.4), or to use green as a color or word (green initiatives) to show ecological concerns. This trend may continue for years to come, but it is likely to take many forms. (See also Figure 6.5.)

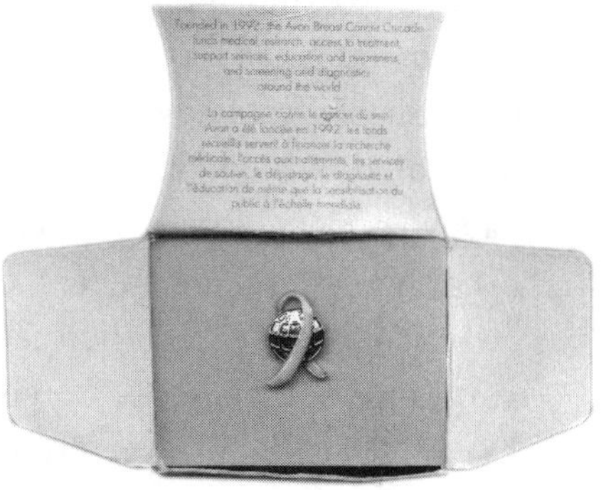

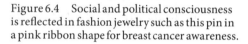

Figure 6.4 Social and political consciousness is reflected in fashion jewelry such as this pin in a pink ribbon shape for breast cancer awareness.

Promotions

Promotions refers to every tactic that pushes a product, designer, or fashion line into the public eye, resulting in increased visibility and sales. In the narrower sense, **promotions in business** is a term that encompasses special sales events, specialized advertising approaches, and a whole range of practices that involve placing "something to be sold" into a position of public recognition.

For example, having a fashion show at a shopping mall is a promotional activity. Sending press passes to

Figure 6.5 Heart disease awareness fused with fashion in a series of word-play ads characterized by the word "RED."

133

fashion journalists may result in a mention of the fashion show or a particular designer or trend in their publications. Hiring floor models to wander around the cosmetics or perfume section of Bloomingdale's and handing out makeup samples or small vials and cards with a new scent is a form of promotion. Requiring a model to actually wear the makeup or skin product she (or he) is selling is taking the promotion a step further: The model is then coached to exhibit (and describe) how the product acts and feels.

Promotion, as a communications concept, is neither easily contained nor clearly distinguishable from advertising and public relations. It is often interwoven with the fabric of a company's established effort to gain attention. That attention can happen through a happy accident, as when a well-known, well-respected person makes public claims about his or her fashion preferences, or when a journalist becomes particularly impressed by the quality or effect of a certain fashionable item. More often than not, however, promotions are crafted and planned. Television comedian Jon Stewart's *The Daily Show* (2007) carried a small byline banner crediting Polo Ralph Lauren's "Black Label" in Stewart's wardrobe. In the same year The Weather Channel showed catalog giant L.L. Bean's logo on all of its hurricane-battered weather reporters.

Branding

Branding is of major concern to all the players in the fashion game, including clients, marketers, advertisers, graphic designers, publicists, promotions experts, and magazine editors. It is the buzzword of the century, and it has enormous relevance for the fashion industry and for fashion communicators. Alina Wheeler defined branding in her book, *Designing Brand Identity*, one of the most thorough discussions of branding ever published:

Brand is the promise, the big idea, and expectations that reside in each customer's mind about a product, service, or company. Branding is about making an emotional connection. People fall in love with brands—they trust them, develop strong loyalties, buy them, and believe in their superiority. The brand is shorthand: it stands for something and demonstrates it. . . . A strong brand stands out in a densely crowded marketplace. Translating the brand into action has become an employee mantra. There is substantial evidence that companies whose employees understand and embrace the brand are more successful. What began as corporate culture under the auspices of human resources is fast becoming branding, and the marketing department runs the show. (Wheeler, 2003)

Branding involves naming, taglines, values, signage, uniforms, typeface, product essence, and moods. It is reflected in a word or words, in a name or names, and in storylines. From Banana Republic to Balenciaga to Victoria's Secret to *Cosmopolitan* magazine, branding is intimately tied to fashion success. By its very nature, branding involves masterful communications approaches and constant vigilance to ensure the strength and integrity of the brand. Branding is not something that is determined overnight. It is carefully developed . . . and legally researched (See the Legal Brief in Box 6.4). Wheeler quotes Andrew Welch of Landor Associates as saying, "Branding is a journey, not a destination."

OLD CODES AND NEW CODES

In marketing, sales, advertising, public relations, and promotions, it is important to observe the basic principles and goals that define good business practices. Seeking to target one's market appropriately, making a profit, having effective advertising, managing public opinion, and exciting the public by creatively exhibiting in the marketplace are all common business practices designed to ensure a brand's success. Communicating messages across the media environment is an integral component. This information promulgation appears in business-to-business publications, smartphones, trade magazines, television, billboards, radio broadcasts, after-runway parties, and professional associations.

The relatively new phenomena of reality TV shows (*Project Runway, America's Next Top Model*, etc.) and shopping channels such as QVC have opened up some broad new avenues for fashion marketing. This chapter's profile of *Project Runway* contestant Marla Duran (Profile 6.1) explores how reality TV has affected a real designer.

One aspect of marketing that is often overlooked pertains to workers within the system, and their codes of behavior as they serve to support a marketing **campaign** of any description. When it comes to putting one's product "out there for all to see," fashion frequently has a timeline that must be honored, and that timeline may well demand **confidentiality**. In such a dynamically creative industry, where it counts to be fresh, new, exciting, and different from the rest of the pack, not sharing the details of an ad campaign or a promotional tool until the timing is right is not just only highly valued; it is sometimes a written requirement. A legally binding confidentiality agreement may already be in place in a company, or one may need to be written in order to prevent damaging leaks to other companies, individuals, or the press.

(continued on page 141)

BOX 6.4

LEGAL BRIEF: HOW TO OWN A NAME

In a *Business Week* article titled "Brands: Namestorming," Jeremy Quittner describes the fun and creative challenge of coming up with a brand name. Helpful brainstorming tips and corporate anecdotes are a strong part of this article. Quittner also discusses something else that is vital to branding, how to avoid stepping on someone else's toes. Federal law provides protection for fashion brand names and logos that are properly registered, which is why naming a line of clothing or accessories can be complex and costly. However, the rewards are usually well worth the time, money, and legal consultation. Quittner writes:

> The game isn't over when you find a name you like. You have to make sure you have the right to call it your own. To avoid potentially costly missteps, hire an intellectual property lawyer. Expect to pay your attorney up to $10,000 for all the searches and filings. That might seem like a lot, but according to Ilene Tannen, partner at New York law firm Jones Day, the costs of disputing a lawsuit for trademark infringement, along with lost goodwill, advertising, and packaging costs if you have to change your name, can run to tens of thousands of dollars.
>
> After narrowing the field to half a dozen names, see whether any have been trademarked. Start with the [U.S.] Patent & Trademark Office [PTO] database, which lists all names filed with the federal government for the purpose of doing business. The owner of a name registered with the PTO trumps anyone who comes afterward, as a federal trademark holds throughout the country. You can search this database yourself at no cost, but an intellectual property lawyer can do a better job. . . .
>
> Next, you'll need to consult state registries. . . . No free, central repository exists for the state registries, so for this leg of the journey, you should hire an intellectual trademark attorney. Most charge in the range of $400 an hour. Trademark specialists will also search databases such as CT Corsearch and CCH for so-called common-law names. Although these names, which specialists cull from trade magazines, local publications, and other sources, have not been registered, trademark law gives precedence to the first user. . . . And be aware that if a business owner can prove he has been using a state-registered or common-law name nationally before you filed for a federal trademark, you could lose your right to the name. (Quittner, 2007)

LIFE BEFORE AND AFTER PROJECT RUNWAY: INSIDE THE STUDIO WITH MARLA DURAN

The role of the media and technology in fashion communications is undeniable. Bravo Network's *Project Runway* is a prime example of how television programming reflects a public interest in the world of clothing and propels that interest forward at lightning speed. *Project Runway* is a reality TV series set in New York City at Parson's the New School for Design. It features a group of designers competing to create the best pieces of apparel with limited materials in a small amount of time. Describing the onset of the show's burgeoning popularity, Virginia Postrel wrote in *Forbes* magazine in March 2006 that *Project Runway* (then in its second season) "attracts more Wednesday night viewers in the U.S. than any other cable show," with viewers of the eighth episode of that season reaching 2.3 million.

It is increasingly important for people in the fashion industry to have a finger on the pulse of modern media interests and on the new ways of staying connected. Those who foresee their careers intersecting with the fashion business, whether working directly with textiles or in an administrative position, can greatly benefit from the infinite public relations possibilities available in television and media journalism. That means actually watching TV, contacting the right people, keeping up with e-mail, learning to write and speak coherently, and investing in a smartphone. Access to instant communication is vital whether you are a designer or a vendor. There is always a product at hand and the ultimate goal is to sell that product. For those on the creative end, selling product means public appreciation of one's work or display and the resources needed to keep creating. For sellers, it means company profit and professional (and sometimes public) recognition of one's success.

Fashion designer Marla Duran.

(*continued on next page*)

The following is an interview with atelier Marla Duran, a contestant on the second season of *Project Runway*. She describes how all the publicity from the show affected her, personally and professionally. Her remarks suggest she is still finding her own voice in the fashion industry. She acknowledges the media assumed a role in helping her define and deliver her message. More important, her experience with television and media communications has prompted an awareness that her life and business are plugged in now more than ever.

What is strong about your design approach?

I think I have a sense sometimes about what's coming, and I don't necessarily act on what I pick up on. I think sometimes, God, if I was maybe in—I don't know what the right environment would look like—and have access to maybe more resources? I just think that I have a knack for sensing things that are coming before they come.

How has your experience on *Project Runway* had an effect on what you've become or what you're doing now?

I certainly have a lot more recognition, and there have been people who come in specifically to see me because I was on the show. I'd say people are more impressed with me. Sometimes I kind of go, "Wow! I was one of the people picked for that show. That's pretty cool." But if I'm trying to get my foot in the door somewhere, it makes people sit up and pay attention.

How do people contact you? Do they call you up and say, "I'd like to visit you and be your customer?"

Yes! These people called me a few days ago and said, "What are your hours on Thursday? We want to come and see you." And yesterday this couple from Toronto—their son is at the local Velodrome, biking—just wandered in, and I don't think the woman expected to find what she found. She was exactly my kind of target customer, and so we had fun. She was perfectly nice, trying on things. . . . She's the kind of person who needs some help in putting it all together, and her husband likes clothes, too, and so we had fun. That's how I like it to be.

It is inspiring that you have fun at work!

One of the things I'm good at is working with my customers. I'm enthusiastic about what I do. And I think my clothes need to be tried on to really be appreciated, and when I get somebody who's willing to do that, it's just fun. It's fun for me, and it's fun for them.

So you enjoy the personal touch?

Yes. I do. And I don't ever assume that someone's going to like my clothes. I am always flattered and grateful when people find my stuff. It's like, wow, thank you. I do these craft shows in cities like New York,

LA, Chicago, San Francisco. . . . People become your customers, repeat customers, and they collect your clothes, and that's a lot of fun. The personal touch is a big part of what I do.

Appearing on *Project Runway* has certainly increased your recognition in the outside world. Has it changed the way you think about and recognize yourself?

One of the things Tim Gunn [the show moderator] told me was that I should have more confidence in my own ideas. So, I've probably heard myself say this too many times, but I'd like to see myself spend more time hands-on, being creative, and trusting my own ideas more often. The full experience of being there was what was most amazing. Being in the workroom with other creative people, and then having Tim come around and critique my work, I really, really liked that.

> ## "I'd like to see myself spend more time hands-on, being creative, and trusting my own ideas more often."

You liked having the critique part?

I liked having the feedback.

Talk about your work—aside from *Project Runway*.

Oh, I'm happy to talk about it. I mean, that's [Project Runway] all anyone wants to talk about.

Well, television is only one aspect of communications. You also have a Web site, *www.marladuran.com*. You were meeting with your Web site guy earlier, you talked about making it more inviting, more active, more friendly.

Yes, I was looking forward to my meeting with him. The Web site was getting dated.

You were describing the changes you wanted to make, one of them being making it more interactive.

Yes. You know what, I feel like I get kind of overwhelmed with all the stuff I have to do, and so sometimes I just push things aside. And I realized that this is one of those things that I just can't push aside anymore.

(continued on next page)

Duran at work in her atelier studio.

A signature creation of designer Marla Duran.

You've got your studio and store space, so you're open to clients coming in off the street. But you're also creating art, new fashions, at the same time. You're doing an awful lot at once.

I know. Part of me feels like I should remove myself, sometimes, like when I hear myself saying, "I can't create." So, I took this one month away from my business where I was doing all sorts of gardening stuff. [Laughs] And I'm not a gardener! I was just sort of whacking away at stuff . . . and then I just said to myself, "You can do anything you want right now." I'd been pushing myself so much, I just had to leave some room for my-self to just have no agenda. Just to get back to finding my voice.

Do you write?

Occasionally. [On a stool nearby is a neat pile of loose-leaf pages, looking lusciously full of fabric swatches and drawings and intriguing handwriting.] That, over there, is what I need to remind myself to do. I'm thinking of just getting outta town. Say, Max [speaking to one of her dogs], we need to go on a road trip.

You must feel that you are constantly connected. A couple of times when I e-mailed you to get in contact, you used a BlackBerry right away. Tell me about the BlackBerry as a means of communication. Do you depend on it?

Well, I rely on my phone a lot. I forward all my calls from work to my cell because I'm not here a lot, and this way people can reach me. I like it because it keeps me in touch. It's probably paid for itself in just being able to be on top of e-mails I receive. And I don't tend to go online with my laptop all the time, so this keeps me connected.

Customers like to contact me, so I definitely find it worthwhile. I may have made some sales quicker and more solid because I was able to respond.

Did you ever miss an opportunity because you didn't respond quickly to your e-mail?

Yes. I got an e-mail from a woman who works for NBC, who's a Project Runway *liaison, and she sent me and everyone else an e-mail asking, "Tell us what you're doing. We want an update," and I never got back in time. That's just pure stupidity on my part. I did get back to her, but I think it was late. . . . It was for* New York *magazine. . . . That's like free PR.*

You have to get back to the press right away, right?

Yup. There's no excuse for that. I should know better. The truth is, though, Project Runway *is not the be-all and end-all of my career. It's really about the clothes I make. Having been on that show changes the perception . . . that's it! People's perceptions of me change, whereas I'm doing stuff that I always did! It's about the clothes I make, and the hard work I put in, and the relationships I build.*

(continued from page 135)

In recent decades, fashion communicators working in marketing, advertising, PR, and other career areas that formerly operated separately from one another have found themselves working together because all aspects of product visibility are tied to a common branding goal. (See Box 6.5 for some of the shared terminology.) Every aspect of the fashion product, every word, image, font size, label, and Web design element, is scrutinized and weighed against a brand concept in order to attain as seamless a picture of the product as is possible. Marketing people find themselves communicating with photographers. Designers hire public relations consultants to prepare them to appear on talk shows. Graphics editing software and digital image programs have created crossovers in talent abilities, so that it is no longer rare for an art director or photo editor to write captions for a fashion spread. The roles and goals of these professionals shift and redefine themselves in response to:

BOX 6.5

FROM GUTTERS TO WHITE SPACE

There is a language peculiar to media that all involved must master sooner or later. Here are just a few of the colorful terms that are used in design studios and layout meetings:

- **Bleed:** when a designated color or type runs (bleeds) to the edge of a given page. Important as a design element for overall effect. Sometimes a bleed can present technical problems in printing and alter costs.
- **Gutter:** the inside edge of a magazine or catalog page. If a designer forgets to account for a wider margin in the space where the magazine gets bound, the entire ad or article could be "lost" in the gutter.
- **PMS:** refers to PMS colors (trademarked by Pantone Matching System) that are an industry standard when printing. The exact color chosen for branding and advertising can be perfectly matched every time, by any printing company, using the PMS number.
- **White space:** the negative space in an ad or layout of any type. Allowing for white space usually results in a layout that is less cluttered and more visually appealing.

- improved facility with computer graphics
- easy access to equipment that was once too technical or too expensive for anyone besides experts to own
- increasing sophistication with words and images, in many dimensions
- ongoing exposure, practice, and training in communications methods
- expanding ability to interact quickly with people all over the world

In the face of all this rapid change, terminology is changing as well. When it comes down to getting "out there," fashion communicators direct their discussions toward such concepts as **presence**, **relativity**, and **currency**.

Presence

Presence—A combination of being, being seen, and being appreciated.

- "Does this _____ [item/label/brand/trend/wording/image] carry presence?"
- "Which qualities define, enhance, and express (its) presence?"

Relativity

Relativity—How a fashion item or trend makes sense or has context, and how it connects or does not connect with people, elements of society, place, and purpose. Relativity answers such questions as:

- "Why?"
- "Why not?"
- "Who should or will care?"

Currency

Currency—The timeliness of all aspects of a fashion item, look, personality, or image, as well as its present value and its projected value, and its ability to draw concrete dollars for what it represents. Some questions for analysis include:

- "Will this _____ [person/garment/silhouette/material/paragraph, etc.] have currency with the public?"
- "Should it?"
- "How much currency does it have?"

Communication = Democratization

There is good reason for inventing new language to manage new phenomena in the fashion industry. In past centuries, fashion applied strictly to those of privileged rank and class. The democratization of fashion has changed all that. And as technology continues to be a liberating force in society, fashion communications will become increasingly liberated as well.

PRACTICE: EXPLORING THE DO'S AND DON'TS OF GETTING OUT THERE

The following assignments allow you to explore the different aspects of marketing fashion.

Explore the "Oops" Effect

There is an old saying that goes "All publicity is good publicity." Is this true or false? Does bad publicity count positively simply because it puts a brand name on people's tongues? What constitutes good publicity?

Find examples of where this saying has been true or false in the fashion world. Examine various aspects of fashion, including makeup, apparel, accessories, and hairstyles. Look especially at designers, celebrities, athletes, or politicians. Some examples you might consider include: Donna Karan and media attention to sweatshop labor, Nicole Kidman and her work on behalf of the United Nations, football player Michael Vick and his canceled Nike contract, and Senator John Edwards's $400 haircut. Presentation tips:

- Discuss the pros and cons, as a group or class; *or*
- Write an essay or create a PowerPoint presentation, after researching more about the meaning and manifestations of this saying; *or*
- Interview a public relations professional regarding his or her personal experience and thoughts regarding this adage. Ideas for presenting results: Write the transcript and present it in an article or essay, or present it in a live interview on a college radio station.

Keep a Group's Activities Secret

New fashion is all about surprises and being fresh. Therefore, keeping confidences is a valuable tool in the business, at all levels, from brainstorming ideas to creative design phases to media exposure and "look launches." Editorial, promotions, advertising, and other creative work in a professional corporate environment constantly requires that teams of individuals hold fashion secrets close to their chest until it's time to let the new style or layout or product debut.

Here is a two-week, fun assignment that requires minimal energy but maximum coordination, to practice and test out confidentiality skills within a group of people:

First, assemble in small teams of at least four to six people. A random group within a class is best. For this exercise, it is important to avoid cliques.

Second, meet privately with the group to brainstorm a plan to dress in a certain way two weeks from this starting date. The goal of the activity is to have all members of the group dress uniformly with a fashion theme in mind. This theme must remain a complete secret until the chosen date so that other groups will not have a clue about the plan.

Be as creative yet reasonable as possible. In other words, group members should not have to spend money unless it is a very small amount—such as $5 for a "tiara" or $3 for matching "belts" made of rawhide from a hardware store. Themes should involve some thought process that the group can present to the rest of the class. For example, if the group discovers that all of its members have a habit of changing into heather-gray sweatpants after classes, then a common theme of "casual studywear" emerges, and the group may wish to assign everyone to wear heather-gray sweatpants to class. If a group discovers a favorite movie in common, that movie may provide inspiration for the group uniform. Naming the group's look is a good creative challenge.

As a group, devise a system to uncover potential leaks. In other words, discuss how the group can maintain secrecy and prevent the group's secret fashion plan from becoming known to rival groups.

At the end of the two weeks, on the day when all groups present their theme looks, be sure to discuss whether spying or leaks occurred. Have an informal vote on which group kept the best secret, and which group had the most interesting/crazy/adoptable fashion.

Surf for Resources

There are numerous professional associations for people who are interested in or are already active in the career paths discussed in this chapter. For example, in public relations, the Public Relations Society of America (PRSA) is one of the most active societies, and it has a student association that offers many benefits. (See *www.prsa.org* for full details.) Using a librarian's help, or just surfing with the "dot-org" mindset, locate a variety of professional groups, and write a list of them with a response to each. Explain why or why not a Web site looks or sounds inviting and helpful. Using a checklist approach, include whether or not each organization has:

- a publication
- a membership form online
- a "Jobs" section
- an events calendar
- conference information
- press releases

For communications careers in general, many options for professional associations exist, including the National Communication Association (*www.natcom.org*), and specialty groups like Women in Communications International (*www.wici.org*).

Brand It

Attempting a branding project is an ambitious undertaking. It may be small and shallow—such as coming up with a Web site name. Or it may be the beginning of a long-range project that is personally compelling (e.g., designing a store name, a clothing or accessory line, etc.). A branding project may be short or ongoing through the semester, depending on the focus of the fashion communications class. Think about the kind of branding project that would be most challenging to you. Would it be a new fashion magazine? A radio show on fashion? A television program? A new line of perfume? A line of business suits? Formal wear for a red carpet event?

KEY TERMS

advertising
allure of fashion
B2B
blogs
brand equity
branding
campaign
complementary fashion item
confidentiality
copy platform
cross-promotion
currency
demographics charts
direct mail
fashion weeks
focus groups
layout
loyalty programs
marketing
media kit
point of purchase
positioning
presence

primary research
product placement
promotional events
promotional theme
promote
promotions in business
publicity
public relations (PR)
relativity
retail salesperson
sales
secondary research
slogan
sponsorship
surveys
tagline
target audience
teamwork
terminology
testimonial
trunk show
visual merchandising
zeitgeist

part iii

FASHION COMMUNICATIONS—
REPRESENTATION IN THE MEDIA

THE VISUAL-VERBAL ELEMENTS COMPRISING FASHION SEE THEIR MOST consistent expression in media outlets, a term that requires regular redefinition, given the explosion of burgeoning options for communications.

Chapter 7, *The Big C: Creativity*, sets the stage for all communications with its focus on creativity. It explores the power of originality, using real-life examples and offering tips to students for attaining authentic creative expression, whether as graphic designers, style innovators, copywriters, artists, or problem solvers. While fashion speaks for itself, there is always a practical need for human expression using images and words to communicate that physical manifestation.

Chapter 8, *Evolution of the Fashion Magazine*, examines the beginnings of mass fashion consciousness, following the historical evolution of both women's and men's magazines, with illustrations that serve to contrast and compare the print media of yesteryear with more current representations.

Chapter 9, *Dynamic Wordingó The Art of Describing Fashion*, asks: How can words best serve the fashion world? It isolates the art and practice of wordsmithing, exploring the realm of possibilities with relation to description through examples (e.g., adjective-oriented, verb-oriented, storyline, emotion-charged, etc.) to discuss a fashion. The range of writing for fashion embraces the spoken word (e.g., radio, runway, TV); typed and fonted words (e.g., magazines, newspapers, advertising, logos, Web sites); scripted indications (e.g., film, theater); dreams-to-paper (e.g., designers' thoughts at the inception of new fashion); translations of inspirations (e.g., nature, fabric/pattern/line/form, makeup and other fashion expression); and observations (e.g., translating "seen on the street" to words that capture the concept).

Chapter 10, *Visuals That Speak*, delivers a wide overview of the basics of graphic design in print media, along with core concepts of image literacy. It examines how fashion is visually represented across the media, with a focus on placement, position, mood, lighting, silhouette, and other key factors. The art director, photo editor, photographer, stylist, and other visual agents all engage in creating visuals that speak.

Chapter 11, *With This Page (Ad, Script, or Whatever!), I Thee Wed!*, introduces trends regarding the successful marriage of words and images. This marrying-up is a balancing act of the highest order, which, as public sophistication grows, increasingly leans toward simplicity, with a dependence on the public's perception of cultural codes to derive meaning. Advances in communication technology become more and more accessible across the spectrum of society, suggesting a fuller democratization of fashion in years to come.

UNCOVERING VOGUE'S
the Wizard of

OZ

Photographed by
Annie Leibovitz

THE POWER OF
STORYTELLI/\G
Fashion Wizardry at Vogue *Magazine*

In December 2005, *Vogue* captured the attention of thousands of people outside the usual fashion audience. Online, in print, and in conversations from New York to Sydney, celebrity bloggers and art critics alike talked about this imaginative issue. Photographed by Annie Leibovitz and featuring actress Keira Knightley, the 20-page spread took cues from the iconic 1939 movie *The Wizard of Oz*. Modeling alongside Knightley were such art-world luminaries as Chuck Close (the Wizard), Jasper Johns (Cowardly Lion), and Jeff Koons (winged monkey)—not the standard high-fashion models. Storytelling, or narrative, is a driving force in features, even without text. Narrative frequently serves as inspiration for communicating fashion, and thematic elements with moody dramatizations readily engage readers in fantasy.

"We're off to see the wizard/The wonderful Wizard of Oz/We hear he is a whiz of a wiz/If ever a wiz there was"

"Oh, you cursed brat!
Look what you've done!
I'm melting! Melting!
Oh, what a world,
what a world!"

"There's no place like home."

CHAPTER SEVEN

The Big C: Creativity

"The only real elegance is in the mind.
If you've got that, the rest really comes from it."

DIANA VREELAND
legendary magazine editor

CHAPTER OBJECTIVES

The information presented in this chapter is designed to help you understand:

- The five basic elements of creativity: inner vision, curiosity, inspiration, ability, and environment.
- How seemingly unrelated disciplines (philosophy, architecture, anthropology, etc.) are connected to fashion expression.
- That a lifelong commitment to creativity is a goal for all fashion communicators.

Ideally, after reading this chapter, you will:

- Be equipped with tools for creative **brainstorming**.
- Expand your personal range of creative abilities.

What does it mean to be creative in fashion? How is a look created? Does it just happen? What do the words "original" and **originality** mean? Is everyone creative? Are there un-creative people? Can people become more creative? Can **creativity** be taught? If so, is there a limit?

In truth, there is ample evidence that creativity starts exactly the way this chapter starts, with questioning and curiosity. Other aspects of creativity include burning desire, intuition, or the compulsion from within to do something that has never been done before, to put one's unique stamp on the world in an expressive manner.

There is a mysterious element to creativity and the creative process, but being open to learning is also an important element of the creative process. Julia Cameron, author of *The Vein of Gold* and *The Artist's Way,* is a leading expert on the creative process. She writes and lectures extensively about creativity as a universal trait that everyone naturally possesses and can develop. Peter London, author of *No More Secondhand Art*, is another advocate of developing personal creativity. This scholar and author encourages people to overcome their fears and resistances to creativity, and he describes ways in which everyday people can discover original expression within themselves.

FUNDAMENTALS FOR FASHION

Creativity exists at all levels in the fashion industry, not just in the design houses (see Box 7.1). Fashion communications not only employs creativity but it depends directly on creative input for its existence and effectiveness. It is very important for the fashion communicator to strive toward achieving higher and higher degrees of personal creativity, and it is often a lifetime goal.

The concept of having a lifelong commitment to creativity seems obvious to some people. Other people find themselves filled with anxiety when they are faced with having to be creative. For whatever reason, some people define themselves in their own minds as distinctly un-creative, and they are fond of saying things like "Leave creativity to the designers and just let me write the press release," or "The most creative thing I do is pick out eye shadow at the cosmetics counter." A close analysis reveals these people are fooling themselves. If a press release required nothing more than raw information, a computer could write it. Every communications director knows that a well-crafted, lively press release requires not only thought but also original thought. It involves imagination and searching for the right word choices to convey the exact message intended for the reader. Likewise, selecting eye shadow requires stepping back mentally to determine exactly which product

BOX 7.1

FASHION FOR AVATARS

Journalist Andrew Lavallee's article in the *Wall Street Journal* from September 2006 covered a fascinating new outlet for fashion creativity—clothing worn by avatars (computerized representations of people). In his essay titled "Now, Virtual Fashion: Second Life Designers Make Real Money Creating Clothes for Simulation Game's Players," Lavalee writes:

In the real world, fashionistas are recovering from the spring collections in New York. . . . But in the fast-growing virtual world of Second Life, many players are too enmeshed in the game's online fashion community to dissect what Vera Wang or Baby Phat sent down the catwalk in New York. Some players are buying up high fashion for their online graphic incarnations, known as avatars. Others, armed with Adobe Photoshop instead of a needle and thread, are creating their own clothing lines, pitching their designs to style editors, selling their creations, and—in some cases—even earning a living.

Second Life is a simulated world with more than 700,000 "residents," or players, who sometimes refer to their offline existence as their "first life." . . . Residents chat, shop, build homes, travel, and hold down jobs, and they are encouraged to create items in Second Life that they can sell to others or use themselves. The items and services are virtual, but real money is involved. Second Life's in-game currency, Linden dollars, is based on U.S. dollars ($1 U.S. buys about 280 Linden dollars). . . . Many virtual items are bought and sold in Second Life, but clothing has emerged as one of the hottest categories. Real clothing makers, including American Apparel Inc. and Adidas, sell items in Second Life that mimic apparel they sell in the real world. Thus, players can dress their avatars in some of the same clothes they wear themselves. Because Second Life creators own their products and can sell them, the game has attracted both professional and amateur designers, says Linden spokeswoman Catherine Smith. That has led to a thriving fashion scene that includes not just dressmaking but also jewelry, hair and even skin design, as people purchase the elements to create a look for their online alter egos. . . . (Lavalee, 2006)

would be most engaging, effective, and appropriate for the outfit and purpose at hand. Considering which colors and shades to apply on one's eyelids requires imagining how they would actually look. In other words, some amount of creativity is actively working inside that shopper's brain as she is choosing her product.

Creativity and Originality

Taking a broader view of creativity requires taking a closer look at the historical meaning behind the words *creativity* and *originality*. According to *Merriam-Webster's (10th Edition 1993)*, the verb *create* comes from the Latin word *creatus*, a past tense of the verb *creare*, which is most closely connected in meaning to the Latin *crescere*: "to grow," or "to bring into existence." Use of the word *creative* as an adjective dates back to 1678. It means "marked by the power or ability to create." In other words, it means having the ability to bring something into a state of being. The noun *creativity*, which emerged somewhere around 1878, is defined as "the quality of being creative" or "the ability to create." To summarize, creativity is an intangible that causes, enables, and possesses the potential for producing a result, whether that result is an idea, a painting, or the newest trend in fashion.

Creativity is not the same thing as originality, although the two terms are closely related. The root word behind *origin* goes back to the Latin verb *oriri*, "to rise." According to *Merriam-Webster's* (10th Edition, 1993), *origin* "applies to the things or persons from which something is ultimately derived and often to the causes operating before the thing itself comes into being." An *original*, used as a noun, is "the source or cause from which something arises" and is also "a work composed firsthand." As an adjective, *original* means "of, relating to, or constituting an origin or beginning," and "not secondary." Therefore, originality is defined as "the quality or state of being original [not secondary]." Two other definitions are: "freshness of aspect, design, or style" and "the power of independent thought or constructive imagination." So, words identified with originality include:

- Power
- Beginning
- Independent thought
- Imagination

From a sheer philosophical standpoint, creativity and originality are part of everyone's lives to varying degrees. To be sure, there are individuals throughout fashion history who can be justifiably called creative geniuses, creative legends, or even one-of-a-kind originals. Designers like Coco Chanel, Bonnie Cashin (see Profile 7.1), Yves St. Laurent, photographer Richard Avedon, and editor Carmel Snow appear to have been endowed with creative gifts above and beyond the norm. Appropriately, their originality has been a source of **inspiration** for many thousands of others in the fashion industry. (See Box 7.2 for information about the legal ramifications of unscrupulously turning that "inspiration" into an illegal knockoff.)

Some argue that being in the right place at the right time has much to do with great accomplishments and original expression. Landscape photographer Ansel Adams, who has been labeled a creative genius, held this conviction: "Chance favors the prepared mind." Adams was paying homage to Louis Pasteur, whose exact words were "Chance favors only the prepared mind." His words remind fashion communications professionals of the importance of discipline and talent as integral parts of creativity. Being in the right place at the right time, on the other hand, is a concept that relates back to the mystery inherent in the creative process.

No matter how creativity functions, it can safely be concluded that there are varying levels, degrees, and definitions of creativity. Making creative variations on an original concept or design is fundamental to the workings of the everyday fashion world. Finding fresh solutions to problems is also fundamental. Finding just the right word to go with the right image in a handbag ad involves creativity. Devising ways to make a label stand out involves creativity. Writing a 30-word lead to grab TV viewers' attention for *Project Runway* requires imagination. Putting together a resume for a job, whether as an assistant designer, photo editor, head buyer, or visual merchandiser, requires creative input in terms of selecting the right type font, the right paper, and the perfect wording. Writing e-mails, runway scripting, proposing a line of clothing, and tracking trends to keep up with the zeitgeist all involve creative thinking. Bills of lading, customs declarations, and listings in the *Yellow Pages* are about the only items related to the fashion business that allow fashion communicators a break from near-constant creative engagement.

WHAT ARE THE ELEMENTS OF CREATIVITY?

To understand the creative process, it is important to bring into focus, or uncover, all the elements that contribute to it. While each person has a uniquely individual experience with his or her creativity, learning how creativity works for others and how this intangible force

· Profile 7.1 ·

THE GLOBE AS HER PALETTE: THE LEGENDARY BONNIE CASHIN (1908–2000)

One of Bonnie Cashin's most famous sayings is: "Chic is where you find it." A beloved and well-known American designer, Cashin was not only a prolific writer but was an avid reader who loved poetry and inspirational essays (Henry David Thoreau was a favorite). Wherever she lived, she created a "graffiti wall" where she wrote inspirational quotes from her favorite thinkers, including Einstein.

Cashin's original drawings, designs, and writings are housed in the Department of Special Collections at the University of California–Los Angeles (UCLA) Charles E. Young Research Library. Portions of Cashin's work are presented online in an archive called "Chic Is Where You Find It."

Note the following description, a rather academic, museum-style form of writing, used to introduce Cashin in the special collection:

Bonnie Cashin.

Bonnie Cashin (1908–2000) was one of the foremost American fashion designers in the second half of the twentieth century. At the vanguard of her field for nearly forty years, she had an enormous influence on twentieth-century design. Her oft-stated credo "Chic is where you find it" sums up her belief that designers should possess "a habit of wonder" and an ability to connect the fashion world with objects and ideas not usually associated with it.

In the summer of 2003, the Department of Special Collections in the UCLA Charles E. Young Research Library acquired the Bonnie Cashin Archive as a gift from the Cashin Estate. In addition to Cashin's personal papers, the Estate provided an endowment to establish the Bonnie Cashin Lecture Series. The series brings to UCLA gifted individuals from a variety of disciplines to celebrate the creative process, and to preserve the legacy of Cashin's remarkable life and work. (UCLA)

Cashin's parents encouraged their daughter's creativity. Her mother, Eunice, a gifted dressmaker, gave textile swatches to her young daughter as playthings. Having this firsthand, tactile experience with fabric proved to be a huge asset in Cashin's ability to visualize her garments' construction. Eunice Cashin remained an important force in her daughter's life, even stepping in later to personally guide seamstresses who were having trouble figuring out how to execute some of her daughter's designs.

Bonnie Cashin's designs.

"What makes Cashin unique was her extraordinary ability to connect the dots."

Cashin saw the people, places, and costumes around the globe as her palette. Wherever she went, she wrote, drew, photographed, and remarked about what she saw. These recorded materials were later translated into fashion. Her journals and drawings reflect her keen observation skills, sense of humor, and unabashed love of discovering innovation in the world around her. Captions from the Cashin Collection reveal the profound influence she drew from other cultures, travels, and encounters:

(continued on next page)

The Japanese kimono in an un-Japanese fabric—double-faced wool—bound in black kidskin. (Bonnie Cashin for Sills and Co., Spring 1960)

Run around in Russian knickers pushed into boots and tie yourself into a bush country sort of jacket—all leathered—with a cashmere turtle. (Bonnie Cashin for Sills and Co., March 1968)

A shirty coat—like a Portuguese fisherman's—canvassed—firmed with leather inside. (Bonnie Cashin for Sills and Co., July 1968) (UCLA)

In Manhattan, the United Nations, with all its colorful, differently dressed ambassadors and staff members, became a source of inspiration as well. Cashin's journals make references to inspiration she derived from observing the costumes of passersby in the streets below her apartment.

Always a visionary, Cashin even turned her eye and heart toward America's indigenous peoples, and her collections included "an homage to Native American clothing construction in each ready-to-wear collection" from 1957 on, according to UCLA. Throughout her career, Cashin appears to have consistently given credit where credit was due, providing a role model for other fashion innovators.

What makes Cashin unique was her extraordinary ability to connect the dots. Millions of people have recorded materials, from sketchbooks to journals to digital diaries, but Cashin appears to have very quickly made links from concrete images, to design concepts, to material goods, and, finally, to fashion.

has been discussed over time can be a valuable way to boost one's own creativity factor. Five key elements of creativity include the following:

Inner Vision

Whether it is called spark, intuition, imagination, dreamscape, or spiritual direction, **inner vision** is central to being inventive. Yet many experts believe that developing inner vision is less a project of *doing* than it is of *being*. It is allowing and opening the mind to receive messages about what is already inside oneself, and being willing to explore those messages more fully. Inner vision is not strictly visual. Creative direction coming from inside the self may be experienced with all of the other senses. It is said Mozart heard the music he created in his mind. Many writers see the words on an imaginary page in their minds before they write them down. Many designers imagine how a garment feels on the body.

BOX 7.2

LEGAL BRIEF: A LEGAL LOOK AT KNOCKOFFS

When radio broadcast journalists investigate fashion topics, they tend to choose edgy, controversial, interesting subjects that explore questions we all want answered. Knockoffs, unauthorized copies or imitations, are something shoppers wonder about. Is it okay to take someone else's popular design, copy it, and sell it?

An NPR (National Public Radio) story aired on September 18, 2003, by contributing correspondent Rick Karr, used six minutes and 31 seconds of prime radio time to talk about knockoffs in what was to become one of Karr's "most e-mailed" stories, entitled "Fashion Industry Copes with Designer Knockoffs." The subhead for the story is: "With Copyright Protection Elusive, Copies Are Common." He writes:

> If you find yourself attracted to, say, a handbag in an upscale Soho boutique but it costs too much, head a few blocks south to Canal Street. You'll probably find the design that caught your eye on a table on the sidewalk selling for a lot less: A knockoff of a $600 Prada bag, for example, goes for around 100 bucks. (Karr 2003)

Karr discusses Hermes' famous $6,000 (plus) "Birkin" bag, which has been copied more than most accessories on the market, and points out that Hermes' CEO has employed lawyer Joseph Gioconda to aggressively go after retailers producing knockoffs of that handbag and other Hermes creations.

The trouble is that the majority of designers find it far too costly and time consuming to take legal action against the manufacturers of knockoffs, leading to a resigned "acceptance" (on the part of many) of the inevitability of knockoffs in the marketplace.

The fact that knockoffs exist does not mean it is legal to produce them. Karr points out the key to winning a lawsuit against a knockoff manufacturer is based on the following:

> . . . the risk of confusion is the key legal test of whether a knockoff has crossed the line to forgery. Under U.S. law, a company can't copyright a design, but it can register elements of that design as trademarks. If the shape of the bag's flap or the strap across the closure lead a likely Hermes consumer to think the knockoff is genuine, then it's pretty easy to convince a court that the fake violates Hermes trademarks. (Karr 2003)

To catch up on further news on design infringement and legislative moves to protect designs, visit *www.npr.org* and type "knockoffs" into the search engine.

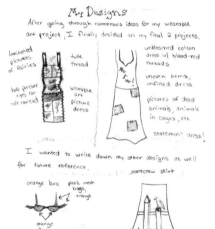

Figure 7.1a and b   A student journal can be a valuable record of creative thought.

Tips for Finding Inner Vision

Tips for finding one's inner vision include:

- Drawing
- Journaling (Figure 7.1a and b)
- Meditating
- Seeking solitude
- Embracing quietude
- Writing down dreams
- Going on retreats that lift the spirit

Curiosity

Curiosity begins with asking, "Why is this like this?" and wondering, "Can this be different?" Some claim that creative curiosity is tied to boredom, and that creative new clothing trends or fashion looks arise from the mind's inability to remain content with what it sees every day.

Other people say that boredom has nothing to do with creativity. They are able to get fresh ideas by engaging with the world around them. The most inspired designers are those who see connections between seemingly unrelated events, readings, and images in their lives. While browsing through recipe books from the 1960s at a yard sale, they might become inspired to reintroduce elements from aprons from the 1950s in their next line of summer skirts. Other people might become inspired by attending church in a nearby town and be impressed by the way the color of the hymnal looks against the color of the pew. The same designer might be inspired by the comfortable silhouettes he or she sees in the church's interior architecture. No matter what motivates curiosity, becoming more curious is key to expanding one's creativity.

Tips for Improving Curiosity

Tips for connecting with one's curiosity include:

- Asking questions
- Challenging the mind
- Looking at the world
- Educating oneself
- Expanding life experiences

Inspiration

Inspiration is the act of drawing in, whether it is by breathing, observing, or experiencing. In ancient Greece, people believed that divine influences or actions on the part of the **Muses** (Figure 7.2) were at the root of all creativity. The Muses were nine sister goddesses who served as guides to inspire the arts and sciences. More recently, painters, writers, and musicians have found inspiration from religious figures, including Jesus Christ, Buddha, and Mohammed. Nature has been a source of inspiration across all cultures. Historical events, ancestors, dreams, **role models**, heroes and heroines (both real and fabled), conversations, and travel are all sources of inspiration. Inspiration is often the bridge between inner vision and outward action.

Figure 7.2   In ancient Greece, the Muses, goddesses or spirits depicted as female figures, were thought to be the source of artistic inspiration.

Finding inspiration is a highly personal process. Never formulaic, inspiration sometimes requires hard work. It can also be the result of pure trial and error or chance. It often seems like it is an unexpected gift. The word *muse* is still used with relation to creativity, but its current interpretation varies with the individual. Andrew Wyeth's paintings of a model named Helga have led people to refer to her as his muse, at least while he was painting her portrait. The reality of the muse is that there is an intangible, or otherworldly, aspect to it perceived by the artist. In that sense, each person's muse can be actively employed in order to become more creative, or for the "un-creative," creative at all.

Figure 7.3   A look from Chado Ralph Rucci.

Figure 7.4   Glass tree trunk, by James Harmon. Harmon is an artist who works primarily in glass. His work has been shown throughout the world, and is in the permanent collection of the Smithsonian's American Art Museum in Washington, D.C. His Web site is *www.jamesharmon.com*.

Tips for Getting Inspired

You can connect with your muse by:

- Watching a runway show (Figure 7.3)
- Listening to a favorite musician
- Reading a good book
- Seeing a powerful movie
- Hanging a picture or poster on your wall
- Browsing through an elegant magazine
- Walking through the woods
- Making a list of things that inspire you and referring to it as needed

Ability

Creativity is influenced by such factors as talent, discipline, and control. Ability describes the physical and mental attributes a person needs in order to complete a task, in this case, to create something (Figure 7.4). A person with a strong photographic ability might not be able to thread a needle, draw a sketch, or plan the layout of a magazine page. The photographer will tend to stick to what he or she knows best, capturing an image in a photograph. That said, the photographer can certainly benefit from learning how to lay out a magazine page or draw a fashion sketch. Many highly creative individuals find themselves multitasking in the areas of designing, writing, sketching, promoting, and leading companies. (Bonnie Cashin, profiled in Profile 7.1, is one such person.)

Ability is not limited to artistry. In life, where thousands of circumstances lie outside the range of one's control, a person who has the ability to be flexible can transcend deficiencies in one area by being resourceful and inventive in others. When it comes to the fashion business, there are numerous anecdotes of real people, many of them quite famous, who moved forward simply because they were creative problem solvers. Fashion giant Kenneth Cole, whose whole story can be found on his Web site, got his start by selling shoes that he designed and had made in Europe. With limited finances, he decided not to debut his shoes in a fancy showroom. Here's what he did instead, in his own words:

> I called a friend in the trucking business and asked to borrow one of his trucks to park in Midtown Manhattan. He said sure, but good luck getting permission. I went to the mayor's office, Koch at the time, and asked how one gets permission to park a 40-foot trailer truck in Midtown Manhattan. He said one doesn't. The only people the city gives parking permits to are production companies shooting full-length motion pictures and utility companies like Con Ed or AT&T. So that day I went to the stationery store and changed our company letterhead from Kenneth Cole, Inc. to Kenneth Cole Productions, Inc. and the next day I applied for a permit to shoot a full-length film entitled "The Birth of a Shoe Company."
>
> With Kenneth Cole Productions painted on the side of the truck, we parked at 1370 6th Avenue, across from the New York Hilton, the day of shoe show. We opened for business with a fully furnished 40-foot trailer, a director (sometimes there was film in the camera, sometimes there wasn't), models as actresses, and two of New York's finest, compliments of Mayor Koch, as our doormen. We sold 40 thousand pairs of shoes in two and a half days (the entire available production) and we were off and running (Cole).

Tips for Expanding Ability

Ways to increase one's ability include:

- Dreaming more
- Learning more
- Practicing more
- Doing more
- Showing more
- Daring more
- Being more flexible

Figure 7.5   Arctic glacier.

Figure 7.6   Nature.

Environment

One's physical surroundings and life circumstances play a critical part in the innovative process. (See Figures 7.5–7.11). Environment includes:

- Everyday, practical factors, like money, work space, information access, time, space, equipment, tools, deadlines, resources, etc.
- Concrete factors such as place (urban or rural), people with whom one interacts, and nature
- Relationships, religion, cultural influences, family attitudes, and approaches toward creativity, etc.

It is impossible to identify what kind of environment is most favorable for promoting creativity. Just as sources of inspiration tend to be highly personal, influences of environment also tend to be personal.

Tips for Making the Most of Your Environment

Ways to identify and use your environment to boost your creativity include:

- Describing various personal environments in a journal
- Imagining dream environments
- Recording intriguing or inspiring settings through drawing, photography, or video recording
- Paying attention to relationships
- Exploring color as a way to boost creative activity
- Staying away from circumstances, surroundings, and people that shut down your creativity

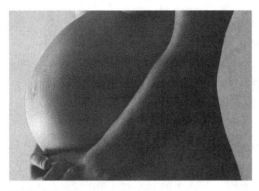

Figure 7.7   Pregnancy.

Figure 7.8   White-tailed deer.

Figure 7.9   Vintage fabric in artwork by Susan B. Faeder.

Figure 7.10   Handmade scarlet feltwork by Kachina Martin.

Figure 7.11   Aerial view of a desert terrain in Morocco.

COMMUNICATING FASHION IN FRESH WAYS

You can probably think of many more contributing elements to creativity. If you have the five elements of creativity we discussed in place, you are well on your way. To be 100 percent successful in communicating fashion in fresh and relevant ways, other factors play support-ing roles. For ideas to become reality, the following considerations also apply:

- Experience—the amount of practice, exposure, and the comfort level one has with relation to a particular creative activity;
- History—one's sense of personal history (see Box 7.3 for Julia Cameron's excerpt on the subject), as well as historical knowledge, appreciation for past events, and perception regarding one's current role;
- Timing—both bad and good, for whatever reasons;
- Patience—when to use it, and to what degree;
- Planning—the discipline to chart a course in the short term and long term, with contingencies factored in;
- Monetary backing—the status of one's job, availability of financial resources, state of career, aspirations, and realities;
- Networking and mentoring—degrees of interaction with others, or whether or not one is mentored or is serving as mentor to another person;
- Confidentiality and loyalty—matters pertaining to investment in a creative project, whether to self or others, and how deep the commitment is (including legal concerns).

All of the above considerations can be discussed and explored further with relation to specific arenas of fashion communications.

Brainstorming

Coming up with fresh ideas on one's own is one thing, but working together with others to create a handbag ad, a description of a new fabric, or a fashion blog on the Internet requires teamwork. Two heads usually are better than one, and before long, someone is bound to say, "Let's brainstorm." Depending on where those ideas take form—in the corporate board-room, a radio broadcast studio, an editorial session, or elsewhere—there are additional con-siderations involved in the creative process. Two key factors are purpose and goals.

BOX 7.3

"WHEN WORDS FAIL ME . . ."

Creativity expert and author Julia Cameron, a creative writer and nonfiction author of *The Artist's Way* and *The Vein of Gold,* writes:

> When words fail me, I turn to pictures. Most specifically, I turn to collage. I keep the ground rules very simple for myself: set a time frame and topic, then tear through magazines, free-associating. When life is very complicated, this simple act of selection immediately calms and focuses me. I don't overthink my choices. I just hold my subject loosely in my mind and then pull together whatever images appeal, whether they seem to be appropriate or not. I am less after art than I am after artifact, or even art-as-fact. My collage is a sort of time capsule: I felt this way then about that. For me, the phrase "make sense" is quite literal, and the sense I often need to use for insight is my sense of sight. (Cameron, 1997)

Purpose

Before a **brainstorming** session, the purpose for the session should be clarified to achieve best results. While a textile laboratory may discover a new fabric accidentally, it may also solicit creative strategies to answer a new need or demand in the market. An ecologically conscious company may brainstorm to find raw materials to use for garments made without using petroleum, as was the case with the corn-fiber company discussed in Box 7.4.

Goals

Identifying the goal of a brainstorming session is also a helpful strategy for bringing focus to the process. Goals vary widely, depending on the situation. Students sometimes work together on a group project in order to meet a portfolio or presentation goal set by the teacher, with an additional goal of trying to achieve high grades. Copywriters work together with designers to create lively, accurate scripts for fashion shows, with an ultimate goal of capturing enough attention to bring acclaim and wealth to the design line. Visual merchandisers for department stores work together with a variety of personnel to determine how they can most creatively and effectively catch the eye of passersby, to draw them into the store to shop.

PRACTICE: CREATING ORIGINAL FASHION AND COMMUNICATING ORIGINAL IDEAS

Taking on a directed creative challenge is a valuable way to explore and develop personal creativity. Exciting approaches to fashion communications emerge when interior vision is sparked by external physical reality.

Brainstorm and Present Ideas

Because inspiration is frequently linked to art and nature, the exercises below include objects and images that are not directly linked to fashion. Using the images presented in Figures 7.4–7.11, begin to brainstorm fashion ideas that emerge. This can be a group or individual activity, and results may be presented in any number of ways:

- Sample page layout
- Text document
- Storyboards
- Sketches, drawings
- Photographs, animations, videography
- CAD-generated garment, accessory, or makeup prototype
- Actual fashion expression or wearable art
- **Collage**
- Descriptive or process essay

To get started on the project, look at each photograph carefully. At first, there might appear to be no connection to fashion or fashion communications in the images. That is a normal response. Simply return to the images, finally selecting the one that seems most compelling. Next, begin to explore the image with fashion in mind. What does it suggest? Is there a garment, pattern, form, or fashion feeling that the image resembles or calls to mind? Why? What is striking about the image? Has any fashion style or line or silhouette been similarly striking? What elements inspire design ideas? What adjectives describe the photograph's mood? What tone or emotion is evoked as reaction? In what way(s) could some aspect of the inspiration be turned into fashion? What do the materials or colors suggest?

BOX 7.4

COMPOST THAT SHIRT

Journalist Bill Ward of the Minneapolis *Star Tribune* recently found himself covering the fashion beat. With everyone focused on sustainable energy and eco-friendly materials, it was inevitable that energy-sensitive approaches to apparel would begin to appear in the media. Ward found that quirky, down-home style stories can make bigger news. His local story got picked up on CBS News and ran nationally.

An excerpt from the story appears below:

Corn can be enjoyed in so many ways—grilled, boiled, broiled, baked, flaked, fried, stewed, popped . . . or on your back.

Yes, corn can be worn. Hopkins-based Mill Direct Apparel is releasing a new line of sportswear made from Ingeo, a material that begins as kernels of corn. It comes from the soil and can also return to it, since Ingeo is compostable. Another eco-friendly aspect: Because Ingeo garments wick rather than absorb moisture, they don't need to be tossed into that power-sucking clothes dryer.

According to its biggest fan, Mill Direct president Dennis Lenz, Ingeo "doesn't shrink, doesn't fade, doesn't wrinkle. It doesn't absorb odor. You can basically shake it dry. The only 'but' is that it's got some heat sensitivity. You can't iron it."

Lenz, who started Mill Direct Apparel in Hopkins five years ago and previously had co-owned the Twin Cities–based apparel agency Klouda-Lenz Inc., almost whispers when he talks about Ingeo, as though he's got this great big secret that's about to make him burst—it's an alternative to the polyester, nylon, and polypropylene clothing made from petroleum-based materials.

"In Brazil, they make everything out of sugar. And so should we [with corn]," he said. "We need to eliminate the use of oil in our clothing. For decades now, the petroleum companies have dictated to us what we're going to use, and we've got to stop that."

Still, the front end of the Ingeo-making process is hardly an ecologist's dream. "Nothing's ever perfect," said Ginny Black, organics recycling specialist for the Minnesota Pollution Control Agency (MPCA). "There are issues. In the process of growing corn, you use gas, you use fertilizer, you use pesticides and herbicides." (Ward, 2008)

During presentations in class, capture the audience's attention by communicating ideas and results concisely, using highly descriptive nouns, verbs, and word combinations with images that reveal the essence of fashion originality.

KEY TERMS

brainstorming	inspiration
collage	Muses
creativity	originality
inner vision	role models

CHAPTER EIGHT

Evolution of the Fashion Magazine

"As for Clothing, to come at once to the practical part of the question, perhaps we are led oftener by the love of novelty, and a regard for the opinions of men, in procuring it, than by a true utility."

HENRY DAVID THOREAU
"Economy," from *Walden*

CHAPTER OBJECTIVES

The information presented here is designed to help the reader understand:
- The evolution of fashion expression through print media, especially magazines.
- How, what, when, where, and why magazines introduce change.
- That magazines have shaped the fashion consciousness of the masses for more than a century.

Ideally, after reading this chapter, students will:
- Be better able to compare and contrast historical images and words with current depictions.
- Know how the balance of words and visuals in print has shifted over time.
- Employ an awareness of art and commerce in relation to fashion.

Human nature is at the root of fashion. Our love of novelty and our desire to be attractive to others (especially to those who attract us) fuels fashion. While being practical counts, utility is not a big part of the clothing equation in our society. If it were, the fashion magazine industry would not exist.

Of course, the fashion magazine evolved over time, with fashion first emerging in newspapers and general interest magazines. The Industrial Revolution in the early 1800s played a crucial role in bringing printed images of fashion to the masses. The advent of cheaper printing presses, and the domestic manufacture of paper and printing ink, paved the way for the United States to become a communications superpower.

Daniel Delis Hill's book *As Seen in Vogue* contains an account of the origins of women's magazines. In it, Hill gives the following list of early magazines devoted specifically to women's interests: *Ladies Literary Cabinet* (1819–1822), *Graham's Magazine* (1826–1855), *Ladies' Magazine* (1828–1836), *Godey's Lady's Book* (1830–1898), *Ladies' Repository* (1841–1876), *Peterson's Ladies' National Magazine* (1842–1898), *Frank Leslie's Ladies' Gazette* (1854–1857), and *Harper's Bazar* (1867–present). (The name was later changed to *Harper's Bazaar.*)

Interestingly, *Harper's Bazar* was the first to publish exclusively fashion. *Vogue* magazine, which began in 1892 with a focus on society and fashion, did not devote an entire issue to fashion until February 1938. Some of the other magazines that first appeared at the end of the nineteenth century included: *McCall's*, *Ladies' Home Journal*, *Redbook*, and *Woman's Day*. During the early part of the twentieth century, a combination of photographs and artists' illustrations (drawings and paintings) commonly appeared in magazines to assert or confirm what was considered to be deemed as fashion-forward (see Figure 8.1). Magazines were **text-dominant**. There was a much larger proportion of words to images. That is, the features tended to be word-heavy, with a visibly larger proportion of words to images on each page. **Space** in a magazine is its gold. Therefore, the editor assumed an enormous responsibility when making decisions regarding how that space was used. It took courage and vision for editors to shift away from long-winded, text-heavy, bookish publications to the image-dominant, design-driven **periodicals** of today. (See Figure 8.2 for an example of photo-dominant design.)

Several significant trends came together, starting in the last half of the nineteenth century, which led to the rise of the fashion magazine:

- Paper patterns for clothing were growing in popularity, having found their way into publication in the late 1860s. In the mid-1890s, *Vogue* was selling patterns by mail order.

- The wider production and availability of ready-to-wear clothing had the effect of making fashion accessible and affordable.
- Advertising started appearing in periodicals after the Civil War. (Before the Civil War, periodicals that carried advertising were not received well by the public.)
- Reports coming back from fashion writers sent to Paris and New York were quickly finding their way into print, energizing the public's interest in style.

It was a remarkable, formative time in the evolution of fashion periodicals. Since several in-depth historical analyses of early fashion magazines already exist, this chapter will focus on fashion magazines as they exist today. (See Box 8.1 for a list of journals to check when researching fashion.)

AGENTS OF CHANGE

Magazines are also called periodicals. The word **periodical** inherently carries a message connected to time, specifically to periods of time. Magazines are created primarily to introduce, report, and reflect on change. They serve as instruments that lead us toward change. They help us, philosophically and emotionally, to get used to change. (See Box 8.2, "The Great Corset Fight," concerning the *Jenness-Miller Magazine*'s attempts to convince women they should do just that.)

Consider these examples of **coverlines** (headlines from magazine covers) and **body copy** (texts printed in magazines). While reading, ask these questions:

1. How is change being introduced (by this coverline or body copy)?

Figure 8.1 A 1933 cover of the *Saturday Evening Post*, featuring tennis star Helen Wills. Sports figures have long held prominence as trendsetters, especially with the advent of the magazine industry.

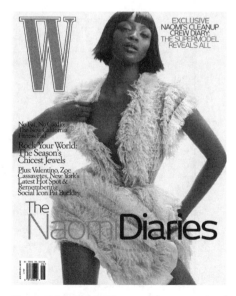

Figure 8.2 Magazine covers have remained unchanged in basic design—title, cover lines, and a central figure. Naomi Campbell is the model on this issue of *W*.

2. What nouns and verbs signal change? What do the writer's word choices say about the target audience?

3. How does the writer persuade the reader? (Tools include humor, a confidential or guiding tone, comparisons, and compliments.)

4. Does the reader have a choice when presented with new ideas?

Examples from June 2007 GQ

Tagline: "Look Sharp/ Live Smart"
Coverline: What a Man Should Wear This Summer
Brief: Go Sockless (headline), p. 56.

You might have noticed that in the warmer months, fashionable sorts prefer the sockless look—even with dress pants or a suit. The question is, do you really want to walk around all day not wearing socks with nice leather shoes? Thought so. Which is why you should buy loafer socks—so low-cut they're essentially invisible. We like the ones at Banana Republic. Buy a bunch. (body copy)

BOX 8.1

ACADEMIC JOURNALS ON FASHION

Research on fashion is published in such journals as:

- *Clothing and Textiles Research Journal*
- *Fashion Theory*
- *International Journal of Fashion Design Technology and Education*
- *International Journal of Clothing Science and Technology*
- *Journal of Fashion Marketing and Management*
- *Research Journal of Textile and Apparel*
- *Textile Research Journal*

As is the case when researching any topic, remember to check with your school's reference librarian for additional help with any topic of interest.

BOX 8.2

THE GREAT CORSET FIGHT

According to Jenna Weissman Joselit's accounts in *A Perfect Fit*, the end of the 1890s saw women's corsets under attack by "dress reformers" who urged women to free themselves from the confinement of lacings and whale bones. Brooklyn doctor Robert L. Dickinson invented a "manometer" which approximated the amount of pressure exerted on a woman's upper body. Dickinson and other physicians declared corsets dangerous, saying they squeezed vital organs and ribs and caused back deformities. Book and magazine publishers got into the fight, urging women to fight the status quo. Editor Annie Jenness-Miller, a dress reformer, published a periodical called *The Jenness-Miller Magazine*, "dedicated to the 'high and holy mission' of dress reform." Alternatives to traditional dress and underdress were proposed, including Turkish trousers and loose-fitting garments (tunic-style).

"Not surprisingly," Joselit writes, "many women had to be coaxed to try this novel form of dressing. Wouldn't they be too cold? Or look untidy? They wondered. 'I am very stout,' said one woman, not too keen on the prospect of relinquishing her corset."

Joselit's fascinating book reports that *American Jewess* magazine "recommended to its readers that when cleaning house, they might consider retiring their corsets for an hour or two." (Joselit, 2001)

Column Copy: Glenn O'Brien Solves Your Sartorial Conundrums (headline), p. 91.

From "Pants in Suspense": The good thing about suspenders is that you wear them under your jacket as a hidden punch line, like a wild lining in a conservative suit, ready for deployment when necessary. If you're not wearing novelty suspenders, then why are you wearing suspenders at all?

Examples from Fall 2007 Elle Accessories, Your Fall/Winter Shopping Guide

Coverline: 6 Trends You Need to Work for Fall: Menswear, Big Belts, High-Waisted Pants
Article: Take Flight (headline), p. 112.

Whether the effect is naughty, haute-hippie, or nice, designers are flocking to feathers this season (subhead)

Popular the world over for centuries—from eagle feathers on Native American warriors' headdresses to opulent plumes on Pimm's-drinking Royal Ascot ladies' hats—feathers lend an ornate and dramatic touch to accessories this fall. . . . Sportmax's downy choker and Eric Charles-Donatien's ring with chicken feathers conjure visions of '30s burlesque costumes, while Ferragamo's burly pheasant bag, Marni's silk bohemian satchel, and Michael Teperson's groovy pink clutch call to mind free-spirited, rebellious '60s rocker chicks like Anita Pallenburg. . . . (body copy)

—Alexa Brazilian (byline)

Examples from December 2007 Glamour

Coverline: 15 Things No One Ever Tells You about Being Married
Article: Julie Klam didn't think saying "I do" would change her life, until she said it.
Subhead: Here's the post-wedding truth she and 14 other women only learned about marriage *after* they tied the knot (p. 164).

When I asked women what seems self-evident about marriage but would be helpful to be reminded about, one of the gals said, "Well, I guess one thing is you can't go out on dates with guys anymore." Good point. Here are more. . . . [Several anecdotes follow.]

—Julie Klam

Examples from December 2005 Vogue

Column: Life with Andre (column name), p. 100.
Headline: "Rock the House!"

. . . **Karl Lagerfeld** is the biggest fashion rock star of today. But **Oliver Theyskens** at Rochas and **Rick Owens** are also both breaking on through to the other side, producing ready-to-wear clothes with a couture sensibility, while aping that rock-star je ne sais quoi that is so mesmerizing. . . . To get a sense of the Owens vibration, think of an American in Paris, working in a garage with concrete floors and exposed lightbulbs—and yet bringing to women's wardrobes a very modern elegance, in the fine French tradition of **Madame Gres** and that Delphic oracle of bias cut and *flou*, **Madeleine Vionnet**. His color palette is strong on concrete, greige, and white sand, and he has a very fine hand for drape and cut. I was amazed by his brilliant bias-cut rocker jackets. *Whooah*, there! Cutting bias in toad, sea leopard, and viper? "I can ship those skins to L.A.," he tells me later, sitting on a daybed of squirrel in his Place du Palais-Bourbon showroom, once the office of **President Mitterand**. (Talley, 2005)

CHOICES, CHOICES, CHOICES

One of the biggest criticisms of fashion magazine journalism is that it avoids criticism. In fact, fashion magazines are unlike any other genre of periodical in that they are heavily dependent on advertisers. The writing in these magazines is showy and informational. There is little or no room, nor is there editorial support, for negative reviews. As Michelle Lee writes in her book *Fashion Victim* (2003): "Fashion, since it holds the tricky distinction of being both art and commerce, leaves some journalists scratching their heads about just how to review it."

When it comes to runway reviews, Lee suggests, silence about a designer's line seems to be the accepted way of saying:

Not cool. . . . There's a time-honored formula for attendance, as with live theater: even if you weren't wowed by the show, don't diss it publicly. . . . Some fashion insiders, like Stig Harder, publisher of the online fashion magazine *Lumiere* and Internet portal *Fashion Net*, don't think it's a fashion writer's job to criticize in the first place. . . . Harder's view is that fashion "isn't important enough of a subject to warrant deep, objective analysis" and "if a designer had a bad season, the lack of good press will encourage him or her to do a better job next time." (Lee 2003)

The lack of critical focus is something that news journalists love throwing at fashion magazine staff writers, sparking debate over exactly how fashion ought to be reported. The readership is always going to weigh in heavily on this score. There are millions of fashion fans who would not trade their favorite magazine for all the critical reviews and up-front blogs in the universe. That's because they are not buying *Allure, Cosmopolitan, Glamour,*

Femina, W, InStyle, or *Lucky* for straight journalism. If they want straight journalism, they read Robin Givhan at the *Washington Post*. People who buy fashion magazines buy them for the eye candy, from features to ads, and for the wealth of ancillary, non-fashion-related articles that meet their lifestyle fantasies. (See Box 8.3 for legal tips on working as a freelancer.)

Fashion magazine readers have more choices than ever today. There appears to be no end in printed versions, and many fashion magazines also have online editions. As soon as a fashion niche makes its mark, it finds its way into print media.

Giving People What They Need

In *Language Power*, Seyler and Boltz describe the **Fifteen Appeals** of advertising according to the psychological needs that drive human behavior. The list is largely taken from the groundbreaking research of Henry A. Murray, a Harvard psychologist. Since fashion magazines depend on advertisers and—to a lesser extent—subscribers (circulation) for financial survival, they necessarily connect with the needs listed below in their features as well as their ads.

The Fifteen Appeals

1. Need for sex (physical affection, sensual appeal)
2. Need for affiliation (sense of belonging)
3. Need to nurture (caring for self, others)
4. Need for guidance (how to, solution-oriented)
5. Need to aggress (aggressive/competitive drive)
6. Need to achieve (in work life, personal life)
7. Need to dominate (control, "craving to be powerful")
8. Need for prominence (prestige, status, "looked up to")
9. Need for attention (desire to be "looked at")
10. Need for autonomy (individual style)
11. Need to escape (adventure, freedom)
12. Need to feel safe (durable looks and goods)
13. Need for aesthetic sensations (pleasing design, layout)
14. Need to satisfy curiosity (informational, looking into another's world)
15. Physiological needs (eating, drinking, sleeping, etc.) (Seyler and Boltz, 1986)

BOX 8.3

LEGAL BRIEF: OF CONTRACTS AND KILL FEES

Detective novels sometimes use the same terms as magazine publishers who invite freelancers to write articles or submit photos. Contracts, killing, deadlines. . . . It all sounds a bit morbid. However, freelance writers, editors, and visual artists do themselves a favor when they obtain to have in place a signed contract that includes kill fees whenever working for a client. A contract establishes what the freelancer will be paid for and when. For example, a writer's contract specifies how much money the writer will be paid per word, how many words are expected, what the topic is, when the article is due, terms for any revisions, and when the payment is to be made. The contract should also give a figure for the kill fee: the amount of money paid if the article is not published for any reason.

For more information on managing the details of being a freelancer for a magazine, see *Writer's Market*, *Photographer's Market* (both are published annually), or other publishing guidebooks.

In addition to advertisements, fashion magazines carry feature articles, columns, Q&A sections, briefs, quizzes, tips, interviews, and profiles that satisfy the majority of the 15 appeals identified above. Only the mix varies. Most successful magazines have a standard lineup, a formula for success, which includes a percentage of pages devoted to various topics. These magazines develop a reputation for having a particular mix, and readers who relate well to that mix begin to identify with it and become regular buyers or subscribers.

In years to come, it will continue to be interesting to see how fashion magazines alter their lineups in response to lifestyles. It will also be interesting to see how the proportion of visuals to text shifts according to people's taste. One thing seems clear: A career that involves working for the most glamorous fashion magazines and Webzines is likely to stay glamorous, and only those who can keep up with the fast pace will survive. (See Profile 8.1 for what it's like to be a fashion magazine writer.)

WHAT'S IT LIKE TO BE A FASHION MAGAZINE WRITER? AN INTERVIEW WITH KAREN BRESSLER

Karen Bressler's list of published magazine articles alone is seven pages long. She has also written for newspapers, books, and Web sites. This seasoned fashion and beauty writer has worked as a freelancer (independent worker) and as a full-time staff writer at major magazines. She has covered runway shows and interviewed famous designers. She has worked with designers, executive editors, art directors, and photographers. In this e-mail interview, Bressler shares her inside story and lends some advice to aspiring fashion writers.

Karen Bressler.

You have been on staff at different magazines, including *Vogue*, *Mademoiselle*, *Seventeen*, and *YM*, and you have written numerous freelance articles on fashion topics for a variety of print media. What is the difference between working as a fashion magazine staffer and working as a professional freelancer?

Working on staff at a magazine gives you a better understanding of the publication's needs and how things operate. When I worked at Vogue, I had access to the fashion layouts and the actual clothes, which helped if I was interviewing designers about their collections. When I worked on staff at Seventeen, we had weekly editorial meetings during which each department reported on what they were working on for each issue, so you really got a good idea of what each issue was going to include.

When you freelance, you are often an outsider, presenting your own views, and it's sometimes difficult to have them fit into what the [magazine] issue is trying to achieve. The best part about working on staff was having a well-known fashion name behind my work. I could have been the janitor at Vogue, and it wouldn't have mattered to some people outside the industry. As soon as I said I worked at Vogue, people were impressed. Not to date myself, but the least enjoyable part was working there during the transition between longtime Editor-in-Chief Grace Mirabella and current head Anna Wintour. With this change in guard, there were many management changes. No one knew what was going on. We had to read the New York Post and Spy magazine to hear the scoop on who was in and who was out. Anna wore sunglasses (it's true!) all day long so you could never read her face. When her assistant called your office (or cubicle) and asked you to come down, you ran through the halls as if you couldn't get there fast enough. It was definitely trying to live through that and do your job at the same time.

What do you like about freelancing, and what don't you like about it?

The best thing about freelancing is that you get to make your own hours, choose your own assignments, and work on such a wide variety of topics at the same time. I treated freelancing differently than many other freelancers I know. Many of them would file their stories while lying on their beds in their pajamas. I made sure I woke up, got dressed, and sat at my desk as if I was going to an office. I also made sure I took a break mid-morning to run out and get coffee. Otherwise the entire day could go by, and I wouldn't see the light of day. Also, being dressed for the day was convenient as I was always running to press lunches or media events around town, so I was always ready to go. During my freelancing years, I had two regular assistants (one year each) to help with the work. They would research stories and arrange interviews so I could just do the story and not have to spend time on all the details. I was also the editor of a fashion Web site at the time and wrote for a local newspaper and was able to get them [assistants] bylines in both so they could have some clips to jump-start their careers. In addition, I ran an intern program through my alma mater, SUNY Binghamton, and I had two or three interns working with me every summer and winter break, so I could introduce them to the industry. It was so much fun teaching them and watching them get excited about the world of fashion writing.

The worst thing about freelancing is trying to get paid. People pay you whenever they feel like it. Even the biggest national magazines took forever sometimes. But mostly everyone paid eventually—it just took millions of phone calls and lots of time to get them to send the check. Since I love what I do, I found it very hard to say no to an assignment, so I ended up working for some smaller publishing companies that went under before they could pay me. Anyway, it was all worth it in the end.

What do you like best about fashion? Did you plan to write fashion? Or did it just happen?

I knew I wanted to write for a major magazine but not necessarily a fashion pub. (I was not the most fashionable person I knew!) But when I graduated from college, there was a job opening at Vogue as an assistant in the bookings department (coordinating fashion shoots, i.e., booking models, hairstylists, makeup artists, locations, and photographers). It turns out I would be reporting to the business manager. It wasn't my ideal writing job but how do you turn down a job at Vogue? My boss knew I wanted to write and helped me interview for an assistant position in the copy department when one opened up. Then I worked on staff as a writer for Seventeen (fashion, beauty, health, fitness, lifestyle) and for YM (fashion, beauty, fitness, entertainment). I believe my stint at Vogue played a crucial role in determining the rest of my career path.

(continued on next page)

Is it tough to do an interview with a big-name person like Oscar de la Renta? Can you talk about that interview [an *Elements* article], or other ones with famous people such as Donna Karan and Michael Kors, and can you describe how you put the piece together?

When interviewing a big-name person, I think it's tough to come up with questions that haven't been asked yet. You want your interview to sound different than everything else people have written about the person, but aside from new projects that he's working on or other timely issues, it's hard to find that extra something special to talk about.

"When interviewing a big-name person, I think it's tough to come up with questions that haven't been asked yet."

How do I put it together? I think of a funny personal anecdote first. For Michael Kors, I said something like "The first time I heard of you was when a coworker and I sent a messenger to your sample sale to pick up a couple of skirts for us since assistants weren't allowed to leave work for it." Or I find a timely statement about the person to use as an intro. Then I weave together his or her quotes with their background info and some info about their brand or company. With Oscar de la Renta, I told him that his was the first fashion show I ever went to and that I was so in awe of him. (I really admired his work.)

Another anecdote: With Jan Patrick-Smith, CEO of Montblanc (they are most well known for their Meisterstuck pen), at the beginning of the interview, my pen ran out of ink. (I always take notes in addition to recording the person, just in case the tape recorder breaks down.) He said he'd offer to help but that they don't stock Bic refills! It was so embarrassing!

What is your educational background? Did it prepare you for a writing career? Have you always been a writer?

I have a B.A. in political science from [State University of New York] SUNY Binghamton, because it was an easy major and there was no journalism major in the curriculum. I minored in communications. There were only a handful of journalism classes to take—intro to journalism, broadcast journalism, and freelance magazine writing to name a few. When I took freelance magazine writing, we had to submit two ideas to real magazines to try to get stories published. I was one of two people in the class who had both our articles published. My first story was about my mom's business (a kosher weight loss business), and it was published in In Business *magazine in Emmaus, PA. For the second story, I profiled the captain of a ship on which I held our sorority's semiformal in college (I was social chairman) in a regional publication called the* Grapevine Press Finger Lakes Magazine.

This class in particular prepared me for freelancing. While I was writing all of my life (I was the loser who created a family newsletter on holidays and had all the cousins contribute articles to it, then passed it out at the Thanksgiving table!), I was on such a high from actually getting articles published that it was then that I decided to be a writer professionally. The year after I graduated, I was excited to find that I had an article published in the same magazine that my magazine writing teacher had an article in. That felt great!

Also, for a few years after graduation, I dated my boyfriend from college. He went on to Columbia Law School, and I thought it would be fun to go to grad school at the same time, so I applied to Columbia School of Journalism. I went through the entire application process (forms, letters of recommendation, writing samples), and then it came time to take a written test on site. The test consisted of about five essay questions, mostly about politics, which was a challenge for me. We had to type the answers to the questions on a manual typewriter. My e *key stuck and my space bar didn't work. I was so frustrated, I walked out without completing the test, so I obviously didn't get in. By the way, I had also asked a million people in the publishing business how important it was to get a master's in journalism and only found one editor at* NY Mag *who had one. It seemed the consensus was that unless you wanted to be an investigative reporter (think Watergate), it was better to get firsthand experience than stay in school.*

About your work with *Seventeen* and *YM*: Is interest in teen fashion going to continue to grow? Do you approach a teen fashion piece in the same manner, basically, as any other article?

I definitely think teen fashion is growing by leaps and bounds. Teens are so aware of fashion these days. I know teenagers who know famous designers, hairstylists, and makeup artists and their work as well as they know their own names. In addition, so many fashion brands are gaining teen celebrity status, and so many teen celebrities are starting their own lines, so there is a lot going on in this market. I would approach a teen story the same way I would approach any other story, but I would try to relate it to their age group by identifying with celebrities they know and referring to things they're into, like the iPhone, texting, blogs, etc.

Do you have any input with regard to the imagery used in your pieces? How is the artwork coordinated? Are you present at photo shoots? If so, what is that like?

I am often asked to call in the artwork for a story I'm working on, mainly because I am the one with contacts to the subject. Usually a fashion company has stock photos of their collection, headshots of their

(continued on next page)

lead designer, and images from their events that they can supply. I have been present at many fashion shoots and worked as the contributing fashion editor of Elite Traveler *magazine for three years, during which time I coordinated their fashion shoots. It's a lot of detail-oriented work, but when you are dealing with big stars and designers, it's fun to be there, especially if you get to interview them on set.*

What advice would you give to students of fashion journalism or students who wish to work for a fashion magazine? Is it hard to get a job?

I definitely recommend taking an entry-level job just to get your foot in the door, as I did at Vogue. *I also recommend freelancing since you need clips [published article samples] to get the job and a job to get clips. But if you write for smaller pubs that need freelancers, you can get clips more easily. I wrote for the* Resident *newspapers (community newspapers in Manhattan) for six years. We made $50–$100 per article, but I made about $6,000 a year (about 10 articles a month). I also bought* Writer's Market *every year and pitched new mags as well as lesser-known publications. I don't think my two ideas for journalism class would have been accepted by* Forbes *and* New York *magazine, but they were welcome at the smaller pubs. I think it's a great idea to get published in different mediums, i.e., college papers, blogs, etc.*

Networking is key. Talk to everyone you know and tell them you want to write. They might know people who need writers in their businesses and don't have a big budget to hire a professional. Also, get out and about. Go to parties and events in your town and other areas. They are usually designed to promote something new (a new store, a new fund-raising initiative, etc.), which are all good subjects for stories.

What is your all-time favorite experience working on a fashion piece?

I produced a photo shoot for Elite Traveler *that we shot on a private jet. We didn't take off anywhere, but it was so much fun setting up the shots and prepping the plane for the shoot. We had clothes from top, top designers, from Prada to Hermes to Armani, millions of dollars' worth of jewelry, including lots of diamonds (that I had to personally pick up from the stores, complete with bodyguard in tow), luggage from the best leather stores, even Frette linens for the bed and tables.*

Also, it was amazing interviewing Oleg Cassini, who sadly passed away a few months after our interview. He is a fashion legend and grew up in the same circles as Grace Kelly and other fashion icons of that time. I felt like I was part of fashion history when I talked with him.

Can you talk about the teamwork aspect of being a writer? Is it important to develop oral communication skills?

It's important to get along with all the different people you might have to deal with on a magazine, which is a challenge since almost everyone in the creative field feels strongly about the way they see things, so compromises don't come easy. Secondly, it is easy to understand what a person is looking for but not always easy to create it. Finally, many creative types don't know what they want; they only know what they don't want. So they have to see something to be able to tell you they don't like it. This often leads to many rounds of revisions.

What about personal style? When you go out into the world, what style considerations cross your mind? Do writers and editors have to dress like they are right off the pages of *Elle* or shopping in Milan?

Many fashion editors/writers think they have to dress the part, but it doesn't always mean expensive designer clothes. A lot of the time, it's the anti-fashion statement they are trying to make, dressing in looks they put together themselves or wearing up-and-coming designers that aren't known to the public yet. Of course, there are always Carrie Bradshaw [character on the TV show Sex and the City*] wannabes who do do the designer thing. One good place to spot the latest fashions is at New York Fashion Week, which I have covered for the past 10 years. Those who wear designer clothes and Manolos to the shows are either top editors or celebrities who want to support a specific designer. Writers, photographers, stylists, and others who are actually working at the shows (you'll see them taking notes, not fanning themselves and hiding behind sunglasses) dress up-to-date but often have to run to more than 100 shows during the week, so they can't wear stilettos and dresses with gigantic flowers pinned on the front. They'll be dressed a bit more practically, but still look fashionable.*

What would be your ideal job—your dream job?

I have experienced my dream job—working for top magazines; interviewing celebrities; seeing my byline on the newsstand in an average of four national magazines a month; authoring books; or, better yet, seeing my book, A Century of Lingerie, *in the window of a bookstore in Milan (in Italian!); getting to travel around the world and writing about it; and helping others get into the writing business. Now, as a mother of two, my dream job is watching my children grow up and helping them learn everything they need to know in the world. Who knows? Maybe they'll be writers someday!*

PRACTICE: UNDERSTANDING MAGAZINES AS AN INTERSECTION OF ART AND COMMERCE

These exercises are designed to expand your knowledge of fashion magazines and their function.

Pursuing the Philosophy of Fashion Magazines

The excerpt about advertising below may be used as a starting point for discussion or as an essay topic. Some questions to ask after reading it include:

- To what extent do ads influence life?
- How do fashion magazines reflect Williamson's thoughts about advertising?
- What is the role of **symbolism** in fashion photography?

Advertisements are one of the most important cultural factors molding and reflecting our life today. They are ubiquitous, an inevitable part of everyone's lives: even if you do not read a newspaper or watch television, the images posted over our urban surroundings are inescapable. . . . Obviously, it has a function, which is to sell things to us. But it has another function, which I believe in many ways replaces that traditionally fulfilled by art or religion. It creates structures of meaning. . . . For example: diamonds may be marketed by likening them to eternal love, creating a symbolism where the mineral means something not in its own terms, as a rock, but in human terms, as a sign. Thus a diamond comes to "mean" love and endurance for us. Once the connection has been made, we begin to translate the other way and in fact to skip translating altogether: taking the sign for what it signifies, the thing for the feeling. . . .

Advertisements are selling us something else besides consumer goods: in providing us with a structure in which we, and those goods, are interchangeable, they are selling us ourselves. And we need those selves. (Williamson, 1978)

Getting Real with a Magazine Content Count

What do magazines contain? Choose a popular fashion-oriented magazine. Using any method that works for you (different colored Post-It notes, Excel spreadsheet, handwritten notes on a legal pad, etc.), create a report of the publication's contents by category. Calculate how many pages are full-page ads, half-page ads, feature articles, columns, departments, etc. Compile a detailed listing, labeling, and counting of each fashion article and fashion ad. Look at the balance of text versus images, advertising comparisons (cars vs. jewelry vs. perfume, etc.), and subject areas (fashion, sex, health, beauty, theater and movies, lifestyle, relationships, sports, etc.).

Compare these results with those of classmates. Compare the report you have created with a second magazine (another issue of the same title or a rival fashion magazine). If possible, compare a current report with one from an issue published 10 years ago. Any changes? Interesting discoveries? Predictions about future lineups?

Debate It!

In *By Design*, author Ralph Caplan quotes a statement by Dwight E. Robinson, which appeared in the *Harvard Business Review*: "Fashion is . . . the pursuit of novelty for its own sake." Take sides in class and prove or disprove the opposing viewpoint.

KEY TERMS

body copy	space
coverlines	symbolism
Fifteen Appeals	tagline
periodical	text-dominant

CHAPTER NINE

Dynamic Wording—
The Art of Describing Fashion

"It's a visual art and an emotional sensing. It has to do with feeling good in a second skin, and how others perceive you."

GEOFFREY BEENE

fashion designer (defining fashion in the *Washington Post*, 1987)

CHAPTER OBJECTIVES

The information presented here is designed to help you understand:

- The range of descriptive options in writing fashion copy.
- Visual impressions can be created by "fashion-speak" (industry-related jargon) (e.g., spoken words, scripting).
- The importance of lead-in text.

Ideally, after reading this chapter, you will:

- Improve your abilities to tailor writing to the goal or task at hand, as well as to the type of media.
- Write with a deeper awareness of text as a tool in fashion communications.

If fashion were a queen bee, then words would be her worker bees, devotedly hard at work. Hundreds of words, thousands of words. Too many to count. More work to be done and no end in sight.

In the largely visual and tactile world of fashion, words exist in a symbiotic relationship that runs the gamut from praise to damnation, persuasion to ridicule, and seduction to sarcasm. Words are spoken, whispered, sung, written, catalogued, recorded, repeated, e-mailed, blogged, and printed. They appear on paper as well as on garments, shoes, scarves, neckties, and handbags. In retail, words are employed to describe and define, entice and encourage. In catalogs, words define the specifics, describing the items pictured with flair and detail. In advertising, words usually stay short but say much. On the red carpet of the Academy Awards, chatty journalists (some of them celebrities themselves, such as Joan Rivers) gush, critique, and query actors about their designer gowns and tuxedos, in on-the-spot conversations that are seen and heard in real time by television viewers who are hungry to know more about what they are seeing.

People who write and talk about fashion tend to do so with a specific work order in hand, and that is a crucial element in how words are put together and presented to others. **Venue**—where the words will end up—is everything. Venue—whether media outlet, business, photo shoot, or private salon—dictates the writing and speech; conversely, readers and listeners come to expect specific styles of verbal expressions based on situational factors that are directly influenced by these venues.

Where do words end up? How can words best serve the fashion world? What happens when words have less power than they were intended to have? Can fashion communicators—whose job it is to craft speech, write ad copy, and create magazine and news articles about various aspects of fashion—approach their workload in such a way that it becomes lighter, easier, and livelier with practice?

Because fashion communications as a field encompasses a particularly broad range of expression, the end of this chapter features exercises that involve different styles of fashion writing. The section is designed to stimulate analysis and discussion regarding the importance of **wordsmithing**. Wordsmithing is much more than just writing. It means using words as tools, hammering at them and heating them up and basically doing whatever is necessary to make sure the final written piece accomplishes its intended purpose. (And after all that hard work, it only makes sense that the author retains legal ownership of the piece, as discussed in Box 9.1.)

BOX 9.1

LEGAL BRIEF: WHO OWNS THAT? INTELLECTUAL PROPERTY AND THE LAW

Who owns what? Some cases of ownership are obvious to the average person. A house is the property of the person who bought it. A jacket bought at Nordstrom belongs to the person who purchased it. If a stranger tries to move into a house that is not his, the owner can have the trespasser arrested and prosecuted. If a friend borrows that Nordstrom jacket and then refuses to give it back, the owner of the jacket can take him to court for stealing.

But what about writing, layouts, and other original creations? When someone expends time, energy, and originality to write an article, the laws of intellectual property generally state that this material belongs to the creator. Even without a formal copyright, the philosophy behind intellectual property protects ownership. If someone uses another person's words as if they are his or her own, by not using quotation marks or crediting the source, he or she faces prosecution by the original writer, who can claim monetary damages.

In recent years, intellectual property has become a pressing issue, especially since the rise of the Internet. To learn more about the legalities of intellectual property, see these helpful Web sites:

- The World Intellectual Property Organization (under the United Nations umbrella) *www.wipo.org*
- The Authors Guild (See news and legal sections for updates.) *www.authorsguild.org*
- The Library of Congress, which is where copyrights are lodged and stored in the United States. *www.loc.gov*

WHERE FASHION IS THE FOCUS

Finding just the right words is no easy task. Any fashion journalist, apparel trade editor, fashion magazine editor, or copywriter can attest to that. Just as mystery author Steven King spends hours on end choosing just the right combinations of words to build spine-chilling suspense—a suspense that keeps his readers eagerly flipping pages—fashion communicators are constantly honing their word skills on a daily basis. They live and breathe words as

---

BOX 9.2

COMMON LITERARY DEVICES

Writers use many different techniques to get their point across. Here are just a few common terms to remember and use when writing copy:

- **Alliteration:** The repetition of initial consonant sounds in two or more words that are in close proximity to each other on a page.
  Examples: cool colors; red raspberry relish; vain velvet
- **Assonance:** Words or syllables whose sounds resemble one another. Assonance is similar to rhyme, but not as direct.
  Examples: a shiny time; haute couture
- **Metaphor:** When a word or phrase literally denoting one idea or thing is used in place of another (suggesting likeness).
  Example: Her gown was a summer day. . . .
- **Rhyme:** Words used together that sound similar.
  Examples: blue shoe; mellow yellow
- **Simile:** A figure of speech that draws a likeness between two things or ideas, often using the words "like" or "as."
  Example: His overcoat was like a yoke worn by oxen, heavy and wide across the shoulders.

Challenge: Think of original examples to try out all of these devices.

---

expression, always striving for a fresh turn of phrase, hoping to achieve a perfect capturing of an image (Box 9.2). If they cannot find the right words, some writers turn to a foreign language that says what they are trying to convey. They may even resort to throwing away the dictionary and coming up with a unique word or set of words, when nothing else suffices.

Many fashion journalists lean too heavily on adjectives when they first start writing prose, and they end up alienating readers who expect more than just a rehash of catalog or Web site copy. While a command of adjectives is critically valuable in fashion writing, readers get bored if presented with string upon string of them. Consider the difference between these two sets of text:

"The cream-white, lacy edging sewn at the hem of every plaid skirt in her Fall collection shown in London are retro and racy . . . "

versus:

"Models skipped onto the runway like a runaway pack of Catholic schoolgirls, with creamy lace slips tacked below heritage tartans . . . "

What is the main difference between these two approaches to the same fashion subject? In the first blurb, the visual imagery is set by a telling approach, relying primarily on adjectives. In the second example, the writer uses nouns and verbs to allow the reader to draw his/her own associations, and the writer employs a valuable literary technique called **simile**. (For the definition of simile, metaphor, and other literary terms, see Box 9.2) In fact, the best fashion writing engages the same devices that literary masters use to write novels, plays, poetry, and creative nonfiction. (See Profile 9.1 for an interview with journalist Robin Givhan.)

Words are tools of communication. Because words can be easily misunderstood without proper management, the most successful fashion communicators develop a set of habits with relation to them. Here are some common-sense policies for effective wordsmithing:

1. **Handle with respect.** To do justice to the artistry of fashion design, all words work best when handled with respect. Take the time to check spelling. (Is it "Versacchi" or "Versace"?) Make the effort required to be accurate and precise. (Is that a "kimona" sleeve or "kimono" sleeve?) Use the correct prepositions. (Is the desired phrase "go for" or "go to"?) Respect **grammar** and spelling conventions.

2. **Become brilliant.** Try to know 90 percent more than you *need* to know about every assigned subject. Research first; write second. Do the necessary reading (in print or online); ask credible people for verification; turn to experts (from the atelier to clothing manufacturers); learn the background and history of the subject; check back with colleagues, creative team members, etc., before words are trotted out into the world. Words that get thrown around thoughtlessly are often called back home with their tail between their legs. If an apology is demanded, that means extra time out of everyone's day—plus a loss of personal credibility and worth.

(continued on page 199)

NO FLUFF
AN INTERVIEW WITH ROBIN GIVHAN, FASHION EDITOR OF THE WASHINGTON POST

Robin Givhan, a longtime fashion editor for the *Washington Post*, made history in 2006 by becoming the first fashion journalist to win the Pulitzer Prize for Criticism. The Pulitzer Committee described Givhan's work as "witty, closely observed essays that transform fashion criticism into cultural criticism." In one of her most talked-about pieces, Givhan wrote that Vice President Richard Cheney, who was attending a Holocaust memorial ceremony in Poland in 2005, should have respected the austerity of the occasion and paid closer attention to fashion protocol (see Box 9.3). Givhan's online writing in her regular blog is lively,

Robin Givhan, fashion editor of the *Washington Post*, received the Pulitzer Prize for Criticism in 2006.

provocative, and characteristically humorous in places, as well as intensely sensitive to beautiful form, texture, and design. (Box 9.4 provides some samples of her article ledes.) The following telephone interview with Givhan was conducted on August 10, 2007.

What is your earliest memory or awareness of fashion, or of clothing?

It was when I was five years old, around then. I went shopping with my father, which was unusual. Normally, I would go shopping with my mother. He let me get these white, patent-leather go-go boots. I thought they were the coolest thing ever. And he let me wear them home from the store! That was really a taboo thing; my mother thought doing that sort of thing was tacky. For the next two years, in practically every photo, there are these white boots on me. I think I probably slept with them on. [Laughs.] I just thought they were the coolest thing ever . . . I felt sort of grown-up, I think—going shopping with my father, wearing the boots home . . .

How did you feel about winning the Pulitzer?

Spectacular. It felt spectacular.

How did the different articles get chosen as the submission for the Pulitzer?

The newspaper calls in submissions. The articles were chosen by my editor, other editors, and by myself. The nomination is done by the paper.

I can't help wondering what you wore to the Pulitzer award ceremony!

It was a luncheon. It's a luncheon of journalists, so it's not a Hollywood gown affair. I wore a day dress that I had bought for the occasion.

Do you worry about what you wear in public? That people are scrutinizing you?

I wear what I think is right for a situation. I never feel pressured to dress wearing a certain designer name or shop in a certain place; it's not my personality.

Columbia University President Lee C. Bollinger presented Robin Givhan with the Pulitzer Prize.

What do you think college students should do to become fashion editors? Do you think students need a graduate degree?

I got my bachelor's at Princeton and my graduate degree at University of Michigan. That's the traditional way. For me, going to grad school was really helpful because I didn't really know what I was going to do. At Princeton [as an undergrad] I thought I wanted to go on to med school, but then I was fascinated by art history. . . . I liked to write, but I didn't write for my college newspaper. For a student who writes for their college newspaper, and maybe also does an internship in the field, maybe graduate school is not that important. A question to ask is, do you love writing? Because I have found that the students who ask me how they can become a fashion editor are not that interested in writing; what they're really interested in is styling. You have to make that distinction.

What's your advice then?

Write as much as possible, about anything. The skill translates to all topics. And if you want to do fashion writing for a newspaper, stay at arm's distance from the center of the fashion industry to maintain objectivity. Your goal is not to celebrate fashion but to eye it with respect.

(continued on next page)

A page from Givhan's blog.

Do you write your own headlines for your columns? They're always so good.

I don't write the headlines. We have a copy desk that does that—they're brilliant. They're incredible with those headlines. It's a talent I do not have! Headlines have to be so entertaining, telling, and enticing. . . . Writing coverlines is another skill that I do not have.

Do you write things for yourself—things that are not about fashion?

I took some time off, I wrote about politics. I do some freelancing for fashion magazines— things that are a bit more like essays, personal-essay-driven writing. Sometimes I veer away from fashion here at the Post—*like I'll write profiles every so often.*

How do you stay on top of everything?

[Laughs.] I read the newspaper.

That makes sense! In print or online?

Well, every day I read the Washington Post, *of course. And I read or look at other newspapers, online mostly. I read the* New Yorker, *it's the only magazine I get at home, actually, and I peruse most of the fashion magazines. I read* Ebony *and* Vibe, *too. Some fiction and nonfiction, though there is not too much time for that.*

Can you tell me a bit about your writing habits?

When I am doing a feature, I have more time to work on it, obviously. More leeway, time to research and sit down to write. My column runs every Friday, so I'm on deadline for that every week, and typically it has to go in at the end of the day on Thursday. I don't generally think of finalizing the topic until Thursday morning. It would probably make others happy if I decided on a topic ahead of time.

Why do you wait till then?

I want my column to be as news-driven as possible. By Wednesday I've changed my mind about the topic anyway. It's part of the hallmark of the fashion writing scene that you produce these "evergreen" stories—the ones everyone expects, the ones magazines have to do all the time, the "how to buy a pair of jeans" stories, etc., that get regularly recycled. I don't have a lot of interest in doing those stories. . . . If it's summer and you're buying a swimsuit, white is most popular. I just think it's right for fashion coverage to be as immediate and as much a part of the news cycle as anything else is. It should be alive and organic, not where you pull the story off the shelf.

In general, when it comes to news coverage of fashion, articles are more from a "how to" perspective, or more of a practical focus, like a tool. I don't think that it's really seen as part of the cultural mix. It's seen as something you do so you won't be naked. The color of the seam, the hemline, the top 10 things to buy—these are all consumer-driven. They're about how to make dressing easier. If you look at fashion as a cultural language, there are a lot of other stories to be told.

"I want my column to be as news-driven as possible."

Do you travel often?

Yes, two times a year, for three weeks at a time. I go to Europe for the fall and spring fashion weeks, Milan and Paris.

What about some of the other shows around the world—like India, or Brazil?

I've covered them. It's a little difficult to go from one runway to another. At this paper I am the only one [covering fashion], I'm it. And even if I did, I doubt if readers have a bottomless appetite for that type of thing [focus on the runways]. When it comes to India, the markets are influential, but it's not what they put on their runways, it's the manufacturing that goes on there.

Do you go to museums?

Yes. When I visit other cities, too. I was just in Chicago and went to the Art Institute and saw the photographic exhibits. It's helpful to follow all the pieces of our pop culture.

You were interviewed by Erin Moriarty of the CBS *Sunday Morning Show*. In that segment, you essentially define fashion: "Fashion is what you wear and how you want to present yourself to the world." Would you still agree with that? Would you add or change anything?

It's the way I think about fashion. I write about fashion from the most rarified view to the mass market. We all know the importance of appearance and how we can control it. Appearance also gets into the way we judge people and the assumptions we make. Fashion is about the choices we make depending on the situation. If you are trying to impress someone—if you are going on a first date, for example—you spend time on appearance because there's so much tied up in that moment. We find it troubling that it [fashion/appearance] plays the role that it does. It's that tension that makes fashion so interesting.

BOX 9.3

DICK CHENEY, DRESSING DOWN

Journalist Robin Givhan mixes fashion analysis and politics in a way other fashion editors normally avoid. This story on Vice President Richard Cheney garnered world attention.

PARKA, SKI CAP AT ODDS WITH SOLEMNITY OF AUSCHWITZ CEREMONY

By Robin Givhan, *Washington Post* staff writer

At yesterday's gathering of world leaders in southern Poland to mark the 60th anniversary of the liberation of Auschwitz, the United States was represented by Vice President Cheney. The ceremony at the Nazi death camp was outdoors, so those in attendance, such as French President Jacques Chirac and Russian President Vladimir Putin, were wearing dark, formal overcoats and dress shoes or boots. Because it was cold and snowing, they were also wearing gentlemen's hats. In short, they were dressed for the inclement weather as well as the sobriety and dignity of the event.

The vice president, however, was dressed in the kind of attire one typically wears to operate a snow blower.

Cheney stood out in a sea of black-coated world leaders because he was wearing an olive drab parka with a fur-trimmed hood. It is embroidered with his name. It reminded one of the way in which children's clothes are inscribed with their names before they are sent away to camp. And indeed, the vice president looked like an awkward boy amid the well-dressed adults.

Like other attendees, the vice president was wearing a hat. But it was not a fedora or a Stetson or a fur hat or any kind of hat that one might wear to a memorial service as the representative of one's country. Instead, it was a knit ski cap, embroidered with the words "Staff 2001." It was the kind of hat a conventioneer might find in a goodie bag. (*Washington Post*, 2005).

BOX 9.4

LEADING LADY

These ledes, or leads (opening paragraphs), by Robin Givhan of the *Washington Post* display her entertaining, informational, award-winning writing style.

From "An Image a Little Too Carefully Coordinated," July 22, 2005; Page C02:

It has been a long time since so much syrupy nostalgia has been in evidence at the White House. But Tuesday night, when President Bush announced his choice for the next associate justice of the Supreme Court, it was hard not to marvel at the 1950s-style tableau vivant that was John Roberts and his family.

There they were—John, Jane, Josie and Jack—standing with the president and before the entire country. The nominee was in a sober suit with the expected white shirt and red tie. His wife and children stood before the cameras, groomed and glossy in pastel hues— like a trio of Easter eggs, a handful of Jelly Bellies, three little Necco wafers. There was towheaded Jack—having freed himself from the controlling grip of his mother—enjoying a moment in the spotlight dressed in a seersucker suit with short pants and saddle shoes. His sister, Josie, was half-hidden behind her mother's skirt. Her blond pageboy glistened. And she was wearing a yellow dress with a crisp white collar, lace-trimmed anklets and black patent-leather Mary Janes.

(*continued on next page*)

(*continued from page 193*)

3. **Play by the team's rules.** If a magazine's editorial members are intent on writing a story on a subject that is taboo, those individuals may not survive at that publication. The reasons something may be considered taboo vary. The subject may be too controversial, there may be legal issues, it may be too expensive, or the executive editor may simply be uninterested. Marketing and advertising agencies often have requirements in terms of the amount of space, number of words allowed, and use of industry-related jargon. It is important to follow the organization's policies and style. Corporate PR and other internal communications must also follow company policies and styles. Be sure to consult the appropriate people before releasing any copy or making any statements.

BOX 9.4 (*continued*)

From "Skinny Models and Sheep," posted at 10:16 PM ET, 02/6/2007:

I freely admit that I'm obsessed about the numbers of super-skinny models who have been on the runway. I don't mean the run-of-the-mill size 4 models but the ones who are size 0 or less. There was a presentation Monday morning by the Council of Fashion Designers of America on the issue of the models' health and eating disorders, which I found less than satisfying. No one got a chance to put the designers on the hot seat and ask them why they even hire size 0's. The presentation ended too soon. The president of the CFDA is Diane von Furstenberg, and she must have set a land speed record leaving the scene that was crowded with press as well as a bunch of eating-disorder experts who were close to being on a rampage against the industry.

From "Armani Day," posted at 05:54 PM ET, 02/19/2007:

I arrived in Milan for the fall 2007 women's fashion shows on Sunday afternoon after a complete airline nightmare. Delays, long lines, bad tempers (mine) and power-mad airline employees. But in the Italian fashion capital the sun was shining, the Prada store near my hotel was stocked with spectacular shoes and the Marni shop was calling my name. Life is good.

Excerpted with permission from the *Washington Post*.

---

4. **Avoid pitfalls related to haste and laziness.** Repetition is one problem that happens when people work too quickly, or when writers are too lazy to write fresh text. There are occasions where repetition is necessary, like when it is used to catch the audience's attention in an advertising campaign. Plagiarism is tempting when a writer is in a hurry to produce something. But failure to give proper credit where it is due can result in ruined careers and legal action. Typos and incomplete work can make you look lazy or incompetent, and they can cost the company a lot of money.

5. **Plan well and meet deadlines.** In the fast-paced and ever-changing world of fashion and accessories, timeliness counts.

6. **Pay close attention to style, consistency, grammar, and other copy matters.** Make sure your writing respects the **style** your organization uses. Many news writers use the *AP Style Manual*. Book editors might use *The Chicago Manual of Style*. Many companies also have their own style manual. (See Box 9.5 for more on text style.)

BOX 9.5

STYLISH WORDS

The word "style" doesn't apply only to fashion—it also comes into play in any sort of written communication. From corporate annual reports to magazines and Web sites, every publication has a specific style that its writers, editors, and designers must follow. Adhering to the set style ensures the **consistency**, accuracy, and tone of a written piece. Many of these style decisions are made over time and have a philosophical or legal rationale behind them.

The rules for two standard writing styles are described in *The Chicago Manual of Style* (commonly referred to as "Chicago") and the *Associated Press Stylebook* (AP). These styles differ in many seemingly small (but significant) ways, such as setting book titles in italic type or inside quotation marks and the use of series commas.

In addition to following a standard style, publishers and companies often use a **house style guide**, a set of editorial rules unique to that publication or corporation. Here are some examples of style rules that may be included in such a guide:

- Lists of city names that don't require mention of states (e.g., writers may refer to "Boston" and "San Francisco" but must add the state when referring to "Lowell, MA" or "San Jose, CA").
- Decisions on how to address individuals (e.g., whether to use "Ms." or "Mr." or to simply use a last name or a first name).
- The specific order and presentation of information, especially in catalogs and shopping features (e.g., headings in boldface, followed by descriptions, sizes, and prices).

Publishers also have a **preferred word list**. Being familiar with the preferred word list is important. If you are describing the fit of a hot new brand of jeans, you'd better know if your publication prefers the term butt, buttocks, bottom, fanny, rear, behind, or posterior . . . so that you don't end up looking like a horse's you-know-what.

SHIFTING INTO EXCELLENT GEAR

There are many ways to become better than the wordsmith in the next cubicle. A good way to start is to think deeply about this question: What are the characteristics of good fashion communications? Why do some words and phrases work better than others?

This chapter began with a quote from designer Geoffrey Beene that contains inherent clues for creating fashion writing that is better than average. In defining fashion, Beene says, "It's a visual art and an emotional sensing. It has to do with feeling good in a second skin, and how others perceive you." A **close-reading** analysis (i.e., close examination, word by word) of this quote might read something like this:

Without wasting time, Beene first aims straight at the core of fashion by applying the phrase "visual art." He has thus "labeled" fashion. After all, the eyes are judges; sight is the most critical of all the senses when it comes to fashion. Next, Beene uses the phrase "emotional sensing," which embraces an intangible sixth sense. He continues with a very personal approach that everyone can relate to, referring to "feeling good in a second skin," which evokes positive imagery. Fashion, he asserts, should be so right for the wearer that it has a tactile (touch) effect that is almost as wonderful as one's own epidermis. Finally, he refers to fashion as "how others perceive you." This last reference involves incorporating the outside world and one's relationships into the definition of fashion. It has an overall effect of leading the reader through a mini-journey inside and outside of the self.

What Good Writers Do

Becoming a good writer is no accident. All good writers maintain that practice definitely counts. In addition, the best writers are or do the following:

- **Not lazy.** They never, ever settle for less than the right word. In other words, they may write "red" in the first draft, but their second draft says "crimson." One way to avoid using weaker words is to always schedule in more time for every job or assignment.
- **Inclined to sleep on it.** They write something, think on it, reread it, and sleep on it before settling on a final version.

- **Habitually reading and making notes**. In addition to doing a lot of reading (newspapers, magazines, and novels) and writing (journaling, e-mailing, and scribbling), most good writers keep their dictionaries and thesauruses at arm's reach.
- **Precise**. Clarity is paramount. So, being precise is a goal to strive for.
- **Unpretentious.** Good writers know arcane knowledge—information that no one but a small insider group understands—kills readership. Referring to acronyms, events, and abbreviations that only a select group of people can readily recognize is not an acceptable practice.
- **Complete in scope, without overexplaining**. Copy should only be as complete as it needs to be.
- **Considerate of the audience**. A good writer asks, "Where is this communications piece going to be seen, or aired in public?" If the writing is for a catalog, the writer pretends to be in the shoes of the person who gets it in the mail. He or she thinks: "How do most people read catalogs?" Often, what catches the reader's attention is a commanding phrase or even a single word. Knowing the audience intimately provides focus for a writer's thoughts.

SPOKEN FASHION

When writing fashion scripts for a broadcast audience or for a runway show held in a department store, bridal salon, or other public space, the topics and themes must be as contemporary as possible to attract and hold the attention of listeners and viewers. The writing must be lively, short, engaging, and assertive. Presenters must be well-practiced in the art of public speaking, and they must look polished if they are going to be seen. They must articulate well, so that their words do not slur or falter, but deliver their message with clarity to listening ears. Effective speakers work hard to eliminate fillers, including "like" and "umm." They make sure they know how to pronounce the names of people and of key terms (see Box 9.6). Ideally, presenters and broadcasters also perfect their voices so that they are soothing and pleasant to the ears of their listeners. No one wants to hear a whiny voice speak for more than a few minutes, if that—no matter how wonderful the writing is.

BOX 9.6

DANGER—FASHION FOX PASS AHEAD! (OR *FAUX PAS*, FOR THE SAVVY)

One of the easiest ways a budding fashionista can burn valuable networking bridges is to mispronounce key words of the business. There can be nothing worse than dropping a bomb like "Her-mees" in an interview when one means to reference master silk-and-leather designer Hermès (air-mez). Stumbling through those French and Italian words so amply spread across fashion jargon can jeopardize a career. Imagine if Scarlett Johansson, when asked on the red carpet whom she happened to be wearing, were to reply, "Give-in-chee." The press would be all over it. The ramifications would be horrific for celebrity credibility as well as for product marketing.

To avoid problems, it is wise to invest in a fashion dictionary, complete with pronunciation keys and examples of usage. One great reference is *The Fairchild Dictionary of Fashion*, by Charlotte Mankey Calasibetta and Phyllis G. Tortora. *Merriam-Webster* online also has a pronunciation feature, but not every designer is listed.

The following is a brief list of some must-know words and names. The italicized syllable is generally recognized as stressed. Japanese words ideally do not have accented syllables (i.e., intonation and inflection are more important than stress).

(continued on next page)

Speaking Adjectives

In "spoken fashion," adjectives tend to play a large role in the physical description of garments. For example, in producing a bridal show on a local level, scriptwriters typically will haul out their thesaurus (or synonym finder) and use words like *elegant, romantic, alluring, nostalgic,* and *radiant*. These are exactly the types of words the audience yearns to hear, since the audience is frequently made up of brides-to-be and their friends and family (especially mothers). Gushing, in this case, is a good thing.

BOX 9.6 (*continued*)

Terms

Aesthetic (ehs-*theh*-tik)
Appliqué (ap-plee-*kay*)
Atelier (at-tell-ee-*ay*)
Avant-garde (av-ahn-*gahrd*)
Bandeau (band-*oh*)
Basque (bask)
Boutique (boo-*teek*)
Bourgeois (boor-*zhwah*)
Bustier (boo-stee-*ay*)
Charmeuse (shar-*mewz*)
Chartreuse (shar-*trewz*)
Chemise (shem-*eez*)
Chic (sheek)
Couturier (coh-too-ree-*air*)
Gaucho (*gow*-cho)
Faux Pas (foh *paw*)
Fuchsia (*few*-shuh)
Femme (fem)
Haute Couture (oat ko-*tour*)
Kimono (kee-*moh*-no)
Madras (*mad*-dress)
Mannequin (*man*-uh-kin)
Moda (*mo*-dah)
Outré (*oh*-tray)
Palette (*pal*-et)
Passé (pass-*ay*)
Pique (as in "to pique interest") (peek)
Piqué (as in cotton weave) (pee-kay)
Prêt-à-Porter (pret-ah-pohr-*tay*)
Silhouette (sill-ew-*et*)
Vermilion (ver-*mill*-yuhn)
Voile (vwall)

(*continued on next page*)

BOX 9.6 (*continued*)

Designers

Anna Sui (anna swee)

Balenciaga (bal-lawn-see-*ah*-gah)

Christian Dior (chris-tee-ahn dee-*or*)

Dolce & Gabbana (dohl-*chay* and gahb-*bah*-nah)

Donna Karan (donna ke-*rahn*)

Dries Van Noten (drees van note-*ahn*)

Fendi (*fen*-dee)

Givenchy (zhee-*von*-she)

Hermès (air-*mez*)

Jean Paul Gaultier (zhahn paul gol-tee-*yeh*)

Lacroix (lah-*cwa*)

Louis Vuitton (loo-*ee vwee*-ton)

Ralph Lauren (*lor*-uhn)

Versace (ver-*sah*-chay)

Yohji Yamamoto (yo-jee yah-mah-*mo*-to)

Yves Saint Laurent (eve sanh-la-*rahn*)

Tailor Your Writing to the Task

Fashion is a surprisingly good topic for radio, despite the fact that the clothing and accessories cannot be seen on radio. With interest in fashion on the rise, radio shows are increasingly covering such stories as Academy Awards fashion, a budget-conscious college wardrobe, designer wear for climbing the career ladder, or street fashion. College radio stations are often an ideal place for running a fashion forum, with a main speaker and guests, or a panel of students sharing ideas (Figure 9.1). However, because radio stations must conform to specific rules, broadcasters must familiarize themselves completely with the law so that their shows are in line with FCC (Federal Communications Commission) regulations. For example, a college-run radio station may allow students to discuss and describe particular fashion items that work together for a total ensemble, but it will prohibit students from directly mentioning prices or comparing one store to another by name.

Script work is a specialty all its own, and it is very different from other types of writing. The pace is faster. Communicating poise is very important. Being wordy and long-winded are not valued, while being precise counts heavily.

Fortunately, becoming a skilled wordsmith across many forms of media is more possible than ever before in history. More and more people are texting messages (which is an exercise in editing, since fewer words are better). Millions of people are creating or contributing to blogs, and nearly everyone is directly handling his or her own correspondence. So practice *might* actually make perfect, in this case.

Figure 9.1   A college student at the microphone during a radio spot about fashion on campus.

PRACTICE: DO CLOSE READINGS FOR PLACE AND PURPOSE

There are numerous well-respected avenues along which words travel. Below are contemporary samples from very different types of fashion writing, representative of different fields and media outlets. Read the samples and use them as springboards for discussion, either in class or in a written response such as a paragraph or an essay. Sources are listed where appropriate, to allow for additional research.

Tone, **voice**, style, structure, and word choices all vary from sample to sample, depending on the target audience and the purpose of the communication. In some cases, headlines (hed) and subheads (dek) may be included before the main text.

Writing Sample 1

Exits & Entrances [column]
   Josh Patner [author's byline]
   What's My Line? [hed]
   Only the Most Prestigious Shirtmaker in the World [dek]

In a small office overlooking the Ritz, Jean-Claude Colban sits at his desk for hours on end, selecting various shades of purple and pink, examining endless bolts of cloth and living with his shirt and tie designs as a vintner lives with his grapes. Monsieur Colban is the co-president of Charvet, his family's company, which is to men's style what Chateau Latour is to fine wine.

Colban is an erudite man of the old school, well versed in politics and the arts, finance and business, history and food. He speaks of Proust with great warmth ("Oh, indeed! Swann wears a Charvet tie"). He speaks of the competition with polite disdain ("We cannot ask people in the morning to work slow and then to work fast in the afternoon"). And he speaks of the new generation of "super, super, super-trendies" who have discovered the pleasure of ordering made-to-measure shirts because "custom is ideal for the new, narrower suits where the fit of the shirt is key."

But Colban is above all a haberdasher. He knows about cut: how the torso lies when the sleeve moves. He knows the importance of detail: the pearly cuff link, the dimpled knot, the collar stay. And he knows about color: the proper complement of tie and pocket square is his stock in trade. . . . (Patner, 2006)

Discussion openers: What is the writer's tone? Who is the probable audience? Who is NOT a probable audience? What about voice? Style? Structure? Choice of words? Level of education of the reader? What is the rest of the piece likely to say?

Writing Sample 2

International Designer Fashion and Accessories
(April 4, 2007. New York)

Join us for a celebration of the seasons ahead as our designers open their showroom doors to present Fall Two/Holiday collections at the DoubleTree Guest Suites Times Square, corner of 7th Avenue & 47th Street in midtown Manhattan, May 6th & 7th from 9a–6p, May 8th from 9a–5p.

The focus for Fall and Holiday remains casual, comfortable, great for relaxing, working, travel and parties, but always with a sophisticated sensibility—inspired by nature, but with city style. From wardrobe basics to unconventional accessories, texture and color abound.

Our designers are addicted to color! Plum, wine and aubergine . . . olive and basil . . . cayenne and yam . . . pomegranate and cranberry . . . indigo . . . bark, walnut and French roast form the base palette this season. Anthracite, onyx, silver tinsel and antiqued metallics add holiday shimmer. Platinum and winter white echo the winter palette.

Dichotomy continues to inspire—masculine/feminine, matte/lustrous, casual/sophisticated, natural/man-made. Nostalgia and ecology play a part, with inspiration from retro linoleum patterns to classic picnic blankets to Old Dutch masters . . . including "green" materials, found objects and recycled/repurposed materials.

For further information contact Susan Summa 505.982.9112 or visit us on the web at www.atelierdesigners.com

Discussion openers: What type of writing does this appear to be? What is especially striking about this copy? How do the word choices tie in with the event? What is the author's goal? Analyze tone, voice, style (e.g., abbreviation, punctuation issues), probable target audience, etc.

Writing Sample 3

Passion for fashion [hed]

    High-end boutiques see market grow [dek]

    By Katie Arcieri, Staff Writer [byline]

A $330 pink satin dress seen on actress Eva Longoria hangs neatly on a hanger.

Near the mirror, an oversized gold Francesco Biasia handbag can be slung over your shoulder for $490.

It's not even spring, and designer sunglasses by Fendi and Michael Kors are flying off the shelves.

Even if you don't get the dress, the accessories offered at Annapolis fashion boutique Diva can pull together any outfit.

"With a handbag and a great pair of sunglasses, you could have no makeup and pj's and you'd still look like a diva," says Michele Deckman, co-owner of Diva at 30 Market Space, where high-end brands from Los Angeles, New York and Milan are regularly in stock.

Annapolitans in search of designer labels are fueling a growing unit of fashion boutiques in the city.

"Everyone says, 'Thank God I don't have to drive to D.C. or New York,'" said Julie Buckley, owner of Astrid, a high-end West Street clothing boutique known as a pioneer in the city's burgeoning fashion district. "Now there are a lot of new shops out there. People really want that."

That's true at Diva. Fashion-savvy women swiping credit cards for designer labels have fueled profits each month since the store opened in May, Ms. Deckman said. The J Brand Jeans, favorite with actress Angelina Jolie, are a hit, she said.

Her store has even had a celebrity sighting: Pop star Hilary Duff dropped in last year to buy Taverniti So jeans.

Ms. Deckman, who has also noticed a growing number of Washingtonians in her store, said she expects sales to grow this spring with a Nicole Miller fashion event March 31. . . . (Arcieri, 2007)

Discussion openers: What is the tone in this piece? Who is the readership? How does it differ from Writing Samples 1 and 2? What adjectives can be used to describe this style of writing? What is the author's purpose?

Writing Sample 4

If You Don't Have a 'Do,' Why Wear a Doo Rag? [hed]
White Suburbia's New Import: An Inner-City Hair Tamer; The Urge to Tie One On [dek]
  By Shelly Branch [byline]

In late August, Matt Buehl, a chubby Christian-music fan with a heart-shaped face, traveled from Laconia, N.H., to New York, hoping to wow judges for the popular TV show "American Idol." Sporting a black "R-O-C-K" T-shirt from Wal-Mart and a denim jacket from Old Navy, the 21-year-old chose to top off his audition look with a somewhat risky accessory: a shiny silver doo rag. . . .

    . . . America's embrace of urban fashion has meant big business over the past decade, with the fast-growing hip-hop clothing category estimated to ring up sales of more than $1 billion annually. As a result, suburban kids craving low-rise pants, velour "hoodies," or other emblems of hip-hop culture, don't have to look far: Chains such as d.e.m.o. and Jimmy Jazz carry pricey labels such as Sean John and FUBU, and cater to a customer base that is up to 70% white . . . (Branch, 2003)

Discussion openers: What words capture the reader's attention? What is the target audience, and the tone, style, structure, etc. of this piece? Is it more descriptive or informative?

Writing Sample 5

Posted at 06:00 PM ET, 03/4/2007

Au revoir [hed]

. . . This was the last day of shows, and everybody was practically giddy in anticipation of going home. It seemed as if the houses showing today were extra nice to the guests. All the doors were open on time. Lanvin served fresh macaroons. At Miu Miu, there was champagne and all sorts of savory hors d'oeuvres. Nina Ricci had a beautiful white tent with an enormous window that let the air in as well as a bit of the scenery from the Tuileries gardens. Only Louis Vuitton kept its audience sweltering in a plastic tent that essentially became a greenhouse. But at least I had my first significant celebrity sighting: Scarlett Johansson. She was decked out in a most unflattering shade of mushroom. Such a pretty girl in such a bad color. She was sitting in VIP row next to Bernard Arnault, the chief shareholder of LVMH Moet Hennessy Louis Vuitton, as well as Lee Radziwill, the sister of Jacqueline Onassis.

That about did it for celebs, which was fine. Because whenever a show gets bogged down with celebrities, the aisles get congested, security guards get their panties in a bunch and the shows start ridiculously late.

As I was arriving for the Vuitton show, I saw a couple of old Paris trolleys pull up. I think they dated back to the 1950s. A large contingent of well-dressed ladies disembarked. I pegged them as Vuitton clients since each of them appeared to be clutching a handbag that cost at least $2,000.

I thank everyone for reading the blog. And I appreciate your comments, even the really rude ones because at least that means you're reading. I'm no hater. Love and kisses. But really, people, let's get things straight: Robin Givens—actress. Robin Roberts—"Good Morning America" anchor. Robin Givhan—that would be me. (Givhan, 2007)

Discussion openers: How does the writer use words to set her unique tone and style? What sets this piece apart from other writing samples in this section? What is the media employed (where did this first appear)? Who is the main readership for this author?

Writing Sample 6

Fashion Icon Liz Claiborne Dies [hed]
   AP
   Posted: 2007-06-27 17:13:58
   Filed Under: Business News

NEW YORK (June 27)—Fashion designer Liz Claiborne, whose styles became a cornerstone of career women's wardrobes in the 1970s and 1980s, has died, the company she founded said Wednesday. She was 78.

Liz Claiborne created a collection of fashions aimed at the growing number of women entering the workforce, an approach that revolutionized the department store.

Claiborne died Tuesday at the New York Presbyterian Hospital after suffering from cancer for a number of years, said Gwen Satterfield, personal assistant to Claiborne.

Claiborne founded Liz Claiborne Inc. in 1976 along with her husband, Art Ortenberg, and Leonard Boxer. Their goal was to create a collection of fashions aimed at the growing number of women entering the workforce.

The new approach to dressing revolutionized the department store industry, which had only focused on stocking pants in one department and skirts in another.

The clothes became an instant hit, and the company went public in 1981. By 1985, Liz Claiborne Inc. was the first company founded by a woman to be listed in the Fortune 500, according to the company's Web site. The company, whose brands now include Ellen Tracy, Dana Buchman and Juicy Couture, generated sales of almost $5 billion last year.

Liz Claiborne retired from the day-to-day operations in 1989. (Associated Press, 2007)

Discussion Openers: What is the main topic? Who authored this piece? What is this type of writing called? Where did it first appear? What media delivered this news item? Discuss the style, purpose, tone, structure, etc.

Writing Sample 7

How to Work Out Which Colors Suit You

Go into your wardrobe and pick out the clothes in the colors you wear most often. Don't choose on the basis of whether that item of clothing actually suits your shape or if it cost you an arm or leg. This is about how the precise shade of a color works with your face.

Take the pile to a full-length mirror in good daylight and sort by color. Make a pile of blues, reds, and so on. Taking one category at a time, put each item up against your face—and see what it does. Do your eyes look brighter? Your dark circles worse? Does your skin look radiant or does it go totally flat? You will soon know which shades of which colors are best for you.

Once you have your final pile of shades that suit you best, go to our color charts to find out which section (Cool and Bright, Warm, or Mid-Tones) you belong to. We are not looking for a perfect match here, but you should have at least four of the colors from one of the sections in your pile. (Woodall and Constantine, 2004)

Discussion openers: What is the tone and style of writing? Who is the intended audience? What sort of fashion writing is this, compared to some of the other pieces (above)? What parts of this excerpt are interesting? How are words used to meet the authors' goals?

KEY TERMS

close reading	style
consistency	tone
grammar	voice
house style guide	venue
preferred word list	wordsmithing
simile	

CHAPTER TEN

Visuals That Speak

"In contrast to the written account—which, depending on its complexity of thought, reference, and vocabulary, is pitched at a larger or smaller readership— a photograph has only one language and is destined potentially for all."

SUSAN SONTAG

art critic

CHAPTER OBJECTIVES

The information presented here is designed to help you understand:

- Basic concepts of visual literacy.
- Emerging changes and challenges in image-making.
- How a fashion brand translates to runway, TV, and print.

Ideally, after reading this chapter, you will be able to:

- More capably assess how photography, drawing, digital imaging, and other media are used to depict fashion.
- Be familiar with terms like placement, position, mood, lighting, and silhouette;
- Be familiar with a critical analysis approach to illustration.

In fashion, the visual image is like the Best Actor or Best Actress at the Academy Awards. Words—no matter how marvelous or dramatic or compelling—will only ever be supporting members of the cast, a Best Supporting Actor or Actress at best. Some words end up much like the extras in a movie—valuable because they enhance the scene and set the stage for the main action, bringing validity to the story (Figure 10.1). Clearly, visuals rule.

Visuals are the most important component in most forms of media. Visual images are so ubiquitous, people practically inhale them. To be successful, fashion communicators must always ask, *How do people see fashion? How do they view images, make impressions, and form opinions?* This focus on the "how" of visuals is not easy to explain, but it is worth asking about.

Think of all the ways in which fashion comes into a person's awareness. High fashion may be seen live on the runway, but only by a small percentage of the general population. Many more people might tune into a television broadcast or an online video of a fashion show. (See Profile 10.1 for an in-depth interview with designer R. Scott French [Figure 10.2], whose 2008 Fashion Week runway show was featured on the Bravo Network series *Make Me a Supermodel*.) Or they may attend a fashion show at a store or other venue (Figure 10.3).

In addition to runway shows, people see fashion in many other places. They may admire a department store window, or they may see something they like on an actor in a movie or on television. They may see garments they would like to buy in magazines and catalogs. Without a doubt, the greatest dissemination of individual fashion items and looks is made possible through photography (Figure 10.4). So, the question, restated, becomes: *How do we see fashion when looking at a visual image?*

To figure out the answer, look at an advertisement, magazine cover, magazine spread, or any photograph or home page of a Web site. Next, without doing any deep thinking about the fashion or the person in the picture or the printed words, just pay attention to the route your eyes follow across the page. This is called **visual flow**.

The eyes will be drawn in many conflicting directions if the design is weak.

News Release

June 17, 2008

Office of the Mayor
Richard M. Daley
Mayor

Contact: Mayor's Press Office
(312) 744-3334

Brooke Vane
Department of Cultural Affairs
(312) 742-4983
Brooke.Vane@cityofchicago.org

FASHION FOCUS CHICAGO 2008 CELEBRATES GROWTH OF CHICAGO'S FASHION INDUSTRY
Back for the Fourth Year, October 1 – 8

Fashion Focus Chicago, a weeklong celebration of Chicago's thriving fashion industry, returns for a fourth year in 2008. Running from Wednesday, October 1 through Wednesday, October 8 Fashion Focus Chicago showcases some of the city's top designers, and features five runway shows in Millennium Park, fashion installations, shopping events, student designer events, and industry seminars.

Appearing for the first time at Fashion Focus Chicago 2008 is Clandestine Industries, a clothing line created by designer, activist, and musician Pete Wentz. The Chicago-based creative talent and entrepreneur's line will be featured during Fashion Focus' opening show, *Gen Art's Fresh Faces in Fashion featuring Clandestine Industries*.

"The growth of this exciting industry is a testament to the hard work and dedication of our designers and industry professionals," announced Mayor Daley. "We are proud to showcase the talented designers that call Chicago home as part of Fashion Focus Chicago 2008."

Chase Promenade North in Chicago's world-renowned Millennium Park will be home to five runway shows:

Gen Art's Fresh Faces in Fashion featuring Clandestine Industries – Wednesday, October 1
Chicago Sister Cities International Program *World Fashion Chicago* – Thursday, October 2
All-School Fashion Show – Friday, October 3
The Allure of Couture – Monday, October 6
Designers of Chicago Fashion Show presented by Macy's – Tuesday, October 7

- MORE -

City Hall, Room 502   121 North LaSalle Street   Chicago, Illinois 60602
(312) 744-3334   FAX: (312) 744-2325

Figure 10.1   The press release is a vital piece of communication, whether in print or online.

The eyes will make a direct journey to the dominant area of a strong, well-designed piece.

Visual flow tends to move from:

- Top to bottom
- In a Z pattern
- From upper left to lower right

Figure 10.2   A behind-the-scenes look at designer R. Scott French.

With many fashion magazine covers, the reader's eyes start off at the most compelling portion of the page. If there's a portrait of a model, the reader is often drawn to the model's eyes or face. Following that, the visual flow might skip sideways to the left side of the page, then move up to the top, to the right, down, eventually back to the central figure. The dominant area is not always the center of the page. The focus may be off center, to prevent boredom, or to challenge predictability of the overall composition.

This trajectory that the eyes tend to follow with a magazine cover is not set in stone. Visual flow can vary, of course. But fashion communicators should keep in mind that a compelling cover is sort of like a map of the United States, whose visual journey begins in Chicago (north-central), jumps a red-eye flight to the West Coast (left), then travels up over Montana and eastward (right) toward the Great Lakes, en route to Boston and New York, and from there further south to check out Miami and New Orleans (the type at the bottom of the page) before boarding a nice riverboat up the Mississippi (center), and back to Chicago.

Figure 10.3   The runway.

In television, there is an added kick to visual flow, which is related to motion. When motion happens on screen, the eye jumps toward it and follows it. (Anyone who has ever been annoyed by an online pop-up box can attest to this truth.) If the motion or action is lateral (side-to-side) or vertical (up and down), a sense of realism is imparted. If the motion

Figure 10.4   During Fashion Week, photographs are taken digitally and are uploaded onto Web sites for all to see. Featured in this image from R. Scott French's January 2008 show is Nikki Taylor and Tyson Bedford.

has an inward zoom effect, the viewer feels a sense of impending change. In her essay "Television Graphics and the Virtual Body," which discussed logos in TV, Margaret Morse (1998) explained that "movement along the depth axis is consistently associated with a transformation, be it a change of worlds or condition." Studying the visual effects of film, television, and cyberspace is a valuable venture for the aspiring fashion communicator. (See *www.ejumpcut.org* for more commentary on television images and their effects.)

No matter which form of media is used, the goals of fashion images include:

- Attracting attention and drawing focus
- Allowing the viewer to absorb details and meaning, and appreciate beauty and design expression
- Encouraging the viewer to transfer or project himself or herself into the image
- Provoking a desired reaction (e.g., to pique interest, excite, satisfy, imply fulfillment)
- Creating a desire for purchase

ENDURING DESIGN PRINCIPLES

Keeping these goals in mind, a new question to ask is: *How can fashion best be presented in illustrations that yield desired results* (Figure 10.5)?

Understanding and observing basic principles of design is a useful tool in boosting visual literacy. Artists and designers may argue about the exact number of basic principles, but here are at least four to remember when assessing illustrations:

Balance—this refers to the symmetry or evenness of like objects, colors, values, hues, and concepts in an illustration. Balance also is concerned with issues of contrast and asymmetry (the off-balance aspects of an image), especially concerning the images placed on a page or in a staged setting.

Proximity—The nearness of objects, images, items, colors, or other elements in relation to each other.

Alignment—This pertains to what lines exist (or do not exist) in relation to each other, so that one line continues, or is parallel to another line, or appears at an angle for a desired effect. Alignment helps position objects and images in relation to each other.

Unity—The quality or state of wholeness or completeness of the image or staging. Unity is achieved by using techniques like repetition (or subliminal suggestions of repeating elements), which result in a total effect of harmony, or feeling of oneness on the part of the viewer.

These principles are equally at work in a dynamic garment design; a dynamic visual image—photograph, drawing, or Web site home page; and in a dynamic magazine article, fashion-related script, or print ad.

More terms used in describing, defining, and using visual images include: placement, position, mood, lighting, silhouette, space (negative and positive), **white space**, contrast, texture, scale, detail shot (e.g., close-up of a man's wrist, shirt cuff, and cufflink), and depth of field (range of distance from the camera). In printing and publishing, lingo pertaining to how images are set on a page is common in everyday communication, and includes such terms as **bleed** (where the image extends into an area, unstopped by a graphic edge, such as a tooling line), **gutter** (the inside edge of a magazine page), and **folio** (page numbers). Other terms to become familiar with include career positions most closely tied to production, including producer, assistant producer, art director, photo editor, stylist, writer, and assistant editor.

Writing staff members may seem to be out of place on a photographic set. However, there is often a good reason to have the writer on site or accessible by e-mail or phone. If the content and tone of the writer's words are inaccurately represented while shooting an image, the resulting visual will be incongruous—it will not match or enhance the fashion focus. The writer can prevent problems easily by being available to the photographer. The writer may also wish to see for himself or herself how a garment moves on a model or to observe the mood and intention of a designer's creation, in order to create exciting copy.

A visual image may be so powerful that words are not even needed, except for branding or informational purposes. (See the "W" jewelry ad in Figure 10.6.) In this visually oriented world, visuals often replace words. This trend is radically different from early representations in print, where words played the starring roles, and the photos and drawings were in the supporting cast.

Figure 10.5   A fashion shoot entails creating a look and then selecting a final image for production, including digital manipulation of the image. In these images, created for a modeling portfolio, photographer James Cucinotta of Cucinotta Images must focus on having the clothes come to life on the model's body. The prettiness or uniqueness of a model is secondary. A successful model will usually be chosen for her ability to sell a particular product or look.

R. SCOTT FRENCH AND THE REALITY OF THE RUNWAY: AN INTERVIEW WITH THE DESIGNER

R. Scott French is a contemporary designer of both men's and women's sportswear. While French's garments are sold in specialty shops from coast to coast, the main showroom is located in New York City. According to the company's Web site:

R. Scott French in his New York studio.

> The collection strikes a balance between item-driven diversity and the cohesive development of a designer look with European influences combined with a clean American sensibility. R. Scott French targets the fashion-aware, but not the fashion-consumed. His customer reads "Harper's" & "Vogue" & "L'Uomo Vogue" to monitor the zeitgeist, but reads "Lucky" & "Details" to decide what to buy. (*www.rscottfrench.com/designer.htm*, 2008)

This interview with designer R. Scott French and his PR marketing director Meredith Garcia demonstrates how the combination of inspired design and constant communication fosters success in this American fashion house.

Meredith, tell me a little bit about what you do for Scott French.

MG: *First, I was his publicist, and now I'm the PR marketing director for R. Scott French. I basically handle everything to do with the two, whether it be to meet with editors or stylists, make phone calls, handle different projects here and there, get Scott's name out there, and get involved with different projects. Most recently, we had the runway show, which opened doors to so many other companies that wanted to have that designer name attached to it. I put together marketing packages, pitches, and all that good stuff that comes along with working with Scott. Right now, we're working on the look book with all the images from the show to try to get that second wave of interest . . . send it to the editors . . . make marketing appointments.*

You're referring to the show in Bryant Park during [New York] Fashion Week, when you teamed up with Bravo Network, right? The one where the male models from the reality show *Make Me a Supermodel* walked for you?

SF: *Yes. But, we didn't team up with them. They came to us, actually. We were doing the show regardless, and we were on the schedule for the fourth of February [2008]. And as is normally the case, as things get closer, all these opportunities start popping up, and all these networks realize they need to do something for Fashion Week. You just can't avoid it, especially if you're a business that's fashion oriented, like Bravo is, with* Project Runway *and* Make Me a Supermodel. . . . *Usually they have to do something.*

MG: *Basically, Lauren, over at Tiger Aspects—which is the company that is doing the* Make Me a Supermodel *show for Bravo—called me . . . very nice girl . . . and she asked, "Scott French designs men's and women's [clothing], right?" So I said, "You know, this season we're really focusing on men's . . . why, what's going on?" She was like, "Aw man, we really want to get our models from* Make Me a Supermodel *walking in a show, but it's hard to find a show that encompasses both men's and women's." And because Scott's Web site does have both, we were the first one they called. I was lucky for that. But, since we're really doing men's now, I told Lauren that, and she said, "Okay, I have to convince them now because it means we have to split the teams up . . . split up the men and women."*

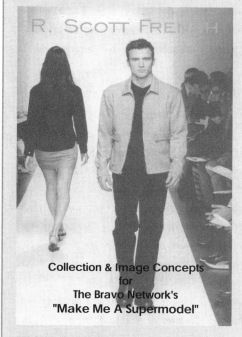

Collection & Image Concepts
for
The Bravo Network's
"Make Me A Supermodel"

Look Books communicate every aspect of a fashion expression.

So, it was my job from there to just keep in communication, to keep up with the people at Tiger and just pitch why they should be in our show. And quite frankly, I think because Lauren and I had such a great relationship from the start, and I was more involved in the process, that Scott's face time and Scott's name was used more in the actual Bravo episode than the women's designers were, because we gave the male models three looks whereas the women only got one.

So, the whole process was basically, one day they called, and the next day it was like, "Can you provide me with a marketing package?" And then, "Okay, provide a little more," and then, "We're making our decision, let's do it." So it was very quick and very good for us, because it's a snowball effect. Once they signed on, then we had more celebrities sign on. Then once more celebrities sign on, more press are interested. Then my job's easy because all I have to do is write the facts instead of making it sound better than it is. Because it's already great.

(continued on next page)

223

SF: *And the location in Bryant Park was so important to our show. The women's show was held off-site at a new museum downtown. This museum had all this buzz around it. It was a happening place, but it just wasn't the right venue for a runway show. As a result of that, it didn't come off that great on TV. They also shot in bad lighting. There was sunlight coming in, and it was a really strange show. Everyone says the design world is just so generic, but there's a reason for it. You just walk down the runway and everything looks so perfect, so vibrant, and everything looks so even because the entire environment is controlled. If the women's show had been on a rainy day, it would probably have been better for them downtown. So, there are all these different things you've got to be careful of when you're doing a show.*

So what really goes into putting together a runway show?

SF: *Many people who aren't in the business don't understand what they're really for, and that they're not about sales . . . directly. The days of the buyer coming to a runway show and sitting there writing down their orders and handing in their order forms as they walk out of the space are long gone. It's really all about the press. You've got to be really, really careful when you're doing a show that, for one, you have something worthy of showing. Many people don't have anything worthy of showing, and they do these shows, and they're bashed in the press. For that 15 or 10 minutes of the show, all eyes in that room are completely 100 percent focused on what you're doing, and you need to make sure that the message you're presenting is so well-honed that there are no misconceptions of what you're showing there, and it can't be all over the place. That's the design theme. Once you have the design theme, you then say, "Okay, here's the design method, here's the look, now let's look at the music. Let's support it with the proper music, proper backgrounds, proper invitations."*

Do you choose the music?

SF: *Yeah. We choose the music. I chose it this season. We have a little session or panel about it . . . I tend to get stuck on a song and it sort of goes from there, get stuck on a color scheme and it goes from there. The music sort of just comes out, as does the theme of the collection. And then we choose the invitations to reflect what they'll see in the show, so that when they get it they'll have some idea—a little hint—about what they're going to see.*

MG: *The thing that was basically Scott's whole inspiration for his designer line this year was this floral print that he made two shirts with, and we used the print for the invitations.*

SF: *Casting the show is really important. It's always a difficult thing. Like, what do you do? How can you find models to communicate your message?*

MG: *Who are you looking for to represent you?*

SF: *Our biggest mistake would be to say, "Yeah, we have a hip-hop following, let's cast only hip-hop models." That's a big mistake for us. That starts putting you even more into a category. At the same time, you have to be mindful of the fact that those are our customers. We can do that through music. We used music in certain sections of the show that was more R&B. We used one of our mu-*

R. Scott French Look Book.

sician customers as the soundtrack for a show. Then there's the lighting that's on display . . . And finally it's a whole . . . it's a show! It's a choreographed show. There are photographers in place. There are videographers in place. If they miss a look, then that look doesn't go out to the press.

MG: *That's what you use as your sales tool. You need that image to send to the stores . . . to put in the hands of your salespeople to show the buyers.*

SF: *With all the images of the show, we edit that down into our look book. We print that out. We send it to all the people who were at the show, and who weren't at the show, for different reasons: one to remind them, and the other to pique their interests. It's really important that there's one consistent message for the season, and for the collection. Not just one season, something that's ongoing.*

Something that's memorable.

SF: *Yeah. So, what makes your collection is that the collection doesn't change. The interpretation for that season—that's what changes.*

Have there ever been any communication breakdowns—bloopers—that you can remember?

MG: *[To Scott] Oh, my gosh, can I say it? In 2006, we had a jacket in the gift bag for the Tony Awards. Now, our official company name is Rieys Industries.*

SF: *It's pronounced "reese," but everyone says it wrong, calling it "rai-ez," "ris," maybe "roos." But we never actually use that name in advertising anyway, ever.*

MG: *So when the Tony Awards sent out their press release to every media outlet, it was "A.M. Rieyes."*

SF: *"A.M. Rieyes Industries."*

MG: *"A.M. Rieyes by noted fashion designer R. Scott French."*

SF: *I don't even know where they got "A.M." from. But that's how our label went out there. It was picked up by wire services . . .*

MG: *It was picked up every day. Everything we did during that time was just like, "A.M. Rieyes by R. Scott French."*

SF: *So we put all this money into marketing the Tony Awards, a substantial amount of money into all the gift bags for the 60th Anniversary Tony Awards. All the presenters got it. It was in the hands of*

(continued on next page)

all these people, and it was the wrong company name. And it was out of our control! We did everything right, and then somewhere along the line someone looked at one of our business cards and just picked it up incorrectly.

MG: *We're just lucky they got R. Scott French right.*

SF: *There was once a time when if a mistake went out in the mail, you would call up and say, "Disregard that," and it went out again the right way. Or, if it was sent out as a fax, you stopped sending the fax and corrected it. But now you don't know where these are going anymore. One e-mail is forwarded to 10 people, then they send it to 10 people—that's 100 people, and you only know the one that received it. You don't know the other 99.* [Laughs]

MG: *It's hard for me because it's my job to make sure everything goes out and I know what's out there, but it really is hard! And once it's out of my hands . . . Someone once asked Scott in an interview, "What do you feel five minutes before and five minutes after a show?" and he said, "Honestly, I've done the best I can and it's out of my hands." That's how I feel, too.*

After the episode of *Make Me a Supermodel* aired, did you start getting more calls coming in?

MG: *We keep track of our Web site traffic, and the increase in hits after the Bravo show has been tremendous.*

SF: *Our show was on a Monday and that episode aired on Thursday of the same week, so there was a very quick turn-around time so it was appropriately shown during Fashion Week. The* Make Me a Supermodel *program is sort of garnering some momentum anyway, but they also did a really good job, starting on Friday, Saturday, Sunday, putting the models in the tents for different events so people were like, "What's going on? What's going on?" So that episode aired on Thursday night with a lot of momentum behind it. We of course did our fair share of e-mailing everyone we know . . . just putting the word out there.*

Did you have any reservations about teaming up with the Bravo series?

MG: *At first we were a little apprehensive . . .*

SF: *The fashion community has a little bit of a snob factor to it and we're thinking we're selling out doing reality TV . . . is that a dangerous thing? But reality is who is most important to connect with, the fashion community or the customer? We felt that the risk was worth it. And* Make Me a Supermodel *was definitely more upscale. It was a really well-done show. Very well edited. Very well funded. NBC is behind it, and the models are living in $20-million brownstones. There's definitely some money there, so we were like, "Okay, this is definitely worth it." Not to mention it brings that celebrity factor to the front row of the show. So the trade-off was there.*

MG: *Plus it brings Scott's name to people who would never really know him otherwise. Everyone is moving in that direction, really. I mean, Michael Kors is on* Project Runway.

What kind of online networking sites do you use?

MG: *I'm currently on Facebook, MySpace, and ASMALLWORLD. Scott's on ASMALLWORLD. ASMALLWORLD is the best thing ever. I'll explain that in a second. MySpace is really just . . . I was really into it about a year ago. Every intern I had in here I was just like, "Do you guys know MySpace? Work on the MySpace." I think it's a dying site, actually. And Scott's going to make fun of me for saying that because I was so into it last year, but it just grew too fast for its own good and it just became advertising. Everyone has a MySpace page. And not only that but there's no control over it, whereas Facebook maintained a control by having just students. MySpace has become so popular so fast that—please excuse me for saying it this way—but more of the "randoms from wherever" are on here looking for dates. That's what it became. And Facebook really is just a tool to keep in touch with people in a network. ASMALLWORLD is an amazing site that is invite-only for people who are in a certain industry.*

"The fashion community has a little bit of a snob factor to it and we're thinking we're selling out doing reality . . . is that a dangerous thing?"

SF: *It's like "creative world."*

MG: *Creative world, yes, but there are bankers on it too. You have to know somebody. . . . Scott and I are both on it, but I couldn't even invite Scott. I had to find someone who had invite access to invite him. So, they are trying to keep it to the name, "it's a small world." It's extremely exclusive, and out of all the sites it's probably the one with the most elite group of people on it: All the fashion designers are on it; all the heads of the PR agencies are on it. Scott has found all kinds of crazy connections on it.*

SF: *You can only see the networks of the people who accept you and if you are turned down three times you're booted off the site. So you've got to be really sure that you are asking for a connection that's real or else. . . . There are some people that I've communicated with several times that are on there, and I still haven't asked them to look me up. When you're on someone else's site you can also search for random people . . . for instance, Ivanka Trump—I'll use her as an example. I don't know how I found out she was on this site, but I clicked on her and you can choose "shortest path to her," and it tells you who you*

(continued on next page)

already know that you can ask to meet her. So it turned out that I'm only one person away . . . we have a mutual friend, and I didn't even know it. And the fact that it's so exclusive and tight, you don't mind asking someone because you are sort of in the club.

MG: *And what makes this so successful is that it's international, first of all—mostly European. It's very much into travel and city life. So, for example, someone who's based in London and is coming for a business meeting in New York will put out on a feed: "Looking for a good place for dinner in New York. Can anyone help?" Then Scott will reply, "Sure, I think you should go here." And then that makes a connection. And who knows if this businessman is coming in to look at a fashion company to potentially buy it. Those are the kind of people that are on the site that are asking these kinds of questions.*

SF: *And you'll see: "Looking to raise $10 million more dollars. I've gotten $90 million already." And, then, literally, you'll read the string and it'll be like, "E-mail me at this e-mail address, and I'll tell you who to call for this." So, it's difficult to fake these things.*

What other kinds of communication do you employ other than these great networking sites?

SF: *You can't not have a fax, you can't not have a phone, and you can't not have a cell phone. But I think that the reality today is—and I've just noticed this in the last two years—the whole switch to Web communication has gone from maybe 25 percent e-mail to 75 percent e-mail. And the phone rings far less today than it did even six months ago, but yet our profile has grown so much more quickly.*

MG: *It actually kind of angers me because despite the ease of just picking up the phone and calling someone to make a connection, 89 percent of the time they'll say, "Oh, can you e-mail me? Can you do that in an e-mail for me?" It would be so much easier if you could just talk about it, but they say, "Oh no, no, no, just put it in an e-mail." It's one way of channeling things to a different location so you don't have to pay attention to it right away, but it's almost putting everything to the back burner . . . when it's ready for them . . . instead of getting into their face. Actually, Scott and I were at an event at Saks about personal e-mails and how to get people's attention in e-mails. I believe it was the Fashion Director at* Harper's Bazaar *giving the presentation?*

SF: *It was Harper's. She brought along e-mails and was saying, "This is the proper way to contact me. Let me read an example. And this is the way not to contact me." E-mail used to be an intrusion. Now it's the accepted way to communicate.*

How much time do you spend using these different modes of communication versus actually creating?

MG: *I will tell you I was on the phone almost every hour of the day right before Fashion Week . . . like a couple months before Fashion Week. After that, you have to get back the attention. For example, [the editorial staff of] multiple magazines are not around. I would call and leave a message. Pick up the* *phone again and leave a message. I would say before the show, all my time was spent on the phone. Now I do more post-work, post-production work, getting things together . . . That way Scott can create the next thing that will get attention.*

SF: *I don't spend a lot of time on the phone. I mean, rarely. I check e-mail every hour. But also, I channel communications to Meredith. So it's a different situation. If I didn't have her, that stuff would take up most of my day.*

You wouldn't be able to create.

SF: *Right. That's part of the problem. You need to create to survive. . . . It's sort of a difficult thing: You can't create if you're doing the little things you need to do to survive!*

Meredith, what happens during your typical day?

MG: [Laughs] *There is no typical day! I mean, today we've actually been having some technical difficulties. The phone and the Internet weren't working this morning, and that's, like, my entire job! And I will tell you right now they're working on an office two or three offices down from us and we think that some of the lines got crossed. If something like that happens, if we lose any outside source, it really impedes my day. My day always starts with e-mails. I come in, and I have to answer e-mails. As much as people say never answer your e-mails at the beginning of the day, I have to. It's a lot of e-mail answering. It's a lot of just getting things together for that day with Scott, meetings . . . I tend to have meetings three, four times a week so it's just getting things prepared for that as well. Right now, we're working on one project and we have to get that finalized before I can jump into anything else.*

SF: *Designing a collection is surprisingly a little amount of work compared to everything else a designer does. At any given time, we're working on several collections simultaneously, so while we're producing spring and summer . . .*

MG: *Right now Scott's sourcing fabrics . . .*

SF: *We're producing Spring/Summer '08, selling Fall/Winter '08, and designing Spring/Summer '09. So it's an 18-month cycle. Mostly you're entrenched in two seasons at a time, and you're doing touch-ups on three at a time. That physical designing is a relatively small amount.*

Scott, your jackets seem to be a very important part of who you are.

SF: *Yeah, they seem to have taken over. It wasn't intentional, but the jackets were a statement that we happened upon. As time went on, suits were taking a back burner and jeans were becoming a hot thing. We were having that whole designer jeans phenomenon. I believe they call them premium denim. The suit jacket just wasn't quite cutting it with the whole premium denim thing. So we hit upon this crazy jacket, the poodle jacket.* [To Meredith] *Do we still have it?* [Meredith finds it on a rack of assorted jackets and lays it on a table.] *This jacket was a pretty basic jacket and we just added a detachable hood to it, and then we put this big poodle on the lining.*

(continued on next page)

MG: *Yeah, so it's a beautiful cashmere blend—cashmere wool—but inside is this.* [She opens the jacket and reveals a large pop-art image of a poodle against a hot pink background.]

SF: *And I cannot remember what possessed me to put that poodle in there, but we did, and this jacket this season was selling five to one over any other jacket. So we're thinking, "Okay, we're on to something here." It kept getting reordered, meaning we had to cut more for the factory, so from there we said, let's see how far we can push this. So, the next thing we did was this patchwork jacket and then we tried to push the envelope a little bit more.* [Scott pulls from the rack a funky pastiche take on the standard blazer; he explains all the elements of it, from the raw edging to the seams that have been turned out.] *It just became this exercise to see how far we could possibly push the limit. And we realized that no matter what we did, we couldn't kill this phenomenon. So our American Chang line really became this jacket resource. Which is a dangerous thing because when you get pushed into this niche market, and the market goes away from that niche, then you're in trouble. We realized that early on. We'll take this and ride it for as long as we can and we'll keep exploring other things to add on.*

Can you explain the different lines you work with here?

MG: *Scott has his designer label, R. Scott French. That's what he's had for seven or eight years now. So, Scott actually is the head designer for three different labels. Actually, one label, American Chang, has three different sub-lines. There's the Ltd part of American Chang, the American Chang part of American Chang. So he's really designing four collections a season, and so that's broken up into his namesake and American Chang. Now it's American Chang, Ltd by RSF, R. Scott French, and Richard Harris Felt. If you combine all of those together, it's something for any type of man who can come in here. You can take any guy, and he's going to find something in the showroom.*

SF: *Richard Harris Felt is a suiting collection: European fabrications with an American sensibility. You can wear it to work, but also it has enough of a twist that you can wear it out. American Chang is what you see here, the really crazy . . .*

MG: *I'm going to say ostentatious.*

SF: *Limited—Ltd by R. Scott French is an upscale American Chang. It's just a little bit better fabrications. More upscale fabrications but still the same spirit of the American Chang. Then, R. Scott French is really European-designer-collection-type. It's real runway, what you see in the magazines.*

MG: *Very editorial.*

Is American Chang influenced by music culture?

SF: [Laughs] *Yeah, it is. We do a lot of musicians. Oddly and thankfully it's been adopted by the . . . I want to call it the fringe hip-hop.*

MG: *R&B.*

SF: *Yeah.*

MG: *The guys who have their finger on the pulse of all the nice fashions right now. They're always in the tailored suit.*

SF: *Akon was up first.*

MG: *Akon and then Sean Paul were the two biggies that we first got when I first started.*

SF: *So they've sort of adopted this whole thing. They've taken it on. And they wear them when they're performing! Big Daddy Kane, when he came in, he saw this jacket right here [gestures] and he says, "Oh my God, that's your jacket? I bought this jacket in Detroit and gave it to Puma to knock off for me because I loved it so much I couldn't find it again!" [Laughs] Because it's very light and identifiable, the music culture can pick up one and wear it onstage.*

It's edgy, but . . .

SF: *It's like edgy-dressy . . .*

MG: *It's for the rock 'n' roller in all of us.*

SF: *We do a lot of red carpet, Grammys . . .*

MG: *MTV Awards, the BET Awards. And I'm very lucky because for some reason I have this core group of stylists who call me for everything. It's a good thing and it's a bad thing, but it's a good thing for most purposes! [Laughs]*

VISUAL DECISIONS

Vogue's Anna Wintour begins her March 2007 "Letter from the Editor" by sharing her thoughts on the most important visual decision a fashion magazine editor makes each month: "Who will be on the cover?" Here is her lead for a fashion theme inspired by "Confidence Women":

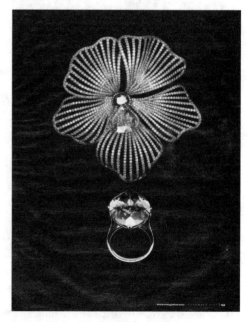

Figure 10.6   Jewelry ad from *W*.

When we considered which face belonged on this month's cover—this is our annual Power Issue—the name on the lips of my editors was Jennifer Hudson. There is no more inspiring example of the power of talent and tenacity than her rise from *American Idol* reject to Golden Globe winner. As André Leon Talley learned when he dressed her for the awards season ("Bringing Down the House"), she's also a style icon whose happiness in her own skin is something we can draw strength from. The question of body image is a current one, and I can't think of a more compelling and beautiful argument for the proposition that great fashion looks great on women of all sizes than the sight of Hudson in a Vera Wang dress on the Red Carpet.

On the cover (Figure 10.7), Hudson is shown with her mouth fully open, laughing, leaning into the camera. Her wine-red dress straps and bodice make a perfect "U" shape, mirroring the lower part of her catchy smile. The reader's eye swoops across the black curls, taking in the top of her left shoulder, traveling up clockwise across the perfect oval arc of her head where her hair explodes into the "O"-"G"-"U" of *Vogue*'s logo, and finally dropping down below the big white "E" to alight on big red capital letters immediately next to Hudson's earring: The words say "THE POWER ISSUE." In white lettering, just below, is "Starring: JENNIFER HUDSON."

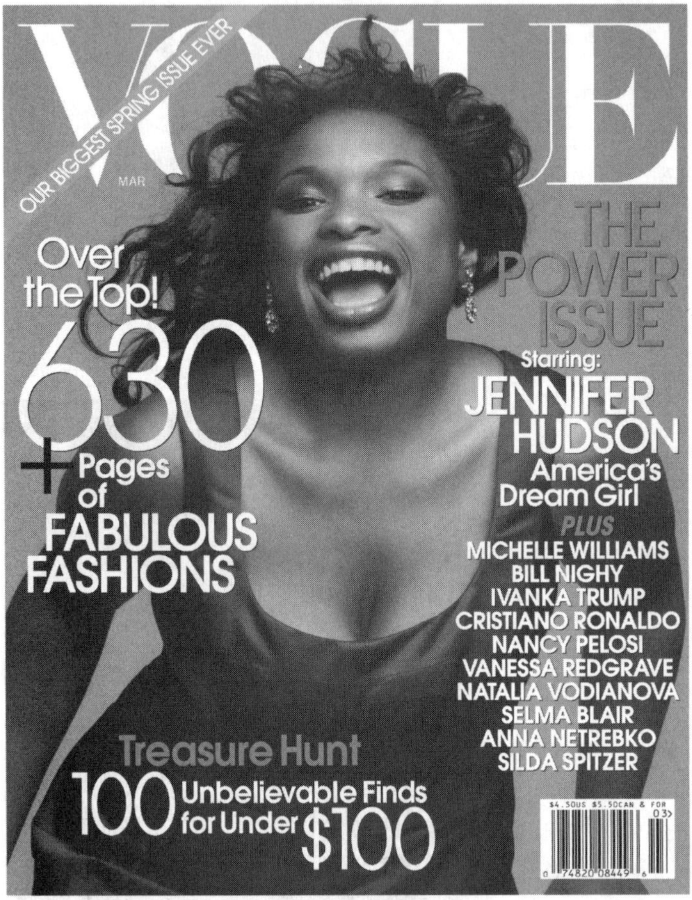

Not everyone can hire Jennifer Hudson as a model. However, it is possible to find good models at established agencies. (Box 10.1 discusses the fact that models are often newsworthy.) Selecting the right model to communicate the mood and feel of the fashion to be portrayed requires a trained eye. Agents can be very helpful in terms of selecting the models a client needs for delivering a particular message. A reputable agency will consider the needs of

Figure 10.7 This magazine cover of Jennifer Hudson is an example of the interconnectedness of different forms of media. Hudson got her first national exposure on a TV talent show, *American Idol*. That was followed by roles on stage and in film, and by plenty of red carpet exposure.

BOX 10.1

MODELS MAKE NEWS

Models have long brought the public's attention to fashion. People are drawn toward the attributes, the beauty standards, exhibited by models—often matching up with a culturally determined "formula" that has to do with symmetry (eyes that are the same size, set at an "acceptable" distance from the nose and forehead, for instance); flawlessly clear skin (at least, made flawless thanks to photo alteration); and a certain appealing spark.

Some writers concentrate their careers on model-related stories, while others might be assigned a feature story. Reporting for the *Wall Street Journal* in the Weekend Edition, February 3–4, 2007, Rachel Dodes's "Strike a Pose, Count Your Pennies" piece discussed the glut of models from Russia and elsewhere, and exposed models' lower fees. "At last season's New York fashion week, the quintessentially American design house of Calvin Klein didn't send a single American down its catwalk," Dodes wrote. "Twelve of the 22 chosen were from Russia and Eastern Europe." Busting commonly held myths about how much models make "in the big time," Dodes's investigative journalism exposed the cruel economics of runway modeling: "For each runway job, which usually takes a couple of hours, many New York designers don't pay at all. In Milan, starting fees are about $650. Models accept the low salaries for the exposure. . . ."

Also hitting news venues are the usual model stories of escapades and excesses, since supermodels have become celebrities in their own right. A reversal of the negative publicity has begun to emerge, however, reflecting the charitable, PC mood of society. AP reporter Samantha Critchell, who regularly covers the fashion beat, wrote up the green political efforts of Lancôme model Elettra Rossellini Wiedemann in April 2007. Apparently, Wiedemann studies environmental conflict in college, and "concerned that her work frequently took her around the globe," she asked Lancôme if the company "would contribute to a carbon offsetting program to compensate for all her flying time." Critchell explains, "Carbon offsetting programs work . . . to reduce greenhouse gases based on an estimate of the amount your actions create." Lancôme actually agreed, and added four more of its famous "faces" to the program—then "decided when it launches its Primordiale Cell Defense anti-aging cream . . . it will plant a tree for the first 10,000 units sold." As Wiedemann herself is quoted as saying, "Is it contrarian to put fashion and the environment together? I don't think so."

In this case, a model becomes a role model.

the customer and use that information to select the best models from its roster to suit the customer's needs. This saves the customer, and the models, considerable time and expense.

Finding Images

The works of fabled fashion photographers are available for viewing online and in art books. All fashion communicators should be familiar with the works of such famous photographers as Richard Avedon, Helmut Newton, Francesco Scavullo, Irving Penn, and Annie Liebowitz.

Illustrating fashion successfully depends on such factors as reasonably generous budgets, good business connections, a well-defined sense of purpose, manageable deadlines, viable media outlets, and access to talented image-makers. **Stock photos,** a collection of images made available by an image service or **photo agency** at varying costs, are generally unsuitable for fashion articles, unless a historical focus is called for; fresh images, with fresh faces, in fresh photo shoots is the order of the day. (See Box 10.2 to view "Photography in a Legal Light.")

If a product is being promoted without the need for a model, the manufacturer or designer or distributor often supplies its own images. These images (and sometimes the products themselves) are sent directly to select fashion columnists. Captioning such images accurately is the responsibility of the writer or publisher of the printed piece. It is crucial to keep good records of images, including any photo credits, and to return any original art in a timely manner if requested to do so.

For the most part, images are transmitted digitally through e-mail as jpegs or TIF files, but an editor must always be sure to check with the photo editor, printer, or art director regarding the reproduction resolution of the image.

Sticking with What Works

Fashion communicators tend to work with visual artists whose style matches the look and feel of their company, store, product, or line. That's because it can sometimes take years to discover a photographer or other illustrator who embodies a certain fashion feel. Jill Smith, creative director of Paul Fredrick MenStyle, explains why she has come to completely depend on a certain photographer: "He knows what we are. Sometimes I think he might know us even better than we know ourselves" (Abbott and Smith,

---

BOX 10.2

LEGAL BRIEF:
PHOTOGRAPHY IN A LEGAL LIGHT

It's often a shock when the average person discovers two important legal aspects about photographers and the images they take with their cameras:

1. A photographer owns the copyright. He or she may be hired to take glamour shots for a modeling portfolio, or be a paparazzo hoping to catch a glimpse of an actress wearing Stella McCartney. It doesn't matter: The photographer owns that image. Unless a photographer or digital-image artist has signed a corporate employment contract that specifically relinquishes copyright (which is not common), or signs away rights to image ownership and usage via a **Work for Hire** agreement, he or she owns the negative or the digital image, and holds proprietary interest in all aspects of that image and its reproduction.

2. Photographers often handle legal details that clear the way for image-making and image usage. Professional photographers and studios charge high prices not just for their artistic eye, sense of timing, and publication-quality imagery, but because they manage many hidden legal aspects of image-making. For example, photographers may handle **Model Release Forms**, assuring the buyer that the model's consent is in place. Without a release form, a photograph would have to be pulled from consideration for print. Photographers also purchase ample insurance to secure liability against costly on-location accidents that could occur—whether it's a person who is injured (e.g., the photographer, the stylist, props person, key grip, model, bystanders, etc.) or to cover costs of equipment and products that may get damaged or stolen (e.g., custom gown, Rolex watch, Galliano bag, etc.).

2007). Consequently, her favorite photographer's name is a closely guarded secret at her company.

A talented photographer can gain huge celebrity in a glamorous fashion magazine. At *Cosmopolitan*, editor Helen Gurley Brown created a legend with her famous magazine covers by hiring photographer Francesco Scavullo. Julian Bain, writing up an interview he did with Scavullo in 2001 (three years before the photographer's death), reveals some of the behind-the-scene dynamics, in Scavullo's own words:

In 1965 Helen Gurley Brown called me . . . and she said that she would like me to do the covers. I didn't even know what *Cosmo* was. I had never seen it. She said, "I know all the magazines you work for, but I want you to do all my covers." I said, "So let me do a cover and we will see what happens." . . . She was wonderful to work with because she never said, "I want to see the rest of the take." She either said "I love it" or "No way," and if she said "No way," then you could have sent her a thousand more photos and it wouldn't have mattered. If she didn't like the dress or the girl, then it was out. I did the covers for *Cosmo* from 1965 to 1995, thirty years. (Bain, 2001)

More recently, the work of photographer Annie Liebowitz has been garnering widespread attention in the fashion world as she lends her creative genius to *Vogue*'s fashion features. Taking dramatic cues from Madrid's bullfights to *Alice in Wonderland* and *The Wizard of Oz*, Liebowitz places her models in elaborate, emotionally evocative settings (see Color Insert).

Photographer and curator Ken Bloom, director of the Tweed Museum in Duluth, MN, observes that photographers are paying closer attention to drama and contrast in their compositions in order to stir reader response:

The technical components of image construction count. But there is a much heavier weight these days in atmospherics to which, in fact, the graphic elements fall in behind. . . . Photographers are paying closer attention to drama and contrast in their compositions to stir reader response, a natural consequence of this media-driven, image-savvy era. . . . It's simply a matter of an expanded range of competing image sources, along with opportunities of digital media and the dramatic range of game design. To capture the eyes of the young, designers are competing in staging, positioning, and the impact of introducing fashion. Envision, for example, an angular-featured tall blonde in an extravagant gown surrounded by the exotic trappings of ancient Egyptian pyramids and camels, or framed by the moody atmospherics of the subway underground—all for the purpose of exaggerating the fine by surrounding it with the raw. Urban imagery and hip-hop has also become increasingly fused with fashion. (Bloom, 2008)

As these influences merge with additional global, technical, edgy, youth-driven expressions, fashion photography dutifully reflects it all, much the same way as a mirror does.

PRACTICE:
SHARPENING VISUAL SKILLS AND UNDERSTANDING

Becoming trained in imaging software is increasingly valuable for fashion work sites. In addition to actively learning and practicing image management in the computer lab, students may improve their visual literacy skills with the following exercises.

Tracing the River

To practice finding visual flow, find three or four compelling advertisements or magazine spreads. Using individual sheets of tracing paper and a pencil, trace each ad's visual flow, marking the dominant point first and then the subsequent areas to which the eye is drawn. The result will be a map of lines that lend clues as to how the designer planned the layout.

Challenge: Swap the ad with another student and do the same exercise with a fresh sheet of tracing paper. Compare results. Do the lines (maps) match up? Why or why not? Discuss the results.

Digital Pix—Blindfolded

Using a digital camera, shoot several pictures throughout the course of an hour or day without looking. A blindfold is not necessary. Stabilize your posture, and click (press the button) with your eyes closed. Compare the results by downloading them on to the computer. Assign labels to each photo, much like a high school yearbook assigns labels to students like "most likely to succeed" or "most beautiful," etc. Which image is most surprising? Most boring? Most intriguing?

This exercise forces the intellect to drop back and the instincts to take over, often resulting in new creative directions and deeper awareness of space and composition.

Create a Hangtag and Bag

Plan, design, and make a hangtag and shopper's bag for an imaginary company or for an original garment, shoe, or store. Spend time brainstorming ideas, writing, sketching, coloring, and playing with type fonts. An original font may also be used, as long as it expresses the brand concept.

Make a Cover!

Create a mockup of a magazine cover using stock photos, complete with coverlines and all the standard elements of a fashion magazine. This may be a group project or an individual challenge. It may take from one week to one month, depending on how original the concept is.

Extra: In class, present the magazine covers for judging. (This may be by anonymous judging or by an open scoring system.) How closely does the cover reflect the magazine's mission? How does the cover appeal directly or indirectly to the target audience?

Tip: Note the lack of punctuation on magazine covers, and the use of different sizes in type based on story prominence.

Design a Magazine or Catalog Page Spread

Create a mockup magazine (or catalog) spread or lay out a whole feature article on a fashion topic. This requires time and planning, and is a long-range project. Consult with the instructor for direction and specifications about such a project. *Important:* Be careful to use original wording and captions to avoid plagiarism.

Initiate the project by writing a proposal or brief describing the purpose of the project, with details regarding the inspiration, potential images, and research sources. Describe the tone of the writing and the style and mood of potential illustrations.

Keep in mind this tip from visual communication expert Paul Martin Lester, Ph.D.: "Perception of the importance attached to words or pictures in publications is often communicated by the size, position, and proximity of the words to the visuals." To read more of Lester's work, see his "Syntactic Theory of Visual Communication" and other writings online at the California State University at Fullerton Web site *http://commfaculty.fullerton.edu/lester/writings*.

KEY TERMS

alignment

balance

bleed

folio

gutter

model release forms

photo agency

proximity

stock photos

unity

visual flow

white space

work for hire

CHAPTER ELEVEN

"With This Page (Ad, Script, or Whatever!), I Thee Wed"

"The goal in marriage is not to think alike, but to think together."

ROBERT C. DODDS

cleric, psychologist, marriage counselor

CHAPTER OBJECTIVES

The information presented here is designed to help you understand:

- The interplay of words and images in fashion communications.
- Design considerations with respect to space, budget, and intent.

Ideally, after reading this chapter, you will be able to:

- Critically assess the **rhetorical situation** of online media.
- Access a practical checklist of rules for combining verbal-visual elements when constructing dynamic messages.
- Think across the media spectrum as you plan magazine spreads, runway shows, media campaigns, and style-themed Web sites, so as to maximize impact in communicating fashion.

Successfully marrying words and images is the primary job of fashion communicators. The visual fashion image that is exhibited and physically seen will—inevitably—come together with spoken words and written expressions. Thanks to the enormous range of imaging technologies and word-dissemination avenues in the twenty-first century, today's fashion communicators can actively demonstrate their skills showcasing the everyday interconnectedness of our information-savvy, information-saturated society.

WORD AND IMAGE VOWS

For a solid pairing to occur, fashion journalists and copywriters alike can use the following checklist to make sure there's a happy ending in store. Just like a wonderful couple, words and images should do the following:

- **Enhance** each other. Some couples know each other so well that they finish each other's sentences. In advertisements, Web site presentations, TV scripting, and every other type of fashion communications, the goal is to enhance, to **complement** (to add to, fill in where something might be missing—not to be confused with com*pli*ment).
- **Explain** each other (but only when necessary). "My wife can't talk right now. She's crying because she's so touched that you sent us tickets for an anniversary cruise." Just as conversation helps explain human behavior, words and pictures shore each other up—frequently with the image delivering the strongest initial message and the words serving to deepen the fashion experience, via written thought.

    It is equally important to know how much to tell or show about a fashion item or trend, and how much to leave unexplained. People are independent creatures: They like to draw their own conclusions and not be clonked over the head with too much information (TMI) either through imagery or words. They want to think that they made a decision based on the information at hand. On the other hand, if a fuller description is needed to draw a full enough picture for the audience, the creator of the fashion communication needs to take the time and space required to make sure the meaning is clear. Doing so solidifies the audience's understanding a trend, a look, a fashion faux pas (a "no-no"), or a fashion must-have. The "Aha! I get it!" moment provided by a great combination of words and images is extremely satisfying to inquisitive human beings. It also is critical to promoting, selling, and appreciating fashion.

- **Exhibit** each other. When a loving, confident couple enters a room, heads turn. People seem to sense the chemistry between them. "Wow! What a pair!" people will say. That is the idea behind strong word-and-image presentations. The words and images are supposed to show each other off. Have you ever noticed how television news teams tend to dress in a way that promotes other individuals on set? That is no accident; it is fashion communications at work. A wardrobe stylist who is on his/her toes will make sure that the main news anchors, the meteorologists, sports desk, and other media presenters do not all wear black suits on the same show or dress in a manner that greatly overshadows or undercuts the style of another team member. Think of how disconcerting and visually unappealing it would be if a lime green blazer was seated next to a hunter green sports jacket, which was adjacent to a tennis-ball-green necktie, when the news team assembled to say "good night" at the end of the show. The negative impression created could have lasting consequences for the TV station's ratings.

  Similarly, when assembling copy and images, the type fonts used for headlines, text, and even captions must exhibit respect for the accompanying photographs and drawings. All sorts of graphic elements and text content decisions need to merge happily, so that the audience can bounce back and forth between text and images in the most enjoyable, comfortable manner possible. Factors that contribute to the cooperation between words and images include color, size, tone, volume, rhythm, flow, shape, overall composition, and choice of media. If the words and images do not work together, the audience becomes bored or confused, and the message is not delivered. In cases where the image is deemed more important than accompanying words, the words must still be bright enough to shine on the image.

- **Excite and entertain** each other. The sexiest couples do not necessarily blow their whole budget at Victoria's Secret. Just a smoky look or a hand gently placed under a lover's chin can keep a good marriage cooking. Great writers find something to get juiced about in their work—something creative and fun and different—no matter what they are working on. Photographers who are not running on autopilot (i.e., mechanically shooting products or merely pulling random stock to illustrate an article), but who inject themselves creatively into the artistic process will be more productive and infinitely happier with the results.

A visually appealing and effectively written magazine advertisement or fashion blog is contagious. It gets people to act or to buy products. An effective fashion communication shows that the people behind the scenes cared enough to bring together the best combination of words and images that would suit the media's purpose. In other words, they created an appealing, compelling example of good fashion communications in action.

TRENDS IN VERBAL-VISUAL INTERPLAY

In fashion information, and its presentation and management, there exists a newly defined need for simplicity. In the current information explosion, people often hunger for things that are clean and simple. Even setting out to produce a two-page spread featuring new swimsuits, for example, requires a simpler, possibly theme-focused approach in order to catch the audience's eye. To arrive at simpler but strong solutions, fashion communicators can make their job infinitely easier by first:

- Defining the goal of the communication.
- Deciding on **scope.** The scope is the range of the message. Do you want to use one form of media, or many different forms of media? It is important to understand that your message cannot be all things to all people in all media. It is especially crucial to avoid "scope-creep," which is what happens when the vision of the project keeps expanding beyond the budget, staffing or artistic capabilities, or media venue.
- Taking a cue from the Internet. Fashion presented online represents an excellent area of study when it comes to attaining simplicity across the media spectrum, since successful sites stay alive only if they adhere to the realities of online viewing. How people surf the Internet influences how they read and respond to other forms of media. Consider the facts listed in Box 11.1, "How People Read—or Don't Read—Online." (For starters, researchers estimate that nearly 80 percent of people scan a page on the monitor, rather than absorbing text word for word.)

Rather than worrying about whether or not people will still read (the phenomenal popularity of the *Harry Potter* books provided reassurance that print is *not* dead), aspiring fashion communicators can best stay ahead of the game by embracing the influence of new technologies, and learning what works and what does not work to hold an audience.

A CRASH COURSE IN WEB SITE EXCELLENCE

Having dual master's degrees in digital media and marketing, with all its current crisscrossing between media and brands, would be ideal for anyone attempting to begin a career in fashion. Add a fine arts degree to that, and then some computer-aided design (CAD) and graphic design and writing courses, and maybe, just maybe, an individual could be expected to put together an outstanding Web site. There is a wealth of information available for the mastering (see Box 11.2 for necessary legalese). Realistically speaking, though, most people do not launch a Web site with all of the aforementioned educational tools. They hire people to help them, or they are self-taught, or use that tried-and-true method of trial and error. When success happens online, it usually is connected to a well-constructed, clearly defined rhetorical situation. Rhetorical situation refers to the particular set of circumstances in which language is being used. (See Box 11.3 on the origins of this term.)

Web Site Pre-Construction Checklist

Whether constructing a Web site or analyzing the presentation of words and images in existing Web sites, the fast track to simplicity lies in figuring out, defining, and then establishing firmly the:

- Task(s) of the writer and image-creator
- Purpose of the writer and image-creator
- Audience (who exactly is the site's core audience or target viewer?)
- Rhetorical stance (credibility, attitude, knowledge and preconceptions, degree of information accuracy, etc.)
- Genre and language (tone, special wording, style of wording)
- Anticipated challenges to online rhetorical situations (how to handle the responses to the Web site)

Examining Successful Sites

In this chapter's profile (Profile 11.1), fashion blogger Michele Obi shares about herself and the Web site she started, *www.myfashionlife.com*. At the cornerstone of her venture has been a strong sense of her own identity, which directly contributes to a well-defined rhetorical stance. **Blogging** offers a unique opportunity for simplifying the presentation of fashion information.

BOX 11.1

HOW PEOPLE READ—
OR DON'T READ—ONLINE

The rise of the Internet as an environment for information, entertainment, shopping, and news has led to a slew of research studies endeavoring to discover exactly how people absorb online communications. Here are some preliminary discoveries:

- The vast majority of viewers—79 percent—simply scan online text; only 16 percent read closely, according to Web usability experts Jakob Nielsen and Carol Pernice (2008).
- It takes people 25 percent longer to read something on a computer than it does to read something on paper (Cameron, 2008).
- According to a study of news sites, people's eyes are not usually drawn first to the photographs, but rather to the words in headlines, especially if a headline is placed in the upper left or right side of the screen (Outing and Ruel, 2008).
- Words have about one second to impress a viewer and convince him or her to keep reading (Sandler, 2006).
- Web site description techniques that help readers find material via search engines are important to visibility for obvious reasons: Someone surfing the Internet may never go deeper than the first page of search results on his or her screen. In the past, metatagging, a technique of search engine optimization, was used widely to select or tag words using HTML code, so that the most pertinent, well-targeted phrases would rise to the top of the results on a search engine. To keep abreast of the best ways with which to capture the attention of potential viewers, technical marketing assistance may or may not be helpful, depending on technological shifts. The main thing to remember is that competition for viewers is fierce and will only become fiercer—so keeping on top of technological developments makes good business sense.
- Emotional connection counts: "What consumers want now is an emotional connection," states Kevin Roberts, CEO of Saatchi and Saatchi Worldwide in the PBS special *The Persuaders*. "They want to be able to connect with what's behind the brand, what's behind the promise" (*Frontline*, 2004). It stands to reason that words, colors, and images all invite longer viewing sessions if they have been crafted to appeal (however subliminally) to the viewers' emotions.

(*continued on next page*)

BOX 11.1 (*continued*)

- People are turned off by small fonts or unreadable type, and will quickly leave a site if the text is not clear and large enough to read easily. Teenagers are even less prone to reading closely than other viewers, unless there are stimulating interactive features (like quizzes), visuals, and clean design *(www.useit.com/alertbox/teenagers.html)*.
- After scanning, once they decide to read a text, readers tend to keep on reading that particular piece.
- When shopping online, "43 percent of readers have been frustrated by the lack of information they encounter . . . [and] 32 percent have been confused by information they have found online during their shopping or research . . . [while] 30 percent have been overwhelmed by the amount of information they have found online while doing online shopping or research" *(Pew Internet and American Life Project)*.

BOX 11.2

LEGAL BRIEF: WHAT IS ALL THAT VERBIAGE?

Online publications look straightforward at first glance. They are glitzy, attractive, and exciting to look at. They often contain more images than words. There are also important legal sections loaded onto every Web site. Written in legalese, they govern the company's "Terms of Use." Since protecting against litigation is an important part of any business, these policies spell out very clearly what the company accepts as its responsibilities to the public and its subscribers.

To see exactly how long and detailed a "Terms of Use" document can be, look for the words "Terms of Use" or "Site Map" (frequently located at the bottom of the home page). Other legal issues are addressed in a Web site's "Privacy Policy" and under headings like "Disclaimers."

For example, on the *Essence* site, the "Terms of Use" page includes such headings as: Subscriber and Member Agreement, Definitions, Monitoring, Disclaimer of Warranty, Trademarks, and Subscription Terms. Lawyers for the magazine's parent company typically draw up and update agreements like these.

See *www.essence.com/essence/termsofuse* for details.

> ## BOX 11.3
>
> # RHETORICAL SITUATION— A DECONSTRUCTION
>
> *Rhetor* (Latin and Greek)—to communicate with words; to speak.
>> Rhetoric—the art of using language effectively and persuasively.
>> Rhetorical—of or relating to rhetoric.
>
> *Situs* (Latin)—location (site)
>> Situation—the way in which something is positioned in relation to its surroundings; the set of circumstances.
>> Rhetorical Situation—The particular set of circumstances in which language is being used.

Other fashion sites worth mentioning include those that have won Webby Awards. At *www.webbyawards.com*, stellar sites are categorized in a variety of ways, including a "Fashion" category, as well as "Magazine," "Blog," "Beauty and Cosmetics," "Best Copy/Writing," "Best Navigation/Structure," etc. (See Box 11.4 for more information.) Winners to learn from include *www.style.com, www.elle.com*, DKNY, which won a "Best Home/Welcome Page, " and Gucci, with its "Best Visual Design—Function."

The creators of all of these sites ensure excellence in the following ways:

- Each image on each page is carefully selected to grab and hold the viewer's attention.
- Whatever words or letters appear are carefully designed in terms of content, symbolism, placement, size, font, color, and effect. Cleverness in headlining counts, but is not at all mandatory. The words that appear with a design in mind are much more important.
- Text and images obey the "laws" of a good marriage: enhance, explain, exhibit, excite, and entertain.

(continued on page 250)

· *Profile 11.1* ·

MICHELE OBI ANSWERS QUESTIONS ABOUT HER POPULAR FASHION-ZINE

Editor Michele Obi has redefined the boundaries between a Web log and an online magazine with her site, *My Fashion Life*. Michele manages to retain the opinionated tone and credibility of a blog while incorporating interviews and articles typically associated with an online magazine. Based in the United Kingdom, *My Fashion Life* is regularly updated with industry news, exclusive interviews, reports on the latest trends, and diary dates for exhibitions, shows, and sample sales.

Fashion-zine editor Michele Obi.

What was your first real awareness of, or interest in, fashion?

My mother was a big influence in my interest in fashion. She was very stylish and extremely fashion conscious. While at university, she'd work all through summer in retail, and she saved every penny so she could buy a high-end designer bag (this was before the whole "IT bag" craze). Her motto was quality over quantity. She always had a copy of Vogue *or* Elle *lying around and I'd find myself flicking through, soaking up all the information. By age eight, my interest in fashion started to manifest itself in my designs. I'd spend afternoons drawing gowns (always with big puffy sleeves) . . . looking back they must have been hideous! Then I started making clothes from plastic bags. I had no material, but I figured I could make a top and a skirt using plastic bags . . . and I did. Finally, I moved on to cutting up my old clothes and making garments with my handheld sewing machine. In the end, I fell into fashion journalism.*

When did you invent *myfashionlife.com*?

I founded My Fashion Life *in 2003 when I first discovered the concept of blogging. I knew immediately that I wanted to blog about fashion.*

(continued on next page)

A page from Michele Obi's Website.

The name of your site is simple and personal, yet what you do appeals to a large audience. Did you have other names that you were considering?

Funnily enough, the name of the site came easily. I originally started as My Fashionable Life, but a friend advised that I shorten it to My Fashion Life.

Is this how you make your living? Do advertisers support your Web site?

The site makes its income solely from advertising, and I was finally able to go full-time as a professional blogger in 2006. After many years slogging away, this is finally how I make my living.

How large is your audience? What kinds of mail do you receive?

My readership fluctuates from 150,000 to 200,000 unique readers per month. I recently started using Google Analytics to track my audience. I get sent e-mails about everything . . . from readers wanting me to track a "must have" item to readers saying how much they love the site. I also get a ton of press releases every day.

How would you describe your site's design elements—its look and feel?

I have always been a fan of clean blogs/Web sites, i.e., the less clutter the better, and I try to incorporate that into My Fashion Life. Easy navigation is also very important. Your readers should be able to find what they want as quickly as possible. Most of the design is in the detail.

Who manages the graphics on your site? Do you have any staff?

I had the site designed professionally, and I recently took on three writers.

Where do you get your images? Do you worry about copyright issues?

I source images everywhere from www.style.com to flickr.com, To avoid copyright issues, I always link back to the source, which is also the general accepted etiquette when it comes to using images online.

Do you ever wear pajamas (or an evening gown?) while you are working on *www.myfashionlife.com*?

Well, I guess one of the perks of the job is that you don't have to worry about what you wear! However, I try not to work in my pajamas if I can avoid it (only if I'm unwell and have to work from bed). I usually try to behave as if I'm working from an office. I wake up early, shower, dress, then hit my desk.

Your style of writing is so engaging and accessible, yet it also seems as though you pay a lot of attention to getting your story straight. What writing training do you have? Any visual education or training? Is it easy for you to "marry" your words and images?

I pay a lot of attention to both the words and images. I believe each is as important as the other. For me, it's easier to find the images first, then I write the story. I started off as an amateur writer, and blogging was just my hobby. With time and practice, my writing has improved a lot. As soon as I knew that this was what I wanted to do for the rest of my life, I changed my degree major to Philosophy in the hope that all the essays would help improve my writing style. Aside from that, I have no visual education or training. I tend to use my intuition most of the time.

"I pay a lot of attention to words and images. I believe each is as important as the other."

What advice would you give to college students who are seeking careers in fashion? What should they pay attention to, when it comes to being good communicators?

Understand Photoshop! Grammar is very important. If you want to own your own Web site, then learn the basics of HTML, and bookmark a couple of tech blogs to read on a weekly basis, as it's important to keep up to date with what's happening in the tech world. Read constantly, everything from magazines to blogs. Have your own writing style, and always be concise.

(continued on next page)

You present a more global approach to fashion than do most fashion influencers. For example, you cover the Korean photographer Kim Yong-ho on your site just as you might cover a Milan or Paris designer. Some people say that Asia, South America, India, and the Middle East are not worth following when it comes to fashion. What are your thoughts on this?

I think the West has been guilty of ethnocentricity for a long time now; however, due to a number of reasons, in particular the state of the global economy, we have been forced to change our way of thinking. For the past couple of seasons there has been an obvious Eastern influence on the catwalks. In addition, India and Hong Kong fashion weeks are garnering more and more attention each year. Also, just recently Elle *sent a representative to cover Dubai fashion week for their blog, which is a real breakthrough. In my opinion, if you cover fashion online, you have a responsibility to cover fashion on a global level, as your readership is a global one.*

What's your prediction regarding the future of fashion online?

Well, I think the future of fashion is online. The Internet is extremely influential now, and most industry insiders have been forced to sit up and take notice. Most magazines have Web sites and/or blogs that are just as important as the magazine itself. Fashion blogs are commanding attention, and brands are now eager to send sample products in the hope of a review.

Do designers court your attention?

Designers are much more approachable today. Where before I would have to be extremely active in contacting designers for interviews, etc., they are now making an effort to get in touch with me. It's also definitely much easier these days for me to get tickets for Fashion Week!

(continued from page 246)

- Copy blocks tend to be shaped according to size—with short summaries that entice deeper reading via hyperlinks (live links that, when clicked on, take readers to a fuller text or sets of words and images). Summary-style copy is called **chunks**; writing these blocks of copy is sometimes called **chunking**.
- "Scope-creep" or an excess of information and imagery is avoided.
- The viewer's satisfaction—related to his/her purpose for visiting the site—is of the utmost importance.

BOX 11.4

THE WEBBY AWARDS

The Webby Awards are exactly what they sound like: They are prizes for outstanding contributions in Web design. How does one get one of these elite feathers in the cap? Here are some insights from Webby Award Executive Director David-Michel Davies.

Are there specific elements of Web site design that always seem to emerge or tend to emerge as standard (recurring) elements of great design, when it comes to selling and communicating fashion?

The basic criteria we use to evaluate Web sites—Content, Structure and Navigation, Visual Design, Interactivity, Functionality, and Overall Experience—are a great starting point. Whether you're interested in making a fashion site or an insurance site, these are the key ingredients and criteria to use when evaluating and making a good Web site.

But beyond that, and in fashion in particular, taking care to effectively communicate the overall brand experience is tantamount. Fashion is so much about emotion. Clothing is, above all else, about how it makes you feel. A site whose primary purpose is to sell or market fashion should try and communicate the feeling of its brand directly through the site.

Do you have any color tips? For instance, are there colors that ought to be avoided? Or, if not avoided, should they be handled carefully and/or backgrounded properly to convey the intended message, whether it's a dress or a type font?

There are no hard and fast rules. Design is a solution-based discipline. A Web designer is trying to do something—make a site that sells clothing, or make a site that showcases a new collection.

Color is an important tool for the designer to use, and a lot of the palette should be chosen based on the feeling of the collection, its season, or as a complement to the palette of the individual collection it may be trying to present.

Obviously, doing things like using light fonts on light backgrounds or dark garments on dark backgrounds is usually not wise as it's difficult to see on the screen. The subtlety that you may find with gray on black in printed form can be completely lost on the computer screen.

(continued on next page)

BOX 11.4 (*continued*)

Why is there a fee to submit a design entry for the Webbys?

Entry fees support the administrative, technical, and promotional costs associated with orchestrating and operating the Webby Awards.

For college students interested in Web design, would you advise seeking an internship somewhere or going on to grad school after getting the bachelor's degree?

I think it really depends on the student. For a long time the best way to learn about Web design was to start making Web sites. It was so new, the curricula available to a would-be Web designer in the academic world paled in comparison to what you could learn by working at a smart interactive shop or Internet company. Obviously, that's changing as time goes on and academic institutions build out programs.

Today "Web design" doesn't mean much because the field is so vast, and the types of knowledge in that field are becoming more and more specialized. Internships can be particularly valuable in helping students figure out what in the world of "Web design" really interests them. Do they want to focus on information architecture, or are they more interested in motion graphics? Or any other of the disciplines that fall under the broad-based idea of "Web design."

In any event, getting some experience as soon as possible is a good rule of thumb. Whether someone chooses to pursue graduate school versus the workforce has a lot to do with what type of learning the individual prefers and is ready for.

How did you first get involved with the Webby Awards and what do you see as the future for the site?

I started at the Webbys as the Academy Coordinator in 1999. Because my job was to coordinate the judging for the Webby Awards, I learned a lot. It was sort of like being paid to go to graduate school. I got to read and sit in on all the discussions the judges had about the sites being considered, and really develop a sense of what makes a great site. Later I took those skills and started my own consulting practice in Paris, which I operated for three years before coming back to the Webby Awards in 2005 as executive director.

As for the future of the Webby site, we'll see! Ultimately, our site is about promoting Webby winners and showcasing the best of the Internet. So, we try and focus our growth and Web presence on those goals.

(continued on next page)

BOX 11.4 (*continued*)

Who serves as judges?

The Webby Awards are judged by the International Academy of Digital Arts & Sciences, a 600-plus-person member organization made up of leading Internet, entertainment, and media professionals, including musicians David Bowie and Beck, Virgin Group founder Richard Branson, Internet inventor and Google Chief Internet Evangelist Vinton Cerf, Simpsons creator Matt Groening, Real Networks *CEO Rob Glaser,* Huffington Post *founder Arianna Huffington, and AKQA Global Creative Chief Rei Inamoto. Members also include writers and editors from publications such as the* New York Times, Wired, Forbes, Details, Fast Company, Elle, *the* Los Angeles Times, Vibe, *and* WallPaper.

What has not been done before with Web site design in the fashion arena? In other words, do you see a certain predictability in design that could be upended, or is that not important?

Well, I think it's important to not get turned off by what has been done before. As I mentioned, Web design is a solution-based discipline. Companies in the fashion industry have a lot of the same requirements—promoting a brand, or selling merchandise, etc. Looking to how others have been successful is smart and a good practice.

But what many industries overlook, and fashion especially, is asking what other problems our Internet presence can help us solve. As a customer, I can tell you there are dozens of problems with the current retail experience, yet I don't see retailers even thinking about using the Internet to solve these problems. The in-store experience is completely disconnected from the Internet! Why?

How do you attempt to keep your own personal vision fresh? Do you personally depend on Web site scanning, or are museum trips, movies, certain magazines, or events important in your sense of the zeitgeist?

The Internet is, in the end, a popular culture medium, so having a sense of what's happening in the world is important. And you can never underestimate the amount of inspiration you can get from other forms of art and design. Everything we do at The Webbys—especially at the event—is inspired by popular culture. But the most important zeitgeist for me is what our judges are doing. I've found that if I can get some sense of what our 600 members are doing—they are so diverse a group—that it's a really interesting and valuable view of what's going on in the world.

With thanks to Gita Chandra, for interview coordination.

WHERE WOULD YOU WEAR THAT?
The Mary Baskett Collection

June 2–August 12, 2007

cincinnati ● art museum

Figure 11.1　With its striking red Issey Miyake dress on the cover, this exhibition catalogue from the Cincinnati Art Museum exemplifies a perfect pairing of words and images.

The Four C's

Finally, lessons to be gained from the Web include this simple set of criteria for evaluating how well words and images work together online. Ask the following questions:

- **Clear**: Is the meaning clear? Or is it obscure? Or too cluttered?
- **Captivating**: Do the words and images sing, seduce, or otherwise transfix the audience?
- **Concise**: Are there too many, too few, or just enough words and images to communicate the intended message? Do the words and images say what you mean and mean what you say?
- **Complete**: Viewers sense that a totality of words and images online accomplishes the intended purpose of the communication.

CAREERS IN FASHION COMMUNICATIONS

The demand for communications skills is on the rise. In job descriptions, the phrase "must be a good communicator" is probably the single most common denominator put forth by potential employers. For the fashion industry, good communications has always been a vital predictor of success.

Job fairs for the fashion industry can be valuable, and Web sites such as *www.style.com*, *www.wgsn.com*, and *www.fashioncareers.com* are worth following. To check out fashion jobs involving communications (including internships and apprenticeships), read over the full range of job titles. The communications components of the jobs are often hidden within the job descriptions. Classified advertisements in trade publications like *WWD*, *FN*, and *Apparel News* are continually updated for the fast-moving job market.

Careers that offer a more journalistic bent on fashion include positions within newspapers, magazines, Web sites, and other publishing outlets. (See Box 11.5 for advice about improving your resume.) A valuable site to consider visiting is *www.journalismjobs.com*. Radio, television, video, film, and virtual fashion (games) ventures offer still more adventures in fashion communications.

In a totally different arena—the museum—fashion frequently appears in exhibits (See Box 11.6.), requiring not only curatorial expertise but a range of visual, verbal, and spoken communications skills (Figures 11.1 and 11.2).

The door is wide open. Remember: Wherever people walk, fashion walks, too.

PRACTICE: BECOMING AN EXPERT MATCHMAKER

These challenges and project descriptions serve to round out the individual's set of communications skills. They feature research as well as practice in marrying images with words to create a seamless whole.

Taking Aim at Consistency

Examine the concept of communications consistency by collecting a set of printed materials (at least five pieces) from a company, fashion designer, fashion item, or fashion television show (*Project Runway* or the Miss America pageant, for example). Include press releases, annual reports, and catalogs whenever possible.

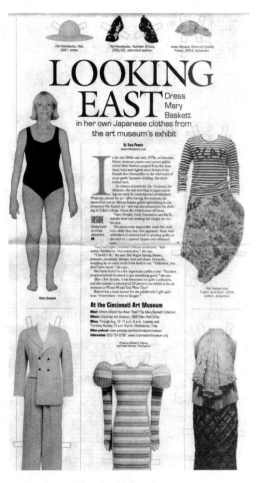

Figure 11.2 The *Cincinnati Enquirer* ran a playful, paper-doll-themed story by Sara Pearce showing the collector, Mary Baskett, with her Japanese designer pieces.

Describe the function and effect of each media exposure. Define the branding, and explain how it evolves over the different forms of media. Describe how writing and visuals "match up" in terms of tone, placement, and physical representation. Has the product/company stayed consistent in its focus and expression?

Lastly, make a prediction for any future cross-marketing or PR ventures that are likely to occur. Be sure to point out the consistencies and inconsistencies between the different types of media coverage.

BOX 11.5

NOT JUST ANOTHER LINE ON THE RESUME

On every superior resume is a heading called "Professional Organizations" where aspiring job applicants list the professional groups to which they belong. A potential employer will look for just such memberships, because the engaged fashion professional is one who communicates with his or her peers and benefits from their associations with them.

Professional associations are communication avenues. They are great for socializing and networking, career development, information sharing, and mentoring. They lend a feeling of kinship. Professional associations give job seekers and established professionals alike credibility within their respective fields. Some of the organizations are open for anyone to join. Others are strictly invitation-only, based on demonstrated accomplishment. For example, the Council of Fashion Designers of America (CFDA) is highly selective and requires nomination and voting for entry. Fashion Group is based on business experience and also requires sponsorship. With chapters in all the major cities in the country as well as international offices, Fashion Group is very supportive of students, offering seminars and design competitions. Color Association of the United States, International Textile and Apparel Association, Costume Society of America, Retail Merchants Association, Public Relations Society of America, the Authors Guild, college alumni associations, and many other groups exist. Many provide internship opportunities, sponsor scholarships, offer student memberships, and feature various design and communications competitions. Their conferences generally occur annually.

BOX 11.6

FASHION IN 3-D

There are various stages in the life of a great fashion designer or a unique fashion statement. The look emerges, then it gets copied and adopted, and next—if it has truly lasting value in an artistic and cultural sense—it enters the exhibition stage. When fashion goes on display in a museum setting, the textile and costume curators are frequently the persons responsible for setting up the show, coordinating all the details, and making sure the garments' labeling and signage is accurate, clear, and appealing to museum-goers. Moreover, there may be a catalog or book produced for the show, which requires photographing the display items, writing copy, and getting a graphic designer involved to lay out the publication, and so forth. Since the typical museum has dues-paying members, docents and donors, and all sorts of people who expect an invitation to the show's opening, this communication, too, must be properly worded, designed, and produced. Along the way, the museum's Web site must be updated to stay current, and the media must be contacted to gain coverage for the show.

A discussion of the Cincinnati Art Museum exhibit of Japanese fashion designers is included in this chapter, showing an innovative approach to both the exhibit topic and its media coverage. It provides an example of strong communications efforts from the curators, news media, and community.

In two interviews combined below, curators talk about the importance of good communications networks. The initials "JA" refer to Dr. Jacqueline Atkins, the Kate Fowler Merle-Smith Curator of Textiles at the Allentown Art Museum. "DB" refers to Dilys Blum, the Jack M. and Annette Y. Friedland Curator of Costume and Textiles, at the Philadelphia Museum of Art.

When you are preparing for an exhibition, what methods of communication do you employ in order to coordinate with your staff (internal communications)?
    DB: Internal planning meetings.
    JA: Face-to-face, e-mail, and telephone.

(continued on next page)

BOX 11.6 (*continued*)

What kind of role does e-mail play on a day-to-day basis?

DB: We use e-mail for general discussion, and find it makes it easier to set up meetings.

JA: If you mean the general public, e-mail is the correspondence method of choice these days, it seems. I get several requests a day for information about the collection and exhibitions and from people asking how to care for their textiles or wanting to bring in textiles/costumes for identification and information. Some of these may be initiated by phone, but follow-up is almost always by e-mail, and more and more are coming in directly by e-mail. I often feel I spend at least half the day answering e-mails, both internal and external.

How about those that you use in order to contact and draw in the public?

DB: [The] Marketing and Public Relations [department] has standard protocol for advertising exhibitions, including press releases, interviews, etc.

JA: This is really more the provenance [origin, source] of the marketing staff, and they use all kinds of media, from press releases and media kits to targeted e-mails to info on the museum Web site to billboards to PSAs [public service announcements]. I have individual discussions with many people, including curators at other museums, local faculty whose students might find exhibitions of interest, and textile-related groups, such as a local couturiere [dressmaker's] group for whom I write a monthly newsletter entry on textiles. I have also done talks on specific exhibitions to various groups who have related interests in order to draw their broader membership into the museum for the exhibitions. I give media interviews (newspapers, radio, TV), but these are usually arranged by our marketing department.

What is the importance of press releases to the media?

DB: Vital—that is what stirs interest.

JA: Extremely important. They help get attention to the local and regional media, who, if their interest is tweaked, then request more information or interviews with the curators. Press kits, sent by mail or hand-delivered, are more effective, as they contain more information and visuals, but the distribution is smaller simply because of the cost.

(continued on next page)

BOX 11.6 (*continued*)

The language of fashion from antiquity to the present: How does that impact verbiage in museum fashion exhibitions? Is today's average audience sophisticated enough to understand fashion terminology, and, if not, do curators find themselves working hands-on with texts to make sure they appeal to visitors? Or do they hire outside writers, editors, and graphic designers to do that?

DB: *Curators write their own labels, which then are edited by our label editor. It's unnecessary to use fashion jargon to communicate.*

JA: *Outside hires largely depend on budget, and [it] is rarely or never done in our museum. The curator is the point person in making sure exhibition text is understandable by the audience, and if [non-jargon] terminology is not readily understandable, then other terms are used. If it is important to include less recognized terms, then it is the curator's responsibility to define the term carefully and without condescension so the audience understands the exhibit and gains a bit of additional interesting knowledge in the process. This also holds true for outside, or traveling, exhibitions that are brought into the museum. Although text done by the originating institution comes with traveling exhibitions, I feel I still have a responsibility to check the wording carefully to make sure it will be understood by our audience and, if necessary, provide any additional explanation that might be needed, so our audience will have the best possible experience with the exhibition. If, for example, an exhibition was originally created for an expert audience already familiar with specialized terminology, it is highly likely that some of that terminology would require adjustment or further definition for a novice audience to be able to appreciate the exhibition objects to the fullest.*

Could you share with me a communication breakdown that you have experienced? What was its impact?

JA: *Do you mean like a spelling mistake in the title of a show in a gallery brochure? Luckily, that one was caught before being put out to the public, but it did cost us money and time in reprinting the brochure. In another case, a magazine review of a photograph show gave the number of works on view as "50" when in fact only 14 works were on view. In that case, we had supplied the right number, and the writer was at fault, but some visitors were disappointed to find fewer works on view than they expected.*

(continued on next page)

BOX 11.6 (*continued*)

Is it important for you to know how to write coherently, or is that more important for editors and marketing people at the museum?

JA: This is an extremely important skill to have. If you cannot write coherently, can other people really make it coherent for you? Yes, good editors are important to help clarify and add elegance to your work, but they need to be able to understand what you want to say to begin with—and they don't always have the luxury of time and proximity to take you step by step through your thoughts to get it right. I put clear writing at the top of the list, and coherent speech next. (And, I clearly need an editor to cut my verbiage in half!)

To learn more about the fashion/costume collections at these two museums, see: www.allentowartmuseum.org and www.philamuseum.org.

Four C's Web Site Analysis

Select a store, designer, magazine, or product to explore, and print out its Web site home page or a portion of the Web site for a fashion words-images analysis. Imagine that you are the site's editor, and can substitute other words for at least three of the headlines to see if they work at all—or if the site functions best as it is. Discuss the results in class.

Using a clustering technique, refer to the section's primary words and images and how they relate to each other. For example, if the home page has "Tops" in large bold letters, scroll over the lettering to find the font and size. Write that on a plain piece of paper, or use an online drawing tool. List other words and word blocks in a free-form manner, and then draw lines tying words together. Do they relate? Are they repetitious, or do they enhance the page? How?

Lastly, create an outline for an essay or PowerPoint presentation that shows whether this particular site section adheres to the **Four C's**: clear, captivating, concise, and complete. Give a letter grade for each category as it relates to the site. For example, a bridal gown site may receive an "A" for being "captivating" because its imagery is powerful and its words are compelling. The same site might get a "D" in the "complete" category because it does not tell you where you can buy the gowns.

Make a Crazy Collage

Create a "Crazy **Collage**" where words get switched around, as illogically or crazily as possible. This is a creative exercise that forces the brain to wander into unfamiliar territory. The best way to do this is hands-on, like a jigsaw puzzle. After trying this once on paper, try doing it using graphics editing software.

The Rules:

- Humor is allowed.
- Working together with friends is okay.
- Allow at least 45 minutes to an hour for the assignment.
- Set up with several sheets of plain white paper, a pair of scissors and glue, and some magazines.

Step 1

Using fashion magazines (men's and women's, if possible), spend several minutes cutting out several random words and images.

Step 2

On blank sheets of paper, arrange the images and words that were *not* originally on the same page in the magazine. Strive for unmatching or crazy concepts. For example, you might pair up an ad of a model wearing a ski jacket with words that come from a jewelry ad. Later, you might decide to add words cut from a completely different page, such as a cooking article.

Step 3

Take a 10-minute break from the project.

Step 4

Finish your collage pages, making final decisions about words, images, and word placements on the page. Paste them down.

Step 5

Share with the instructor and the class.

Journaling

After you have completed the project, or even during the project, if you like, write down your thoughts about the process. Did rearranging the words and images have a freeing effect on you? To what degree should images and words conform on a page?

Do a Fashion Review

Review a fashion show, on TV, online, or live, as a fashion journalist might do. Or write a review of the fashion in a TV show, movie, music video, or YouTube piece. *Suggested word count*: 500–750 words.

   Tip: Avoid reading fashion reviews in these media outlets until after you complete the exercise. Later, check out sites like *www.style.com* or the reviews from journalists who cover Fashion Weeks both in the United States and abroad. Why? Sometimes reading a review first can affect how you react and write about a show. Once you have completed your exercise, read others' reviews to see how experienced fashion communicators covered your event.

Compare and Contrast Web Sites

Either alone or in pairs or groups, examine some of the tips and model sites profiled compared to the tips in *www.websitesthatsuck.com*. Then choose any two Web sites to compare and contrast—one you think is good, and one you think is bad. What makes each site good or bad? Do a rhetorical situation analysis based on the checklist presented in this chapter.

   Major Project: Design a Web site that has a fashion focus, or come up with a proposal for a fashion column or feature for a magazine or community TV station.

KEY TERMS

blogging	rhetorical situation
chunks, chunking	scope
collage	the Four C's (clear, captivating,
complement	concise, and complete)

A Call to Scholarship in an Age of Media Convergence

". . . Laughing on the bus, playing games with the faces
She said the man in the gabardine suit was a spy
I said be careful, his bowtie is really a camera . . ."

PAUL SIMON
excerpted from "America" (sung by Simon and Garfunkel)

In Europe, the fast-fashion, Spanish retail phenomenon known as Zara can reportedly take a fashion concept and have a final product available for sale on its shelves in two weeks. Zara's stock moves in and out so quickly that customers drop by the store on a regular basis just to make sure they haven't missed something, some must-have item for their closets.

When new styles debut on runways around the world, knockoffs are in the works minutes later, fueled by bootleg videos.

During Oscar season, pre- and post-award shows on TV feature talking heads who authoritatively dish their advance scoops and after-carpet thumbs-up/thumbs-down on celebrity garb. In 2008, when a writers' strike threatened to shut down the Oscars, the *Wall Street Journal* ran an article warning of the devastating effect such an action could have on fashion designers.

Paul Simon was right: The bow tie was really a camera.

Cameras are ubiquitous, and talk is, too. All the suggested meanings and non-meanings human beings ascribe to fashion exist in a cluttered, disorganized mess of what is often dismissed as merely pop culture or the reflection of capitalism in material form. Cynics could find it easy enough to say that fashion is here today, gone tomorrow, and later repackaged.

An inquisitive person, one who is always seeking knowledge, does not shut the door on that discussion. An inquisitive person seeks meaning in fashion's manifestations, looking for ways to organize information pertaining to all aspects of fashion's existence. Some of the questions he or she might ask include the following:

- What is the meaning of fashion?
- What is anti-fashion?
- Is anti-fashion fashionable?
- How are fashion trends communicated from decade to decade, and from place to place?
- How do different media contribute to different understandings of fashion?
- What is pop culture?
- How does technology affect pop culture?
- Does an elite fashion mafia exist? Does it promulgate notions of what is desirable in dress?
- Do those in control of mass media dictate fashion?
- To what extent do consumers influence fashion?
- Is fashion becoming democratic?

While looking at magazines, catalogs, TV, and Web sites, students of fashion and journalism often add questions of their own, as they expand upon their knowledge by studying how fashion is covered in the media. These (all actual questions overheard in the classroom) include:

- Who decided that little girls have to look like miniature rock stars?
- Why can't I have the kind of body for a dress like that?
- Is this ad selling clothing or sex?
- Is that bracelet a code for something?
- Why does the color yellow have such a short life in the fashion cycle?
- How often should you change what you look like on Facebook?

- Is stereotyping inevitable?
- How can you keep someone from posting or passing a weird picture of you online—one that might cut you out of a job that depends on your looking great?
- Will magazines die?

Questions like these generate good discussions. To develop a higher-level discussion, to understand the overall picture of how fashion operates within the larger realm of mass communication, students must invest time and research into the study of media theory, communication theory, communication science, cultural studies theory, and related realms of academic inquiry. To comprehend the role of communication in industry, students must take classes that expose them to advertising and marketing theory and practice; to management theory; to political economy theory; and to other important schools of thought.

Theory provides a framework upon which to hang concepts of fashion, dress, and human behavior. For example, those questions pertaining to body image and the portrayal of girls as sexy can be approached from a feminist theory. Feminist theory explores patriarchy, the subjugation of women in relation to men, and gender inequity, among other subjects. Questions about the pace of fashion, consumerism, corporate behavior, and anti-fashion fashion can be explored better by exploring political and economic theory, including capitalism, Marxism, and neo-Marxism. Concepts of civic journalism and the social responsibility theory (which deals with changes in the media following World War II) can help current scholars analyze, and make predictions regarding, politically correct fashion. A study of semiology, the philosophy and meaning of signs, symbolism, and language, and their effects on society and individuals, can yield insights on how shared meaning may be communicated through the media.

In other words, learning about fashion communications can and should be much more than acquiring media literacy skills, much more than enhancing or advancing one's career in the business sense. *Uncovering Fashion* is an invitation—a call—to scholarship in the study of fashion communications.

Resources and Recommended Readings

The lists of resources here are by no means exhaustive. They represent only a sampling of the types of resources that fashion communicators might want to own, access, or subscribe to. The author has vetted all the sources on this list. Students of fashion communications are advised to construct their own lists of information sources.

Books

A fashion communicator's library should contain a range of resources, from biographies to books on communication theory, to titles on history, art, advertising, business, writing, photography, and more.

Baran, Stanley, and Dennis Davis. 2006. *Mass communication theory: Foundations, ferment, and future.* 4th Ed. Belmont, CA: Thomson Wadsworth.

Bly, Robert. 2005. *The copywriter's handbook: A step-by-step guide to writing copy that sells.* New York: Henry Holt.

Caplan, Ralph. 1982. *By design.* New York: Fairchild Publications.

Goldberg, Natalie. 2005. *Writing down the bones: Freeing the writer within.* Boston: Shambala Publications.

Hill, Daniel. 2004. *As seen in Vogue: A century of American fashion in advertising.* Lubbock, TX: Texas Tech University Press.

Jones, John. 2003. *Fables, fashions, and facts about advertising: A study of 28 enduring myths.* Thousand Oaks, CA: Sage Publications.

Joselit, Jenna. 2001. *A perfect fit: Clothes, character, and the promise of America.* New York: Henry Holt.

Lee, Michelle. 2003. *Fashion victim: Our love-hate relationship with dressing, shopping, and the cost of style.* New York: Broadway Books.

Rowlands, Penelope. 2005. *A dash of daring: Carmel Snow and her life in fashion, art, and letters.* New York: Simon & Schuster Adult Publishing Group.

Seylour, Dorothy U., and Carol Boltz, 1986. *Language power.* 2nd Ed. New York: Random House.

Wheeler, Alina. 2003. *Designing brand identity: A complete guide to creating, building, and maintaining strong brands.* Hoboken, NJ: John Wiley & Sons.

Williams, Kevin. 2003. *Understanding media theory.* London: Arnold.

Williams, Robin. 2004. *The non-designer's design book: Design and typographic principles for the visual novice,* 2nd Ed. Berkeley, CA: Peachpit Press.

Williamson, Judith. 1978. *Decoding advertisements: Ideology and meaning in advertising.* London: Marion Boyars.

Magazines

The list of magazines coming into one's mailbox can grow quickly. Below is a list of print media (a short list that is by no means definite or exhaustive) that cover different types of fashion.

Note: Other magazines of a timely nature—like *Time, Forbes,* and *Architectural Digest,* for instance—should not be ignored as potentially valuable resources in the news, money, and artistic arenas.

Cosmopolitan
Elle
Essence
Folio
Footwear News
Glamour

GQ
Harper's Bazaar
Latina
Lucky
Men's Vogue
Pageantry
Seventeen
Teen Vogue
Vogue
W
Women's Wear Daily (WWD)

Web Sites

Building a cyber-library of favorite fashion sites takes time, but is worth doing. The list below is a short one, and does not include the many excellent fashion institute, museum, or art museum sites, nor does it include department store or boutique sites.

American Gem Society *www.americangemsociety.org*
    A way to network with people interested in gems and jewels.
Associated Press Stylebook *www.apstylebook.com*
    The self-dubbed "Journalist's Bible," available in print and in electronic format.
U.S. Census *www.census.gov*
    Government data on workers, industry, and trends.
Color Association of the United States *www.colorassociation.com*
    All about making "the right color decisions."
Fashion Infomat *www.infomat.com*
Fashion Industry Search Engine; information.
Japanese Street *www.japanesestreets.com*
    An interesting source of Japanese seen-on-the-street fashion.
Lucire *www.lucire.com*
    Articles in this self-dubbed "global fashion magazine" are worth checking out.
My Fashion Life *www.myfashionlife.com*
    Michele Obi's cyberfashion site, based in London.

Pantone *www.pantone.com*
>   Pantone publishes beautifully designed color trends reports.

Style.com *www.style.com*
>   A must site for keeping up with the runway scene and fashion predictions.

Tirocci Dressmaker's Project *http://tirocchi.stg.brown.edu/exhibition/*
>   A strong example of fashion with an early-America historic angle.

Mainstream Newspapers

Most newspapers are available both in print and online.

Atlanta Journal-Constitution
Chicago Tribune
Christian Science Monitor
Los Angeles Times
New York Times
San Francisco Chronicle
Wall Street Journal
Washington Post
USA Today

Recommended Viewing

Movies are strong sources for research on costuming, color, and fashion expression, and they have a direct impact on fashion adoption and innovation. From early works like *Gone with the Wind* to such contemporary era-renditions as *Gangs of New York*, movies provide fashion communicators with a cinematic visual background commonly referenced by others. Fashion-themed movies also can amuse and inform, including *Zoolander* and *The Devil Wears Prada*, and many more.

Movie-related media: From exposure in cinema, fashion moves into print media and online viewing as writers analyze what they see. Web sites seem to pop up daily, so the wise fashion communicator will keep abreast of developments regularly. For example, a focus on "Celebrities and Shoes" (spurred by movies) can be explored at the shoe-fanatical *www.shoebunny.com*.

Career Resources

Classified advertisements in trade magazines commonly carry job openings in fashion, many of which require strong communications skills. Attending career fairs can also be helpful. Below are some Web sites that may be useful in career searches:

Apparel Search *www.apparelsearch.com/index.htm*
ApparelNews.net *www.apparelnews.net/TradeShows/2007weeks/may.html*
The Association of Women in Communications *www.womcom.org*
Fashion Writers and Apparel Authors *www.apparelsearch.com/News/Writers/ FASHION_WRITERS_Apparel_Authors.htm*
FashionCareers.com *www.fashioncareers.com*
JournalismJobs.com *www.journalismjobs.com*
mediabistro.com *www.mediabistro.com*
National Communication Association *www.natcom.org*
Public Relations Society of America *www.prsa.org*
Sologig *www.sologig.com*
Style Careers *www.stylecareers.com*
Writer's Weekly *www.writersweekly.com*

References

Chapter 1

Betsey Johnson. www.betseyjohnson.com

Bills Khakis. www.billskhakis.com

ColorTone. www.color-tone.com

Cotton Inc. www.thefabricofourlives.com

Dever, John. Interview by author, July 2007.

Howling Ruth Productions. www.howlingruth.com

K. Gottfried Inc. www.kgottfriedinc.com

Merriam Webster Collegiate Dictionary, 10th ed. Springfield, MA: Merriam Webster, Inc.
   1993.

Sherman, L. 2006. The cult of couture, *Forbes*, June 28. www.forbes.com/2006/06/27/
   haute-couture-fashion_cx_ls_0628feat_ls.html (accessed May 1, 2008).

Thomas, Bill. Interview by author, July 2007.

Chapter 2

Federal Trade Commission. www.ftc.gov/os/statutes/textile/rr.fur.shtml#310.0 (accessed
   January 10, 2008).

Horn, M. 1968. *The second skin: an interdisciplinary study of clothing.* Boston: Houghton Mifflin.

Humane Society of the United States. www.hsus.org.

Khuri, Elizabeth. (2005, September). In the stretch, *Dance* magazine.

Mendels Far Out Fabrics. www.mendels.com/furl.shtml (accessed December 7, 2007).

Merriam Webster Collegiate Dictionary, 10th ed. Springfield, MA: Merriam Webster, Inc. 1993.

Phillips-Van Heusen Corporation. *History.* www.pvh.com/OurComp_History.html (accessed January 2, 2008).

Turtle Fur. www.turtlefur.com (accessed July 21, 2008).

Chapter 3

Bas, Nikki F., Benjamin, Medea, & Joanie C. Chang (2004). Saipan sweatshop lawsuit ends with important gains for workers and lessons for activists. *Clean Clothes Campaign.* January 8. www.cleanclothes.org/legal/04-01-08.htm (accessed March 31, 2008).

Bly, Robert. 2006. *The copywriter's handbook: A step-by-step guide to writing copy that sells.* 3rd ed. New York: Henry Holt and Co.

Greenhouse, Stephen. (2000, June 8). Lawsuit accuses fashion house of running sweat-shops, *New York Times.*

Jordan, Tonia. *Alliteration, assonance, and consonance.* ezinearticles.com/?Alliteration,-Assonance-and-Consonance&id=675686 (accessed June 8, 2008).

National Institute of Standards and Technology. (2004). *Short history of ready-made clothing.* museum.nist.gov/exhibits/apparel/history.htm (accessed May 31, 2008).

National Institute of Standards and Technology. (2004). *NIST's role: Standardization of women's clothing sizes.* museum.nist.gov/exhibits/apparel/role.htm (accessed March 31, 2008).

Naughton, Julie. (2006, November 17). Givenchy zeros in on lipstick with rouge interdit, *Women's Wear Daily,* p. 4

Pallay, Jessica. (2007, June 11). Street cleaning, *DNR,* p. 1.

Sammon, Lindsay E. (2007, October 15). Shoes shine on runway, *Footwear News,* p. 1.

Shaw, Madeleine. n.d. *American fashion: The Tirocchi sisters in context.* tirocchi.stg.brown.edu/essays/shaw_01.html (accessed March 31, 2008).

Thompson, Fred W. and Jon Bekken. 2006. *The industrial workers of the world: Its first 100 years.* Cincinnati, OH: Industrial Workers of the World.

University of North Carolina School of Law. (2000). *Asian-American garment workers: Low wages, excessive hours, and crippling injuries.* www.law.unc.edu/documents/poverty/publications/garmentworkers.pdf (accessed May 31, 2008).

U.S. Government (2006–'07). Occupational Outlook Handbook. www.bls.gov/oco/print/ocos233.htm (accessed March 31, 2008).

Von Drehle, David. 2003. *Triangle: The fire that changed America.* New York: Grove Press. pp. 114–115.

Chapter 4

Bloom, H. (2007, March).Confidential interviews in the fashion field.

Ellis, K. (2008, Feb. 28). "House Passes Andean Trade Extension." DNR.

Morrison, T. and Conaway, W. (2006). Kiss, bow, or shake hands: the bestselling guide to doing business in more than 60 countries. Avon, MA: Adams.

Strauss, C. (©2008 by Claudia J. Strauss)."The Ins and Outs of Email."

U.S. Department of Labor, Bureau of Labor Statistics. "Retail Salespersons." *Occupational Outlook Handbook, 2008–09 Edition.* FIXwww.bls.gov/oco/ocos121.htm.

Wolbers, M. (2009, January). Confidential e-mail interviews with fashion professionals.

Chapter 5

Bell, Maria. 2002. Me and my stalker. *New York Times,* February 20, *Style Magazine.*

CNN.com/SportsIllustrated. 1999. sportsillustrated.cnn.com/tennis/1998/wimbledon/fashion_gallery/1950.html.

Cordarounds.com. 2007. Interview with Chris Lindland by author. *www.cordarounds.com* June.

Crane, Diana. (1999, November). Diffusion models and fashion: a reassessment. *Annals of the American Academy of Political and Social Science* (November) 566: 13.

Hancock, Nanette. 1923. The emerging ear. *The American Woman.*

Ladies Home Journal, January

Lee, Michelle. 2003. *Fashion victim: Our love-hate relationship with dressing, shopping, and the cost of style..* New York: Broadway Books. pp.112–113.

Scarpediem blog. shoesense.blogspot.com/2006/06/shoes-in-movies.html (accessed August 24, 2007).

Sternberg, Fern. 2000. Ball bloomers. www.citypaper.net/articles/051100/nc.loot2.shtml (accessed August 2, 2007).

Chapter 6

Brutico, Rosemary. *www.quintcomm.com.*

Duran, Marla. Interview by author, August 3, 2007.

Jones, John. 2003. *Fables, fashions, and facts about advertising: A study of 28 enduring myths.* Thousand Oaks, CA: Sage Publications.

Magic: The Business of Fashion. www.magiconline.com and lv.fabricshow.com/sourcingatmagic/v42/index.cvn?id=10066 (accessed January 3, 2008).

Quittner, Jeremy. 2007. Brands: Namestorming. *Business Week*, December 14. www.businessweek.com/magazine/content/07_72/s0712048778082_page_2.htm.

Wheeler, Alina. 2003. *Designing brand identity: A complete guide to creating, building, and maintaining strong brands.* Hoboken, NJ: Wiley. pp. 2, 130.

Chapter 7

Adams, A. *www.anseladams.com/content/ansel_info/ansel_ancedotes.html.*

Association for Psychological Science. Aha! Favors the prepared mind. www.eurekalert.org/pub_releases/2006-04/afps-aft040506.php (accessed March 3, 2008).

Bonnie Cashin Special Collection. *Chic is where you find it.* www.library.ucla.edu/libraries/special/scweb (accessed June 14, 2007).

Bonnie Cashin Special Collection. Captions. Retrieved on July 7, 2007, from www.library.ucla.edu/libraries/special/scweb/cashin/cashinlook.htm (accessed July 7, 2007).

Cameron, J. 1992. *The artist's way: A spiritual path to higher creativity.* New York: G. P. Putnam's Sons.

Cameron, J. 1997. *Vein of gold: A journey to your creative heart.* New York: Tarcher/Putnam.

Karr, T. 2003. Fashion industry copes with designer knockoffs. *National Public Radio*, September 18. www.npr.org/templates/story/story.php?storyId=1434815.

REFERENCES

Kenneth Cole. *www.kennethcole.com.*

Lavallee, A. 2006. Now, virtual fashion: Second life designers make real money creating clothes for simulation game's players. *Wall Street Journal,* September. www.wsj.com.

Merriam Webster Collegiate Dictionary, 10th ed. Springfield, MA: Merriam Webster, Inc. (1993).

London, P. 1989. *No more secondhand art: Awakening the artist within.* Boston: Shambhala Publications.

Satie, E. www.humanitiesweb.org (accessed May 20, 2008).

Ward, B. 2007. Don't shuck that shirt. Minneapolis *Star Tribune.* ecowear-usa.com/Documents/Ingeo%20Article%20StarTribune% (accessed June 15, 2008).

Chapter 8

Brazilian, A. 2007. Fall. Take Flight. *Elle Accessories.* p. 112.

Caplan, R. 1982. *By design.* New York: Fairchild Books.

Hill, D. 2004. *As seen in Vogue: A century of American fashion in advertising.* Lubbock, TX: Texas Tech University Press.

Joselit, J. 2001. *A perfect fit: Clothes, character, and the promise of America.* New York: Henry Holt.

Klam, J. 2007. 15 things no one ever tells you about being married. *Glamour,* December. p 164.

Lee, Michelle. 2003. *Fashion victim: Our love-hate relationship with dressing, shopping, and the cost of style.* New York: Broadway Books.

Gentleman's Quarterly. 2007. Go sockless. June, p. 56.

O'Brien, G. 2007. Pants in suspense. *Gentleman's Quarterly,* June, p. 91.

Seyler, Dorothy and Carol Boltz. 1986. *Language power. 2nd ed.* New York: Random House.

Talley, A. 2005. Rock the house! *Vogue,* December.

Thoreau, Henry David. 2003. Walden. In Baym, Nina, ed. *Norton anthology of American literature,* 6th ed. New York: Norton. p. 1818.

Williamson, J. 1978. *Decoding advertisements: Ideology and meaning in advertising.* London: Marion Boyars. pp. 11–13.

Chapter 9

Arcieri, K. 2007. "Passion for Fashion. *The Capital, March 18*. www/.hometownannapolis
.com (accessed June 2007).

Beene, G. from www.washingtonpost.com/wp-dyn/articles/A58495-2004Sep28.html
(accessed March 27, 2008).

Branch, S. 2003. If you don't have a "do," why wear a doo rag? *Wall Street Journal*,
September 9, p. 1.

D'Innocenzio, Anne. 2007. Fashion designer Liz Claiborne dies. *Associated Press News
Service*, June 27.

Givhan, R. Interview by author, August 10, 2007.

Givhan, R. Blog. 2007. Skinny models and sheep. February 6. blog.washingtonpost.com/
fashion/2007/02/skinny_models_and_sheep.htm.

———. 2007. Au revoir. March 4. blog.washingtonpost.com/fashion/.

———. 2007. Armani day. February 19. blog.washingtonpost.com/fashion/2007/02/
armani_day.htm

Givhan, R. 2005. Dick Cheney, dressing down, January 28 p C01. *Washington Post*, January 28.

———. 2005. Leading lady. *Washington Post*, June 22, p. C02

International Designer Fashion and Accessories. 2007. Casual comfort is key from day &
weekend to travel & events in fall two/holiday collections NYC. www.atelierdesigners
.com/go/_press.cfm (accessed June 17, 2008).

Pulitzer Prizes. 2006. *http://www.pulitzer.org/year/2006/criticism/bio/*.

Patner, J. 2006. What's my line? *New York Times Style*, Spring, p. 88.

Woodall, Trinny and Susannah Constantine. 2004. *Trinny and Susannah: What you wear
can change your life*. New York: Riverhead.

Chapter 10

Allen Abbott and Jill Smith. Interview at Paul Fredrick by author, June, 2007.

Bain, J. Scavullo. www.scavullo.com/bio2.html (accessed June 18, 2008).

Bloom, K. Email interview (January 7, 2008) with Ken Bloom, Tweed Museum of Art,
University of Minnesota–Duluth.

Critchell, S. 2007. Lancome model focuses on earth's beauty. *Savannah Morning News,* April 23. savannahnow.com/know/lifestyle/fashion/?from=30 (accessed June 19, 2008).

Dodes, R. 2007. Strike a pose, count your pennies. *Wall Street Journal*, February 3–4.

Scott French and Meredith Garcia. Interview by Hella Rose Bloom, March, 2008.

French, R. S. www.rscottfrench.com.

Lester, Paul. *Syntactic theory of visual communication.* commfaculty.fullerton.edu/lester/writings (accessed January 6, 2006).

Morse, Margaret. 1998. Television graphics and the virtual body: Words on the move. In *Virtualities: Television, media art, and cyberculture.* Bloomington, IN: Indiana University Press. pp. 71–98.

Outing, Steve, and Laura Ruel. The best of eyetrack III: What we saw when we looked through their eyes. poynterextra.org/eyetrack2004/main.htm (accessed March 2, 2008).

Sontag, Susan. www.photoquotes.com/ShowQuotes.aspx?id=82&name=Sontag,Susan.

Wintour, Anna. 2007. Letter from the editor. *Vogue*, March, p. 150.

Chapter 11

Atkins, J. Interview by author, Spring 2008.

Baskett, M. Interview by author, Summer 2007.

Blum, D. Interview by Hella Rose Bloom, Spring 2008.

Cameron, M. 2008. *Why people don't read online and what to do about it.* www.acm.org/ubiquity/views/v6i40_cameron.htm (accessed June 17, 2008).

Davies, D. E-mail interview facilitated by Hella Rose Bloom, January, 2008.

Essence. Terms of use. www.essence.com/essence/termsofuse (accessed March 3, 2008).

Horrigan, John B. 2003. Online shopping convenient but Risky. *Pew Research Center Publications,* February 13. pewresearch.org/pubs/733/online-shopping (accessed February 14, 2008).

Nielsen, Jakob, and Pernice, C. 2008. Eyetracking web usability. *New Riders*, December.

Nielsen, Jakob. 2005. Usability of websites for teenagers. *Useit.com*, January 31. www.useit.com/alertbox/teenagers.html (accessed January 3, 2008).

Obi, M. E-mail interview by author. January 25, 2008.

Outing, S., and Ruel, L. The best of eyetrack III: What we saw when we looked through their eyes. *Poynter Online.* poynterextra.org/eyetrack2004/main.htm (accessed March 2, 2008).

Public Broadcasting Service. 2004. *Frontline. The persuaders.* www.pbs.org/wgbh/pages/frontline/shows/persuaders/view/ (accessed June 19, 2008).

Sandler, J. 2006. July 21). Eyetrack '07: New study probes online and print. *Poynter Online,* July 21. www.poynter.org/content/content_view.asp?id=105035 (accessed June 19, 2008).

Credits

Color Insert	© Annie Leibovitz / Contact Press Images	Profile 2.1	Courtesy of Saga Fur
Part I	© Nathaniel Goldberg / Art + Commerce	3.1	Hulton Archive / Getty Images
1.1	Photo by Ken Bloom	3.2	Photo by Byron / Courtesy of the Kheel Center
1.2	AP Images	3.3	Courtesy of Fairchild Publications, Inc.
1.3	AP Images	3.4	Courtesy of Fairchild Publications, Inc.
Box 1.4	Photos by Kachina Martin / Courtesy of Howling Ruth	Box 3.4	Courtesy of Fairchild Publications, Inc.
Profile 1.1	Courtesy of Bill's Khakis	Profile 3.1a–c	Images courtesy of Museum of Art, Rhode Island School of Design
2.1	Bryan Bedder / Getty Images		
2.2	Hulton Archive / Getty Images	Profile 3.1d	Museum of Art, Rhode Island School of Design / Gift of L. J. Cella / Photography by Erik Gould
2.3	Courtesy of No Contact		
2.4	Courtesy of Fairchild Publications, Inc.		
2.5	AP Images	Part II	© Nathaniel Goldberg / Art + Commerce
2.6	Courtesy of Advertising Archives	4.1	© www.imagesource.com / Veer
2.7	Courtesy of Advertising Archives	4.2	© Floresco Images / Veer
2.8	Courtesy of Turtle Fur	4.3	© Colorblind / Getty Images
Box 2.4	Courtesy of PVH.com	4.4	Veer

Profile 4.1   Courtesy of Claudia Strauss
5.1   © Mary Evans / National Magazines / The Image Works
5.2   © Bettmann / CORBIS
5.3   Courtesy of the author
5.4   Courtesy of the author
5.5   Courtesy of the author
5.6   Courtesy of the author
5.7   Courtesy of the author
5.8   AP Images
Box 5.1   © Paramount / Courtesy Everett Collection
Box 5.3   AP Images
Profile 5.1   Courtesy of Lindland's Cordarounds
6.1   Courtesy of Fairchild Publications, Inc.
6.2   Courtesy of Fairchild Publications, Inc.
6.3   Courtesy of Fairchild Publications, Inc.
6.4   Courtesy of the author
6.5   Courtesy of Heart Truth
Box 6.3   Courtesy of Rosemary Brutico
Profile 6.1   Photography by Jim Cucinotta
Part III   © Nathaniel Goldberg / Art + Commerce
7.1   © Erin Fitzsimmons
7.2   Courtesy of Fairchild Publications, Inc.
7.3   Courtesy of Sara Ashenfalder
7.4   Courtesy of James Harmon
7.5   © Ralph Lee Hopkins / NGS Image Collection / Getty Images
7.6   © Martin Harvey 2008 / Getty Images
7.7   Photo by Ken Bloom
7.8   © Robert Cable / Photographer's Choice / Getty Images

7.9   Courtesy of the author
7.10   Getty Images
7.11   Photo by Kachina Martin / Courtesy of Howling Ruth
Profile 7.1a   Courtesy of Condé Nast Publications, Inc.
Profile 7.1b   Courtesy of the Bonnie Cashin Foundation
8.1   Courtesy of the author
8.2   Courtesy of Condé Nast Publications, Inc.
Profile 8.1   Courtesy of Karen Bressler
9.1   © Masterfile (Royalty-Free Division)
Profile 9.1a   Courtesy of Robin Givhan
Profile 9.1b   Columbia University
Profile 9.1c   Courtesy of Robin Givhan / The Washington Post
10.1   Courtesy of the author
10.2   Paul Warner / WireImage
10.3   Mark Mainz / Getty Images for R. Scott French
10.4   Brad Barket / Getty Images for R. Scott French
10.5   Photography by Jim Cucinotta
10.6   Courtesy of Condé Nast Publications, Inc.
10.7   Courtesy of Condé Nast Publications, Inc.
Profile 10.1a   Brad Barket / Getty Images for R. Scott French
Profile 10.1b–c   Courtesy of R. Scott French
11.1   Courtesy Mark Baskett Gallery / Cincinnati Art Museum / Designer Marc Fuson
11.2   Courtesy Mark Baskett Gallery / Cincinnati Art Museum
Profile 11.1   Courtesy Michele Obi

Index

ability, 162–63
academic journals, 174
accessorizing, 89, 91
Adams, Ansel, 155
adjectives
    command of, 192–93
    superlative, 131
    thesaurus and, 204
adoption, of trends, 105–6
adornment, 28, 29, 32
advertising, 121, 126–35, 173,
    186
    branding and, 134–35, 141,
        146
    business codes and, 135
    fifteen appeals of, 178
    four-theories challenge,
        30–32
    journalistic integrity and,
        57–58
    layouts for, 128f
    magazine revenue from, 116
    online, 248
    press release and, 129–32
    promotions and, 124, 129–
        30, 133–34
    public relations and, 127–28
    taglines in, 13, 30, 124, 174
    terminology of, 124–25,
        142–43
    trade shows, 129–30
    visual flow in, 237
    word-of-mouth, 126
    See also promotion
advertising professionals, 127
Aeon Flux (film), 107f
aesthetics, 29, 92
alignment, 219
alliteration, 61, 62, 192
allure of fashion, 122
Alpha-Beth (A-B) Sportswear,
    86–90
Americana, 17
American Chang (label), 230
American Fashion: Tirocchi
    Sisters in Context (Shaw),
    54–58
The American Woman
    (magazine), 114–15
Andean Trade Extension, 82–83
animal activists, 33
anthropomorphizing, 61
anti-fashion brand, 13
anti-fashion look, 185
apparel manufacturing, 6, 8
    import law in, 82–83
    sweat shops, 44–46, 52
    Triangle Waist Company
        fire, 44–46
appearance, 89, 91, 197
appropriate dress, 91
Arcieri, Katie, 210
The Artist's Way (Cameron),
    152
Asian American Legal Defense
    and Education Fund, 51

ASMALLWORLD (web site), 227

As Seen in Vogue (Hill), 172

Associated Press (AP) Style Manual, 200, 201

assonance, 192

Atkin, Barbara, 59

Atkins, Jacqueline, 257–60

attachments, in e-mails, 77

audience, 203, 204, 242, 259
    blog, 248
    broadcast, 203, 206
    target, 124

authenticity, 16

balance, 218

banner, 50, 53

Bass, George Henry, 39

B2B. *See* business-to-business publications

Beene, Geoffrey, 189, 202

Bekken, Jon, 65

Bell, Maria, 103

Belle de Jour (film), 107–8

bespoke (custom-made), 6

Betsey Johnson, 23

big business, 49–50

bill of materials (BOM), 40

Bills Khakis, 10, 12–19

Black, Ginny, 169

bleed, 142, 219

blogs and blogging, 107, 110, 122–23, 207, 212, 243
    myfashionlife.com, 247–50, 269

Bloom, Ken, 236

Bloomer, Amelia Jenks, 118

bloomers, 118

Blum, Dilys, 257–60

Bly, Robert, 62

body copy, 173

body language, 95, 98

Boltz, Carol, 178

bottom-up adoption, 105

brainstorming, 145, 151, 166–68

Branch, Shelly, 211

brand and branding, 134–35, 141, 146
    anti-fashion, 13
    notoriety as, 111
    ownership and, 136
    target customer and, 92
    thinking-man, 15

brand equity, 124

brand loyalty, 39, 113

Bravo television series, 137, 223, 226

Brazilian, Alexa, 176

Bressler, Karen, 180–85

broadcast audience, 203, 206
    See also television programming

Brown, Helen Gurley, 235–36

Brutico, Rosemary, 130–32

Bryant Park, 223, 224

Buckley, Julie, 210

business practices, 135

business-to-business (B2B) publications, 50, 124

Business Week (magazine), 136

buttons, 26

Calasibetta, Charlotte Mankey, 204

California State University at Fullerton, 238

Calvin Klein, 233

Calvin Klein jeans, 30, 32

Cameron, Julia, 152, 167

campaign, 124
    marketing, 135

captioning, 234, 241

captivating, 254, 260

careers, 47, 254–55
    communications specialist, 35–37, 81
    fashion occupations, 5, 8
    resources for, 271
    retail sales associate, 91–93, 123

career Web sites, 5

Cashin, Bonnie, 156–58

Cashin, Eunice, 157

Cassini, Oleg, 184

catalogs, 14f, 17, 238

celebrities, 204, 212, 223
    designer labels and, 115
    musician fashions, 108
    shoe trends and, 107–8
    supermodels as, 233

cell phones, 37, 92, 140–41
    See also phone communication

Census Bureau, U.S., 7, 63, 269

Chado Ralph Lauren, 162f

Chandra, Gita, 251

change, 13. *See also* trends

Charles E. Young Research Library (UCLA), 156

Chase, Edna Woolman, 56, 57

Cheney, Richard, 194, 198

The Chicago Manual of Style, 200, 201

"Chic is where you find it," 156

Chinese Staff and Workers Union (CSWU), 51

chunks and chunking, 250
Clairol tagline, 31–32
classic fashion, 10
clear, 254, 260
close-reading analysis, 202
clustering technique, 260
Colban, Jean-Claude, 208
Cole, Kenneth, 163
collage, 168, 261
collar, self-folding, 39
college education, 72, 96–97,
    182–83, 195
color choices, 209, 214
    on Web sites, 251, 269, 270
ColorTone, 23
Commercial Standard (CS), 49
communications, 5, 9, 10, 45
    branding and, 134–35
    democratization and, 143
    information and, 5–6
    instantaneous, 90
    "oops factor" in, 75, 144,
        225
    origin of word, 10
    See also e-mail; phone
        communications
communications specialist,
    35–37, 81
company policies, 199
complement, 240
complementary fashion item,
    123
complete, 254, 260
compliance, 47
computer-aided design (CAD),
    243
computer graphics, 141
Conaway, Wayne, 98–99
concise, 254, 260

conclusions, 54
conference call, 90–91
confidence, 97, 139
confidentiality, 135, 144–45,
    166
connotation, 61
consistency, 200, 255
consumer, 29, 197
    hangtag information and,
        4
    See also customer
content count, in magazines,
    186
contests, 90
contracts and kill fees, 179
cooperation, 66
    See also teamwork
copy, 98, 124
    chunking of, 250
copy platform, 124
copyright, 248
copywriters, 167
Copywriter's Handbook (Bly),
    62
Cordarounds.com, 109–14,
    120
Corey, Madeliene, 56
corsets, 175
Cosmopolitan magazine, 235
cotton, 22
cotton jersey, 27
Council of Fashion Designers
    of America (CFDA), 200,
    256
coverlines, 173
Crane, Diana, 106
crazy collage, 261
creative copy, 60
creative gurus, 127

creativity, 12–13, 149, 151–70
    brainstorming and, 145,
        151, 166–68
    Cashin and, 156–58
    commitment to, 152
    elements of, 155, 158,
        160–65
    fashion communication
        and, 166–67
    inspiration and, 155, 158,
        160, 161–62, 164f, 165f
    originality and, 152,
        154–55
Critchell, Samantha, 233
critical analyses, 54, 57
cross promotion, 124
Cucinotta, James, 221
cultural criticism, 194
cultural differences, 37
cultural language, 197
curiosity, 160–61
currency, 143
customer, 94–95, 138
    loyalty of, 39, 113
    salespeople and, 91–93
    tact and patience with, 72
    target, 15, 16, 17
    See also consumer
custom-made garments, 6

dancers, leotard and, 27
Davies, David-Michel, 251–53
deadlines, 200
DeBeers diamonds, 31, 32
Deckman, Michele, 210
deconstructing, 26, 40
democratization, 143, 150
demographics, 123, 124
Deneuve, Catherine, 107–8

denim sales, 60
  See also jeans ad campaign
Department of Agriculture,
  U.S., 48
Department of Labor, U.S., 7,
  8, 72–73
description, 189–214
  adjectives, 131, 192–93, 204
  fashion focus and, 191–93
  Givhan, 194–200, 212
  scriptwork, 206–7
  spoken fashion, 203–4
  style guides and, 201
  writing samples, 207–14
descriptive details, 54
designer bag, 247
designer collections, 229
designer labels, 115, 230
designers, 155, 206, 222
  sweatshops and, 51
  See also specific designer
Designing Brand Identity
  (Wheeler), 134
design principles, 218–19
detail, in retail, 71–101
  attention to, 71, 72
  corporate PR, 83–85
  e-mailing, 73–80, 90–91
  planner and, 93–96
  quiz, 97–98
  sales associate and, 91–93
  supervisor and, 96–97
  trade laws, 82–83
  visual merchandiser, 81,
    86–91
diamonds, 94
  ad tagline, 31, 32
Diana, Princes of Wales, 104–5
Dickinson, Robert L., 175

dictionaries, 10, 34, 154, 204
"Diffusion Models and
  Fashion: A Reassessment"
  (Crane), 106
digital image programs, 141
digital pix, 237
direct mail, 124, 126
Disclaimers, on web site, 245
disclosure, 47
dissection, style, 7, 9–11
DKNY (Donna Karan), 246
DNR magazine, 59–60
Dodds, Robert C., 239
Dodes, Rachel, 233
domain names, 38
double entendre, 61
Draddy, Vin, 39
drama and contrast, 236
dress reformers, 175
Duran, Marla, 135, 137–41

early adopters, 105
earrings, 114–15
ecofashions, 33, 233
eco-friendly materials, 169
editorial space, 58
education. *See* college
  education
electronic mail. *See* e-mail
Elite Traveler (magazine), 184
Elle.com, 246
Ellis, Kristi, 82–83
e-mail, 73–80, 226, 248
  attachments in, 77
  conference call and, 90–91
  ins and outs of, 73–77
  key tips to create, 78–80
  mass, 91, 112, 113
  meetings and, 258

mirroring in, 76
"oops factor" in, 75
phoning and, 75, 77, 84, 85,
  88, 140–41, 228
research by, 63
timely response to, 77, 141
embellishments bank, 20–21
"The Emerging Ear"
  (Hancock), 114–15
emerging fashion centers, 50
emotional freight, 75
employer, e-mail and, 80
employment forecast, 73
  See also careers
English language, 36
enhancement, 240
entertainment, 27, 241
enthnocentricity, 250
environment, 164
ergonomics, 47
erogenous zone, 115–16
etiquette, e-mail, 80
event planning, 84–85
evergreen topic, 115, 196
excitement, 241
exhibit, 241. *See also* museum
  exhibits
experience, 166
explanation, 240
express fashion, 26
extension of self, 28, 29, 32

fabric, 117
fabric bank, 20–21
fabric sourcing, 19
Facebook, 227
face-to-face contact, 84
Fairchild Dictionary of Fashion,
  34, 204

fake fur, 33, 34
fashion, 40
    adoption of, 105–6, 118
    allure of, 122
    classic, 10
    defined, 189, 202
    fast, 263
    language of, 9–10
    musician, 26, 27
    origin of word, 10
    teen, 116*f*, 183
fashion, becoming, 103–20
    Cordarounds, 109–14, 121
    erogenous zones, 115–16
    fashion magazines, 114–17
    trendsetters, 104–8
fashion centers, 49–50
fashion classic, 10
fashion communications, 5, 45
    See also communications
fashion communicator,
    defined, 5
fashion critics, 57
fashion dolls, 104
fashion editors, 56
Fashion Group, 256
fashion industry, evolution of,
    46–50
fashion information. *See*
    information
fashion magazines, 114–17,
    122, 268–69
    as agents of change, 173–74
    content count in, 186
    covers for, 217, 238
    evolution of, 149, 171–87
    philosophy of, 185–86
    wordsmithing in, 53–62
    See also trade publications

fashion news journalist, 54
fashion occupations, 5, 8
fashion photography. *See*
    photography
fashion plate, 104
fashion review, 262
fashion scripts, 203
fashion shows. *See* runway
    shows
Fashion Victim (Lee), 115, 177
fashion weeks, 122, 185, 228,
    233
fashion workforce, 50
    See also labor issues
fashion-zine, 247–50
fast fashion, 263
faux fur, 33, 34
faux pas, 204
Federal Communications
    Commission (FCC), 206
Federal Trade Commission
    (FTC), 34
feminist theory, 265
Ferro, Charles, 35–37
fieldwork, 65
    See also research
flow, visual, 216–18, 237
flow of information, 50
focus groups, 123, 124
folio, 219
footwear, 58–59, 163
    celebrities and, 107–8
Footwear News, 58
Forbes magazine, 6, 137
foreign language, 97
form and function, 25, 26,
    28–30
four C's of web sites, 254, 260
freelance contracts, 179

freelancing, 181
French, F. Scott, 216, 222–31
fur, 35–37
    faux (fake), 33, 34
FurVision (trade show), 35

Gallante Uomo, 23
gallery brochure, 259
Garcia, Meredith, 222–31
garment industry, 4, 51
garment profile, 11
garment workers, 8
    See also labor issues
Gioconda, Joseph, 159
Givenchy lipstick line, 60, 61*f*
Givhan, Robin, 194–200, 212
Glamour magazine, 176
globalization, 106, 250
goals, 167
Google (search engine), 113
government
    retail forecast, 73
    See also under U.S.
GQ (Gentlemen's Quarterly),
    174
grammar, 193, 200
Grammy Awards fashion, 108
graphic design, 243
graphic elements, 241
    See also visual imagery
graphics software, 141
Gucci, 246
Gunn, Tim, 139
gutter, 142, 219

haberdasher, 208
hair coloring, 31–32
hair styles, 104–5
Hancock, Nanette, 114–15

hangtag, 4, 237

Harmon, James, 162*f*

Harper's Bazaar (magazine), 172

haute couture, 3, 6

headline, 131, 196, 207

Henning, Arthur, 109–14

Hermes "Birkin" bag, 159

high fashion, 6, 49, 216
    See also haute couture

Hill, Daniel Delis, 172

hip-hop fashion, 211, 224, 230–31

history, 9, 12*f*, 117, 166
    garment industry, 44–46

Horn, Marilyn, 28

house style guide, 201

Howling Ruth Productions, 24*f*

Hudson, Jennifer, 231, 232*f*

Humane Society of the United States, 34

human nature, 172

identity, 29

illustrations, 234
    See also images; photography

"An Image a Little Too Carefully Coordinated" (Givhan), 199

image literacy, 150

images and imagery, 168, 202, 235
    description, 192–93
    digital, 141, 237
    finding, 233
    publicity and, 132
    words wedded to, 150
    See also photography

imaging software, 237

impressions, 197

improv theater, 93

individuality, 49

Industrial Workers of the World (Thompson & Bekken), 65

industry associations, 50

information, 3–24
    accessing core, 5–11
    communication and, 5–6
    disclosure of, 47
    flow of, 50
    research (*See* research)
    revolution in, 4
    style dissection and, 7, 9–11, 22–23

information age, trendsetting in, 105–6

Ingeo (eco-friendly fiber), 169

inner vision, 158, 160

insight, 45

inspiration, creativity and, 155, 158, 160, 161–62, 164*f*, 165*f*

instantaneous communication, 90

intellectual property, 191

intercultural communication, 98–99

interfacing, 78

International Academy of Digital Arts & Sciences, 253

Internet, 37, 242
    avatar fashion, 153
    literary techniques on, 62
    occupation search on, 7
    research on, 7, 38, 244
    trendsetting and, 105
    troubleshooting on, 113–14
    See also e-mail; Web sites

internships, 91, 97, 252, 256

interviewing, 54, 108
    protocol for, 81, 100

intranet, 92

inventory management, 81

jacket design, 229–30

Japan, erogenous zones in, 116

JCPenney, 17

jeans ad campaign, 30, 32

Jenness-Miller, Annie, 175

jersey fabric, 27

job openings, 5, 7
    See also careers

Johnson, Cass, 83

Jones, John Philip, 121

Jordan, Tonia, 62

Joselit, Jenna Weissman, 175

journalism, 177

journalistic integrity, 57–58

Kalinsky, Jeffrey, 58, 61

Karan, Donna, 51, 246

Karr, Rick, 159

Kemble, Fanny, 118

Kenneth Cole Productions, 163

khaki pants, 10, 11*f*, 12–18

Khuri, Elizabeth, 28

kill fees, 179

kimono, 116

King, Steven, 191

Kiss, Bow, or Shake Hands (Morrison & Conaway), 98–99

Klam, Julie, 176

Klint, Dorte Lenau, 37

knockoffs (copies), 159

Kors, Michael, 182

label information, 4, 20
  fake fur and, 34
labor issues, 43–67
  fashion publications, 53–62
  looking into, 65–66
  standard sizing and, 48–49
  sweatshops, 44–46, 51–52
  terminology in, 47
  Triangle Waist Company
    fire, 44–46
Ladies Home Journal, 116, 117*f*
Lancôme, 233
language, 9
  target customer and, 15
  See also terminology
Language Power (Seyler &
  Boltz), 178
Lauren, Ralph, 162*f*
Lavallee, Andrew, 153
layout, 124, 127, 128*f*
lede (lead), 58, 199
Lee, Michelle, 115
legal briefs
  contracts and kill fees, 179
  intellectual property, 191
  knockoffs, 159
  online publication, 245
  photography, 235
  product placement, 115
  trade laws, 82–83
  trademark, 136
legal ownership, 190–91
Lenz, Dennis, 169
leotard, 27–28
Leotard, Jules, 27–28
Lester, Paul Martin, 238
Levi-Strauss and Company, 52
Liebowitz, Annie, 236
lifestyle, 179

Lindland, Chris, 109–14
linen, 22
lipstick line, 60, 61*f*
literary devices, 192
literary techniques, 61–62
Liz Claiborne Inc., 213
London, Peter, 152
look book, 225
"Loosen up my buttons," 26
Los Angeles, 52
loyalty, 39, 113, 166
loyalty programs, 124
Lycra, 28

Made in USA, 19
magazines, 268–69
  covers for, 238
  masthead for, 53
  See also fashion magazines;
    trade publications
MAGIC Marketplace, 129–30
Mail-Order Association of
  America, 48
Make Me A Supermodel (TV
  series), 223, 226
management, 96–97
management training, 72
manufacturing, overseas
  operations of, 51
  apparel manufacturing, 6, 8
  See also garment industry
marketing, 123, 141, 258
  do's and don'ts of, 144–46
  terminology of, 124–25
marketing campaign, 135
marketing strategy, 112
mass e-mails, 91, 112, 113
mass production, 47
masthead, 50, 53

materials, 117
media, 258
  fact sheet, 129
  movie-related, 270
  See also specific media
media kit, 132
media outlet, 50
media representation, 149–50
media spectrum, 239
media theory, 263–65
meetings, 95, 229
  e-mail for, 258
men's wear
  Cordarounds, 109–14, 120
  See also pants
mentoring, 166
merchandising. *See* visual
  merchandising
Merriam-Webster Dictionary,
  10, 154, 204
metaphor, 192
Mill Direct Apparel, 169
mirroring, in e-mails, 76
Model Release Forms, 235
models, 232–34
  health of, 200
modesty, 28, 32
monetary backing, 166
monthly meeting, 95
Moran, Gertrude "Gussy," 118
Morrison, Terri, 98–99
Morse, Margaret, 218
motivation, 16, 118
movies, 270
Murray, Henry A., 178
Muses, 161
museum exhibits, 55, 255,
  257–60
music, for runway shows, 224

musician fashions, 26, 27, 108
    hip-hop, 211, 224, 230–31
myfashionlife.com, 247–50,
    269
MySpace, 227

National Bureau of Home
    Economics, 48
National Bureau of Standards
    (NBS), 48–49
National Council of Textile
    Organizations (NCTO), 83
National Institute of Standards
    and Technology (NIST),
    46, 48
National Public Radio (NPR),
    159
natural fibers, 22
Naughton, Julie, 60
negative publicity, 132
networking, 54, 58, 166, 184,
    227
    public relations and, 128
news cycle, 197
newsletter, 14
    in-house, 85, 90
newspapers, 56, 270
New York City, 163, 213, 222
    fashion show rooms in, 49
    Fashion Week in, 185, 233
    reality TV series in, 137
    Triangle fire in, 44–46
New York Times, 43, 46, 51
    Sunday Style magazine, 103,
    111
Nielsen, Jakob, 244
Nike tagline, 31, 32
No More Secondhand Art
    (London), 152

North America Industry
    Classification System
    (NAICS), 63
note taking, 203
novelty, love of, 172
"Now, Virtual Fashion"
    (Lavallee), 153
NPD Group, 60

Obi, Michele, 243, 247–50, 269
O'Brien, Glenn, 175
*Occupational Outlook
    Handbook,* 7, 8, 66
Occupational Safety and
    Health Act (1970), 47
Occupational Safety and
    Health Administration
    (OSHA), 47
online magazine, 247–50
online research, 7, 38, 244
    See also Internet; Web sites
"oops factor," 75, 144, 225
organizational policy, 199
originality, 149, 168
    creativity and, 152, 154–55
Oscar season, 263
outreacher, 83–85
    See also public relations
    (PR)
Owens, Rick, 176
ownership, 190–91

pacing, 61–62
Pallay, Jessica, 59–60
Pantone Matching System
    (PMS), 142, 270
pants, 28
    bloomers, 118
    Cordarounds, 109–14, 120

jeans ad campaign, 30, 32
    khakis, 10, 11*f,* 12–18
"Parka Ski Cap at Odds with
    Solemnity of Auschwitz
    Ceremony" (Givhan), 198
Pasteur, Louis, 155
patience, 166
Patner, Josh, 208
Patrick-Smith, Jan, 182
PC. *See* political correctness
A Perfect Fit (Joselit), 175
periodicals, 172
    masthead in, 53
    See also fashion magazines;
    trade periodicals
Pernice, Carol, 244
personal database, 9
personal interview, 108
personal process, 161
personal style, 122
personal touch, 139
The Persuaders (TV special),
    244
Phillips-Van Heusen
    Corporation, 39
phone communication, 228–29
    cell phones, 37, 92, 140–41
    conference call, 90–91
    e-mail and, 75, 77, 84, 85,
    88, 140–41
photo agency, 234
photography, 126, 215, 219, 234
    digital, 237
    drama and contrast in, 236
    fashion shoot, 220–21
    legal issues in, 235
    runway models, 222, 223*f,*
    224
    symbolism in, 186

plagiarism, 19, 20–21, 200
planner, 93–96
planning, 166
point of purchase, 124
political correctness (PC), 33, 233
popular culture, 253
positioning, 124
Postrel, Virginia, 137
presence, 142–43
presenters, scripts for, 203
press, interactions with, 84
press kit, 99, 132
press release, 36, 112, 129–32, 216*f*, 258
  creativity in, 152
prêt-a-porter, 4. *See also* ready–to–wear
primary research, 124
Privacy Policy, 245
product placement, 115, 124
professional groups, 145–46, 256
professionalism, 92, 97, 127
  appearance and, 89, 91
projections, 54
Project Runway (TV series), 135, 137–39, 155, 223, 226
promotional events, 132
promotional theme, 124
promotions, 124, 129–30
  in business, 133–34
pronunciation, 204, 205–6
proprietary information, 75
protection and utility, 28, 32
Providence Journal, 56
proximity, 219
psychology, 29
publicity, 132, 144, 233

public relations (PR), 47, 127–28
  marketing strategy, 112
  outreacher, 83–85
Public Relations Society of America, 145
Pulitzer Prize, 195
purpose, 167

Quittner, Jeremy, 136

radio shows, 206
raw materials, 25–41
  communications rep, 35–37
  entertainment and invention, 27–28
  fake fur, 33, 34
  form and function, 25, 26, 28–30
  four-theories ad challenge, 30–32
  See also under fabric
readership, 248
  See also audience
reading, 203
  online, 244–45
  recommended, 267–70
ready-to-wear, 4, 6, 49, 173
reality television. *See Project Runway*
Reinkilde, Per, 37
relativity, 142, 143
repetition, 200
research, 11, 108, 193
  e-mail, 63
  fieldwork, 65
  online, 7, 38
  primary *vs.* secondary, 124
resources, 267–71

retailers, communication with, 16
"retail is detail," 71, 89
  See also detail, in retail
retail sales associate, 91–93, 123
  See also salespersons
rhetorical situation, 239
rhinestones, 23
Rhode Island School of Design (RISD), 55, 57
rhyme, 192
Roberts, Kevin, 244
Roberts family, 199
rock fashion, 26
role models, 161
Rouge Interdit (lipstick line), 60, 61*f*
runway shows, 122, 216, 217*f*
  models, 233–34
  photography, 222, 223*f,* 224
  reviews, 177
  scripts for, 203

safety information, 4
safety regulations, 47
Saga Furs, 35–37
sales, 123, 125–26
  See also detail, in retail
salespersons, 72, 81
  retail sales associate, 91–93
sales reports, 94
sales reps, 15*f,* 18
Sammon, Lindsay E., 58
Scavullo, Francesco, 235
scope, 242
scope-creep, 250
script work, 203, 204, 206–7
secondary research, 124

Second Life (virtual world), 153

The Second Skin (Horne), 28

secrecy, 144–45

    See also confidentiality

self-esteem, 97

self extension, 28, 29, 32

self-folding collar, 39

Seyler, Dorothy, 178

Shaw, Madeleine, 54–58

Sheppard, Eugenia, 56

Sherman, Lauren, 6

shifting erogenous zone, 115–16

shirtmaking, 208

shoes. *See* footwear

shopper's bag, 237

shopping experience, 91

    online, 245

side-to-side adoption, 106

simile, 192, 193

Simon, Paul, 263

Simonton, George, 3

Site Map, 245

    See also Web sites

sizing standards, 46, 48–49

"Skinny Models and Sheep" (Givhan), 200

skit sessions, 93

SKUs (stock-keeping units), 94

slogans, 30, 124

    See also tagline

Smith, Jill, 234

Sontag, Susan, 215

space, in magazine, 172

spandex, 26

special events coordinator, 83–85

spelling, 193

spoken fashion, 204

sponsorship, 124

staff meetings, 95

standards, 47

standard sizing, 46, 48–49

statistics, 54

status, 28, 29, 32

stock photos, 234

Strauss, Claudia J., 74–81

"Street Cleaning" (Pallay), 59–60

"Strike a Pose, Count Your Pennies" (Dodes), 233

style, 104, 122

Style.com, 122*f*, 246, 270

style dissection, 7, 9–11, 22–23

style guides, 200–201

style icon, 231

subheads, 207

Sukley, Bernadette, 35–37

Sullivan, Louis, 25, 26

supermodels, 233

supervisor, in retail, 96–97

surveys, 123

Swarovski crystals, 23

Swartz, Eric, 127

swatches, 15*f*

sweatshops, 44–46, 52

symbolism, in photography, 186

synonyms, 204

taboos, respect for, 199

tact and patience, 72

tagline, 13, 30, 124, 174

Talley, André Leon, 231

target audience, 124

target customer, 15, 16, 17

teamwork, 66, 90, 145, 193, 199

    in public relations, 132

teen fashion, 116*f*, 183

telephones. *See* phone communication

"Television Graphics and the Virtual Body" (Morse), 218

television programming, 217–18

    Project Runway, 135, 137–39, 155, 223, 226

terminology, 123–24, 142–43, 259

    pronunciation, 204, 205–6

Terms of Use, 245

testimonial, 124

text-dominant magazines, 172

textile and apparel workers, 8

    See also labor issues

textile manufacturers

    import law and, 82–83

textiles, 28

    See also fabric

texting messages, 207

Theron, Charlize, 107*f*

thesaurus (synonym finder), 204

Theyskens, Oliver, 176

third-party endorsements, 131

Thomas, Bill, 12–19

Thompson, Fred W., 65

Thoreau, Henry David, 171

tie-dye T-shirt, 23

Tiger Aspects, 223

timeline, 84–85, 135

timeliness, 143, 200

timing, 166

Tirocchi sisters, 55, 57

Tobé Coller Davis, 56–57

tone and voice, 207

too much information (TMI), 240

top down adoption, 105

Tortora, Phyllis G., 204
trade agreements, 81
trade laws, 82–83
trademark, 136
trade publications, 18, 58, 254
    B2B, 50, 124
    literary crafting in, 62
    subscribing to, 64
    wordsmithing in, 53–62
    See also fashion magazines
trade reports, 50
trade shows, 18
    promotional writing for,
        129–30
training, 90, 94, 149
    internships, 91, 97, 252, 256
    management, 72
    See also college education
transparency, 96
trendsetter, 104–8
trendspotting, 106–8
*Triangle: The Fire That
    Changed America* (Von
    Drehle), 44–46
trunk show, 126
trust, 78
Turtle Fur, 33
typos, 200

unitard, 27
U.S. Association of Importers
    of Textiles and Apparel, 83
U.S. Census Bureau, 7, 63, 269
U.S. Congress, 47, 82
U.S. Department of Agriculture
    (USDA), 48
U.S. Department of Labor,
    72–73
    *Occupational Outlook
        Handbook,* 7, 8, 66

U.S. Patent & Trademark
    Office, 136
unity, 219
University of California-Los
    Angeles (UCLA), 156

value, brand and, 16
Van Heusen, John M., 39
The Vein of Gold (Cameron),
    152
venue, 190
verbal description, 6
    See also description
verbal-visual interplay, trends
    in, 242
virtual fashion, 153
visual decisions
visual flow, 216–18, 237
visual imagery, 192–93, 215–
    38, 219
    design principles, 218–19
    words married to, 239–62
    See also photography
visual information, 5
visual merchandising, 123, 167
    specialist, 81, 86–91
visual skills, 237–38
Vivier, Roger, 107–8
Vogue magazine, 56, 57, 172,
    176–77
    power issue, 232
    Wintour at, 180–81, 231
voice, 207
Von Drehle, David, 44–46
von Furstenberg, Diane, 200
Vuitton, Louis, 211

Wall Street Journal, 112, 153,
    233, 263
Ward, Bill, 169

Washington Post, 194, 196,
    198
Webby Awards, 246, 251–53
Web logs. *See* blogs and
    blogging
Web sites, 12*f,* 37, 222, 223
    compare and contrast, 262
    Cordarounds.com, 109–14,
        120
    excellence in, 243–54
    fashion communications
        on, 145–46, 254
    faux fur, 33, 34
    four C's of, 254, 260
    job openings on, 5, 7
    legal aspects in, 245
    listing of, 269–70
    mastheads and, 53
    pre-construction checklist,
        243
    research on, 7, 38
    visiting unfamiliar, 64
    wordsmithing on, 62
Welch, Andrew, 135
"What's it made of?" challenge,
    21
Wheeler, Alina, 134
white space, 142, 219
wholesaling, 72
Wiedemann, Elettra Rosellini,
    233
Wikipedia, 38
Wintour, Anna, 180–81, 231
women, 43
    immigrant, in sweatshops,
        44–46, 52
    marketing to, 13
Women's Wear Daily (WWD),
    53, 60, 61*f,* 64
word choices, 207

word-of-mouth advertising, 126
word origins, 10
wordsmithing
    close-reading analysis, 202
    description, 189–214
    dynamic wording, 149
    in fashion trade publications, 53–62
    on Internet, 62
    policies for effective, 193, 199–200
    rhetorical situation, 246
    visual images married to, 239–62

workers. *See* labor issues
Work For Hire agreement, 235
World Wide Web, 126
    See also Internet; Web sites

Zara (retailer), 263
zeitgeist, 133, 253
zoom effect, 218